Multi-Language Glossary of Social Studies Terms

McDougal Littell

World History

Medieval and Early Modern Times

McDougal Littell

A HOUGHTON MIFFLIN COMPANY

Evanston, Illinois • Boston • Dallas

Multi-Language Glossary of Social Studies Terms

Table of Contents

ENGLISH GLOSSARY

The Glossary is an alphabetical listing of many of the key terms from the chapters, along with their meanings. The definitions listed in the Glossary are the ones that apply to the way the words are used in this textbook. The Glossary gives the part of speech of each word. The following abbreviations are used:

adj. = adjective **n.** = noun **v.** = verb

A

Abd al-Malik n. a Muslim ruler who became caliph in A.D. 685 and made Arabic the official language of government in all Muslim lands.

Abd al-Rahman III n. the eighth emir of al-Andalus, during whose reign al-Andalus reached the height of its power.

Afonso I n. a king of Kongo whose rule began in A.D. 1506. He was influenced by the Portuguese and participated in the slave trade.

al-Andalus n. the area of Spain under Muslim control between the A.D. 700s and 1492.

Allah n. God in the Islamic religion.

alluvial soil n. a very rich and fertile soil deposited by flowing water.

Almoravids n. a North African Islamic dynasty that tried to forcibly convert neighboring peoples, including those of Morocco, Spain, and Ghana.

anatomy n. the scientific study of the shapes and structures of humans, plants, and animals.

Angkor Wat n. a complex of temples in Southeast Asia, built in the A.D. 1100s, that covers nearly one square mile and is the largest religious structure in the world.

anthropology n. the study of humans and human cultures.

aqueduct n. a structure designed to bring fresh water into a city or town.

archaeology n. the recovery and study of physical evidence form the past.

artifact n. a human-made object.

Askia Muhammad n. the ruler of the Songhai empire from A.D. 1493 to 1528, who expanded the empire and organized its government.

astrolabe n. an instrument used to measure the angles of stars above the horizon, thus helping sailors determine their latitude.

Augustus n. the first emperor of Rome, who ruled from 27 B.C. to A.D. 14 and greatly expanded the size and influence of the Roman Empire.

B

Baghdad n. a city, located in what is now Iraq, that was the capital of the Abbasid empire.

Bantu migrations n. a movement, beginning sometime around 1000 B.C., of Bantu-speaking peoples from West Africa to the south and east, spreading their languages and cultures.

bubonic plague n. a disease that struck western Eurasia in the mid-1300s, in an outbreak known as the Black Death.

Buddhism n. a belief system based on the teachings of Siddhartha Gautama, the Buddha, which stress freeing oneself from worldly desires.

bureaucracy n. a system of departments and agencies that carry out the work of a government.

bushido n. the code of conduct of samurai warriors, which required that they be generous, brave, and loyal.

Byzantine Empire n. the Eastern Roman Empire, which was ruled from Constantinople and from the 4th century to the 15th century.

C

cacao n. a tropical American tree whose seeds are used to produce chocolate.

caliph n. a ruler of the Muslim community, viewed as a successor of Muhammad.

calligraphy n. the art of fine handwriting.

Calvin, John *n.* a leader of the Protestant Reformation, who lived from A.D. 1509 to 1564 and emphasized the doctrine of predestination.

capitalism *n.* an economic system based on private ownership of economic resources and the use of those resources to make a profit.

caravel *n.* a type of Portuguese sailing ship with both square and lateen sails, developed for long voyages.

cartography *n.* the skills and methods used in the making of maps.

celadon *n.* a type of Korean pottery, often with a bluish-green color.

Charlemagne *n.* a king of the Franks (from A.D. 768) who conquered much of Europe and spread Christianity in the conquered regions.

chasqui *n.* a runner in the Inca empire who carried messages up and down the length of the empire.

chivalry *n.* the code of conduct of medieval European knights, focusing on bravery, honor, and respect towards women and the weak.

Christianity *n.* a religion based on the life and teachings of Jesus.

circumnavigate *v.* to make a voyage completely around the world.

clan *n.* a group of people related by blood or marriage.

clergy *n.* the people with priestly authority in a religion.

climate *n.* the pattern of weather conditions in a certain location over a long period of time.

Clovis *n.* a leader of the Franks, who conquered the Roman province of Gaul in A.D. 486 and later established a large and powerful Frankish kingdom.

codex *n.* a book of the type used by early Meso-American civilizations to record important historical events.

Columbian Exchange *n.* the movement of plants, animals, and other living things between the eastern and western hemispheres after Columbus' voyage to the Americas in A.D. 1492.

Confucianism *n.* a belief system based on the teachings of Confucius, a scholar who taught moral virtues and ethics.

Constantine *n.* the Roman emperor from A.D. 306 to 337, who ended the persecution of Christians and moved the capital of the empire to Byzantium (later known as Constantinople).

continent *n.* one of the seven large landmasses of Earth—North America, South America, Europe, Asia, Africa, Australia, and Antarctica.

convert *v.* to persuade a person to adopt a new religion or belief.

Córdoba *n.* the capital of al-Andalus.

Cortés, Hernán *n.* the Spanish explorer who conquered the Aztec civilization of Mexico in A.D. 1521.

covenant *n.* a binding agreement.

Crusades *n.* a series of military expeditions from Christian Europe to Palestine between the 11th and 13th centuries A.D.

culture *n.* a way of life shared by a group of people.

D

daimyo *n.* a Japanese lord with large landholdings and a private samurai army, who paid no taxes to the government.

Daoism *n.* a belief system that originated in China around 500 B.C., emphasizing harmony with nature and with inner feelings.

Declaration of Independence *n.* a document that declared the American colonies' independence from Great Britain.

Declaration of the Rights of Man and of the Citizen *n.* a document adopted by the French revolutionary government in 1789, outlining the people's rights.

dissection *n.* the cutting open of plants and animals to study and investigate their parts.

divan *n.* an imperial council that advised the sultan in the Ottoman Empire.

E

elevation *n.* the height of land above sea level.

elite *n.* the superior or wealthiest members of a society or group.

Elizabethan Age *n.* the period of the rule of Queen Elizabeth I in England, from 1558 to 1603.

embassy *n.* an office of one country's government in another country.

emperor *n.* the ruler of an empire.

empire *n.* a group of different cultures or territories led by a single all-powerful ruler.

enlightened despot *n.* a ruler who had absolute power but also paid attention to the political ideas of the Enlightenment and tried to rule in a just and educated way.

Enlightenment *n.* an 18th-century philosophical movement in which philosophers used reason to understand truths about human nature.

epic poem *n.* a long poem that tells a story of heroic adventures.

excavation *n.* the process of digging up historically significant objects for the purpose of studying them.

F

faction *n.* a small group whose interests run counter to those of a larger group of which they are part.

federalism *n.* the sharing of power between an organization or government and its members.

feudalism *n.* the political and social system of the Middle Ages in Europe, in which lords gave land to vassals in exchange for service and loyalty.

Forbidden City *n.* a group of walled palaces built for the Chinese emperor shortly after A.D. 1400 in the capital city of Beijing.

Francis of Assisi, Saint *n.* an Italian who founded the Franciscan religious order in the early A.D. 1200s.

G

Genghis Khan *n.* a Mongol leader who united the Mongol tribes around A.D. 1206 and began a campaign of conquest, forging an empire that covered northern China and Central Asia.

geocentric theory *n.* the theory that Earth is at the center of the universe.

geography *n.* the study of Earth's natural features.

Ghana *n.* a region between the Sahara and the forests of southern West Africa, which was home to many ancient cultures.

glyph *n.* a picture that represents a word, syllable, or sound.

golden age *n.* a period in which a society or culture is at its peak.

Great Enclosure *n.* the largest of the three main sections of the Shona settlement of Great Zimbabwe—likely a royal residence.

Great Schism *n.* a division in the Roman Catholic Church from A.D. 1378 until 1417, which occurred when the Church's two centers of power, Avignon and Rome, split and elected different popes.

Great Zimbabwe *n.* the central settlement of the Shona empire in Africa, enclosed by a large stone wall, covering more than 100 acres, and having a population of 10,000 to 20,000.

Gregory VII, Pope *n.* the head of the Roman Catholic Church from 1073 to 1085, who struggled with Emperor Henry IV for power.

griot *n.* an official storyteller in an African civilization.

guild *n.* an association of people sharing a trade or craft, intended to control the quality and quantity of their production and to protect their interests.

Gutenberg, Johann *n.* a German who, in the mid-1400s, invented a press for printing with movable type.

H

habeas corpus *n.* the right of people not to be imprisoned unlawfully.

haiku *n.* a Japanese form of poem, containing 17 syllables arranged in three lines of 5, 7, and 5 syllables.

harmony *n.* the combining of elements to form a pleasing whole.

heliocentric *adj.* having the sun as center.

hemisphere *n.* either of two equal halves of Earth, as marked by the equator or the prime meridian.

Henry IV, Emperor *n.* an 11th-century ruler of the Holy Roman Empire, who continually struggled for power with Pope Gregory VII.

Hijrah *n.* the move of Muhammad and his followers from Mecca to the city of Yathrib in A.D. 622.

historian *n.* a person who studies and interprets the past.

history *n.* the study of past events.

humanism *n.* a movement in Renaissance Europe, celebrating human potential and achievement and stressing the study of subjects such as history, grammar, literature, and philosophy.

Hundred Years' War *n.* a series of wars between England and France, from A.D. 1337 to 1453.

I

Iberian Peninsula *n.* the southwestern tip of Europe, where the modern nations of Spain and Portugal are located.

Ignatius of Loyola, Saint *n.* a Spaniard who founded the religious order of Jesuits in the early A.D. 1530s.

imperial *adj.* relating to an empire or emperor.

indulgence *n.* a pardon for sin granted by the Roman Catholic Church, allowing a person to avoid punishment by God in the afterlife.

Inquisition *n.* a court established by the Roman Catholic Church in A.D. 1542 to investigate people who may have strayed from the Roman Catholic faith and to strengthen the power of the Church.

Islam *n.* a monotheistic religion based on the teachings of Muhammad.

J

janissary *n.* a member of an elite fighting force of the Ottoman Empire, made up mainly of slaves.

Jesuit *n.* a member of the Society of Jesus, a religious order founded in the early A.D. 1530s by Saint Ignatius of Loyola.

Joan of Arc *n.* a French peasant girl who led the French to victory over the English at Orléans in A.D. 1429.

John, King *n.* the king of England who signed the Magna Carta in A.D. 1215.

Justinian *n.* the ruler of the Eastern Roman Empire from A.D. 527 to 565, who ruled with his wife, Theodora, and reconquered lost territories for the empire.

Justinian Code *n.* a legal code, prepared under the direction of the Byzantine emperor Justinian, that regulated much of Byzantine life.

K

Kabuki *n.* a form of Japanese drama developed in the A.D. 1600s, featuring melodramatic singing and dancing, heavy makeup, and elaborate costumes.

Khmer Empire *n.* the most powerful and longest-lasting kingdom on the mainland of Southeast Asia, centered in what is today Cambodia.

Kilwa *n.* an ancient city-state on the eastern coast Africa, settled by people from Iran and Arabia, that reached its height in the late A.D. 1200s.

kinship *n.* a connection among people by blood, marriage, or adoption.

knight *n.* a highly trained mounted warrior in the service of a noble during the European Middle Ages.

Kongo *n.* an ancient kingdom along the western coast of Africa, settled by the Bantu-speaking Kongo people sometime before the 14th century A.D.

Koryo *n.* a kingdom on the Korean peninsula, established in A.D. 935 after the collapse of the Silla kingdom.

Kublai Khan *n.* the grandson of Genghis Khan who took power in southern China in A.D. 1260 and defeated the Song army in 1279, giving the Mongols control over all of China.

L

labor specialization *n.* the doing of specific types of work by trained or knowledgeable workers.

landform *n.* a naturally formed feature of Earth's land surface, such as an island, a mountain, or a plateau.

latitude *n.* a measure of distance north or south of the equator.

Leonardo da Vinci *n.* an Italian Renaissance painter, born in A.D. 1452, who painted many masterpieces, such as the Mona Lisa and The Last Supper, and also excelled in scientific research.

longbow *n.* a weapon that can shoot arrows able to penetrate a knight's armor.

longitude *n.* a measure of distance east or west of the prime meridian.

lord *n.* a powerful landholding noble.

Luther, Martin *n.* a German theologian, born in A.D. 1483, who was a leader of the Reformation and taught salvation through faith in God rather than through good deeds.

M

Magna Carta *n.* a list of rights written by England's nobility and signed by King John in A.D. 1215.

maize *n.* a type of corn grown by Native American civilizations.

Mali *n.* a West African empire established by the Malinke people.

Manchu *n.* a member of a northeastern Chinese people who conquered China in A.D. 1644 and began the last dynasty in Chinese history, called the Qing Dynasty.

manor *n.* the estate of a feudal noble, usually including a fortified building or castle.

Mansa Musa *n.* an emperor of Mali who made a famous pilgrimage to Mecca in A.D. 1324.

maritime *adj.* relating to the sea.

Maya *n.* a civilization of southern Mexico and northern Central America, which reached its height between A.D. 250 and 900.

Mbanza *n.* the capital city of the ancient African kingdom of Kongo.

mercantilism *n.* an economic policy based on the idea that a nation's power depends on its wealth.

mercenary *n.* a soldier who is paid to fight.

Meso-America *n.* a region that includes the southern part of Mexico and much of Central America.

Michelangelo *n.* an Italian Renaissance artist, born in A.D. 1475, who worked mainly as a sculptor but also painted such famous works as the ceiling of the Sistine Chapel in Rome.

Middle Ages *n.* the period of European history between the collapse of Rome and the Renaissance, lasting roughly from A.D. 500 to 1450.

missionary *n.* a person who travels to a foreign country in order to do religious work.

monastery *n.* a place where members of a religious order practice a life of prayer and worship.

Mongol Ascendancy *n.* the period in which the Mongols controlled all of Central Asia, making overland trade and travel safe.

monotheism *n.* a belief in one God.

Montezuma II *n.* the last Aztec emperor, who ruled from A.D. 1502 to 1520 and was overthrown by the Spanish.

mosaic *n.* a picture made out of many small colored tiles or pieces of glass.

mosque *n.* a building for Muslim worship, designed to face the city of Mecca.

mother culture *n.* a culture that shapes and influences the customs and ideas of later cultures.

movable type *n.* a small block of metal or wood with a single raised character, used for printing texts.

Murasaki Shikibu, Lady *n.* a Japanese writer of the early A.D. 1000s, who wrote The Tale of Genji, considered one of the world's first novels.

Muslim *n.* a person who follows the religion of Islam, accepting Allah as the only God.

Mutapa *n.* an ancient kingdom in what is now the country of Zimbabwe, established by a Shona king around A.D. 1440; also, a ruler of this kingdom.

N

Nam Viet *n.* a Vietnamese kingdom conquered by the Chinese in 111 B.C.

natural rights *n.* the rights that all people are born with—such as the rights to life, liberty, and property according to the 18th-century philosopher John Locke.

Noh *n.* a form of Japanese drama developed in the A.D. 1300s, often featuring retellings of legends and folktales presented by actors in painted wooden masks.

nomad *n.* a person who moves from place to place rather than settling permanently.

O

oasis *n.* a fertile area in the midst of a desert.

Olmec *n.* the earliest known Meso-American culture, which flourished from 1200 to 400 B.C. and was centered in southeastern Mexico.

Omar Khayyám *n.* a Persian-born Muslim poet who usually wrote in quatrain form and was also a great mathematician.

oral history *n.* an unwritten verbal account of events, such as a story that is passed down from generation to generation.

Orthodox *adj.* relating to the Christian church that developed in the Byzantine Empire and is not under the authority of the pope.

Osman *n.* the Turkish leader who founded the Ottoman Empire in the early A.D. 1300s.

P

Pacal II *n.* a king who ruled the Mayan city of Palenque for nearly 70 years (from A.D. 615)—one of the greatest Mayan kings.

Pachacuti *n.* the ninth Inca ruler, who came to power in A.D. 1438 and expanded the Inca Empire.

parliament *n.* a group of representatives with some powers of government.

patron *n.* a person who supports an activity or institution by providing financial backing.

Peace of Westphalia *n.* an agreement reached in A.D. 1648, which recognized the permanent division of western Europe into Catholic and Protestant nations and ended many ongoing religious wars.

perspective *n.* a technique of painting, developed during the Renaissance, that represents the appearance of objects in three-dimensional space.

philosophe *n.* one of the 18th-century thinkers who attempted to apply the scientific method to social problems.

pilgrimage *n.* a journey to a sacred place or shrine.

Pizarro, Francisco *n.* a Spanish explorer who arrived in Peru in A.D. 1532 and had conquered the Inca Empire by 1535.

Polo, Marco *n.* a Venetian trader who traveled the Silk Roads and arrived in China around A.D. 1275. He became an aide to Kublai Khan and later published a popular book about his adventures.

porcelain *n.* a hard white ceramic material, often called china.

predestination *n.* the doctrine that God chooses people for salvation and damnation before they are born and that individuals have no power to change God's will.

primary source *n.* a document or artifact created during a particular historical period.

printing press *n.* a machine for pressing paper against inked movable type.

projection *n.* a way of representing Earth's curved surface on a flat map while keeping distortion consistent and manageable.

Protestant *n.* a member of a Christian group that broke with the Roman Catholic Church during or after the 16th century.

Q

quipu *n.* a counting tool of the ancient Inca civilization, made of cords with knots at various points.

Qur'an *n.* the Muslim holy book, consisting of revelations from Allah that were collected by Muhammad's followers after his death.

R

rationalism *n.* the idea that people should use reason, or logical thought, to understand the world.

Reconquista *n.* the series of campaigns, ending in A.D. 1492, by which Christian armies drove Muslim rulers out of Spain.

Reformation *n.* a movement of opposition to the Roman Catholic Church, beginning in the 16th century.

regent *n.* a person who rules in place of an absent or underage monarch.

religious order *n.* a group of people who live according to a religious rule.

Renaissance *n.* a period of rebirth and creativity in art, writing, and thought from about A.D. 1300 to 1600, beginning in Italy and eventually spreading throughout Europe.

republic *n.* a form of government in which power rests with the citizens, who vote in order to elect leaders.

reunify *v.* to bring together again.

Roman Catholic *adj.* relating to the Christian church of the West that is under the authority of the pope.

S

Sahara *n.* a large desert of northern Africa, stretching from the Atlantic coast to the Nile Valley.

Saladin *n.* a military leader who united Muslims to fight the Christians in Palestine during the 12th century A.D.

salon *n.* a gathering of thinkers and artists to discuss issues and exchange ideas during the Enlightenment.

samurai *n.* a trained warrior of the Japanese aristocracy.

savanna *n.* a flat grassland, with few trees, in a tropical region.

schism *n.* an official split between two groups.

scholar-official *n.* an educated person with a government position.

scientific method *n.* an approach to scientific investigation that involves making careful observations, forming and testing a hypothesis, and drawing a conclusion that confirms or modifies the hypothesis.

Scientific Revolution *n.* a period, beginning in the A.D. 1500s, during which European scholars began to question classical scientific ideas and Christian beliefs.

secondary source *n.* a work produced about a historical event by someone who was not actually there.

Seljuk Turk *n.* a member of a Turkish people that controlled central and western Asia from the 11th to the 13th century.

serf *n.* a peasant farmer in feudal society, who labored for a noble in exchange for protection and certain rights.

Shakespeare, William *n.* most famous English writer of the Renaissance, best known for his plays Romeo and Juliet and Hamlet.

Shi'a *n.* a Muslim group that resisted the Umayyads' rule, believing that the caliph should be a relative of the prophet Muhammad.

Shinto *n.* the traditional religion of Japan, based on worship of and respect for nature and ancestors.

shogun *n.* a Japanese military leader—one of a group that first came to power in A.D. 1192 and ruled on the emperor's behalf but usually in their own interests.

Shona *n.* a Bantu-speaking culture that was thriving in what is now the countries of Botswana, Mozambique, and Zimbabwe by A.D. 1000.

Shotoku, Prince *n.* a regent who ruled Japan from A.D. 593 to 622 and brought elements of Chinese culture—in particular, the Buddhist religion—to the country.

Silk Roads *n.* the ancient trade routes that connected Europe with China.

slash-and-burn agriculture *n.* a type of farming in which patches of land are prepared for planting by cutting down and burning the natural vegetation.

Songhai *n.* a West African people whose leaders created a great empire in the 15th and 16th centuries A.D.

sponsor *n.* a person who gives money in support of a person or project.

standing army *n.* a fighting force that is maintained in times of peace as well as times of war.

stele *n.* an ancient carved stone marker commemorating an important date or great event.

Stoicism *n.* a Greek philosophy that stressed the importance of virtue, duty, and endurance and was especially influential in ancient Rome.

Suleyman I *n.* the sultan of the Ottoman Empire from A.D. 1520 to 1566, who encouraged the arts and organized a legal code.

Sundiata *n.* an ancient ruler of the Malinke people, who captured the capital of Ghana and greatly expanded the empire.

Sunnah *n.* Muhammad's words and deeds, which serve Muslims as a guide for proper living.

Sunni *n.* a member of the Muslim group that accepted the rule of the elected caliphs and did not resist the Umayyads.

Swahili *n.* an African language that blends Bantu and Arabic elements.

T

Tenochtitlán *n.* an ancient Aztec city, founded in A.D. 1325 on a small island in Lake Texcoco.

Thomas Aquinas *n.* an Italian scholar who made a synthesis of classical philosophy and Christian theology.

Timbuktu *n.* a city of central Mali in West Africa, which was founded in the 13th century and was a center of trade and culture.

Tokugawa Shogunate *n.* the rule of Tokugawa Ieyasu and his successors in Japan, which began in A.D. 1603 and brought a 250-year period of stability to the country.

Treaty of Tordesillas *n.* an agreement between Spain and Portugal in 1494, establishing an imaginary line from north to south around the world and allowing Spain to claim lands west of the line and Portugal to claim lands to the east of it.

triangular trade *n.* the exchange of goods and slaves across the Atlantic Ocean between the Americas, Europe, and Africa.

tribute *n.* a payment made by one country to another as a sign of respect.

U, V, W, X, Y, Z

universal gravitation *n.* Isaac Newton's theory that gravity acts on all objects throughout the universe.

vassal *n.* in feudal society, a person who received land and protection from a lord in return for loyalty.

vegetation zone *n.* a region that, because of its soil and climate, has distinctive types of plants.

vernacular *n.* a person's native language.

weather *n.* the condition of the atmosphere at a particular place and time.

wood-block printing *n.* a printing system developed by the ancient Chinese, in which wood blocks were carved with enough characters to print entire pages.

Yucatán Peninsula *n.* an area of southeastern Mexico that extends into the Caribbean Sea and the Gulf of Mexico.

Zen *n.* a Japanese form of Buddhism, focusing on self-discipline, simplicity, and meditation.

Zheng He *n.* a Chinese admiral whose extensive voyages between A.D. 1405 and 1433 greatly expanded China's foreign trade and reputation.

GLOSARIO INGLÉS - ESPAÑOL

Este glosario incluye una lista en orden alfabético de muchos de los términos clave usados en los capítulos, acompañados de sus significados. Las definiciones que se incluyen en el glosario corresponden a los significados de las palabras en el contexto en que se usan en este libro de texto. El glosario incluye información sobre la categoría gramatical de cada palabra. Se usan las siguientes abreviaturas:

adj. = adjetivo   *s.* = sustantivo   *v.* = verbo

SPANISH

A

Abd al-Malik *s.* soberano musulmán que asumió como califa en el año 685 d.C. y convirtió el árabe en idioma oficial del gobierno en todo el territorio musulmán.

Abd al-Rahman III *s.* octavo emir de al-Andalus que llevó a su reino a su máximo apogeo.

Alfonso I *s.* rey del Congo a partir de 1506 d.C. Fue influenciado por los portugueses y participó en el tráfico de esclavos.

al-Andalus *s.* región de España gobernada por los musulmanes entre 700s y 1492 d.C.

Allah / Alá *s.* Dios en la religión islámica.

alluvial soil / suelo aluvial *s.* suelo muy rico y fértil depositado por agua que fluye.

Almoravids / almorávides *s.* dinastía islámica del norte de África que procuró convertir a la fuerza a pueblos vecinos, incluyendo Marruecos, España y Ghana.

anatomy / anatomía *s.* estudio científico de las formas y estructuras de los seres humanos, plantas y animales.

Angkor Wat *s.* complejo de templos en el sudeste asiático de más de 1,5 km^2 de extensión, construido alrededor de 1100 d.C. Es la estructura religiosa más grande del mundo.

anthropology / antropología *s.* estudio del hombre y la cultura humana.

aqueduct / acueducto *s.* estructura creada para llevar agua potable a una ciudad o poblado.

archaeology / arqueología *s.* recuperación y estudio de los restos físicos del pasado.

artifact / artefacto *s.* objeto construido por el hombre.

Askia Muhammad *s.* soberano del imperio Songhai entre 1493 y 1528 d.C., que expandió el imperio y organizó su gobierno.

astrolabe / astrolabio *s.* instrumento utilizado para medir los ángulos de las estrellas en el horizonte y así ayudar a los navegantes a determinar su latitud.

Augustus / Augusto *s.* primer emperador de Roma, que gobernó desde 27 a.C. hasta 14 d.C. y expandió el tamaño y la influencia del Imperio Romano.

B

Bagdad *s.* ciudad ubicada en lo que hoy es Irak, que fue la capital del imperio abasí.

Bantu migrations / migraciones bantúes *s.* movimiento comenzado alrededor del año 1000 a.C. de pueblos de habla bantú desde África occidental hacia el sur y el este, que fueron divulgando sus idiomas y culturas.

bubonic plague / peste bubónica *s.* enfermedad mortal que se extendió por Asia y Europa a mediados del siglo XIV, en un brote conocido como la Muerte Negra.

Buddhism / budismo *s.* sistema de creencias basado en las enseñanzas de Siddhartha Gautama, el Buda, que promueve la liberación del ser humano de los deseos mundanos.

bureaucracy / burocracia *s.* sistema de gobierno dividido en departamentos y organismos organizados.

bushido *s.* código de conducta de los guerreros samurai, que requería que fueran generosos, valientes y leales.

Byzantine Empire / imperio bizantino *s.* Imperio Romano de Oriente, con sede de gobierno en Constantinopla, desde el siglo IV hasta el siglo XV.

C

cacao *s.* árbol tropical americano cuyas semillas se usan para fabricar el chocolate.

caliph / califa *s.* monarca de la comunidad musulmana, considerado sucesor de Mahoma.

calligraphy / caligrafía *s.* arte de escritura manuscrita.

Calvin, John / Calvino, Juan *s.* líder de la Reforma protestante, que vivió desde 1509 hasta 1564 d.C. y promulgó la doctrina de la predestinación.

capitalism / capitalismo *s.* sistema económico basado en la propiedad privada de los recursos económicos y en el uso de esos recursos para obtener ganancias.

caravel / carabela *s.* tipo de embarcación portuguesa con velas cuadradas y triangulares, construida para realizar largos viajes.

cartography / cartografía *s.* conocimientos y métodos utilizados para hacer mapas.

celadon / celadón *s.* tipo de cerámica coreana, generalmente de color verde azulado.

Charlemagne / Carlomagno *s.* rey de los francos (a partir de 768 d.C.) que conquistó gran parte de Europa y esparció el cristianismo en las regiones conquistadas.

chasqui / chasqui *s.* mensajero del impero inca que llevaba mensajes corriendo por todo el territorio del imperio.

chivalry / cavallería *s.* código de conducta de los caballeros de Europa medieval que exaltaba ideales tales como el valor, el honor y el respeto hacia las mujeres y los más débiles.

Christianity / cristianismo *s.* religión basada en la vida y enseñanzas de Jesús.

circumnavigate / circunnavegar *v.* realizar un viaje completo alrededor del mundo.

clan *s.* grupo de personas unidos por vínculos de consanguinidad o de matrimonio.

clergy / clero *s.* personas con autoridad sacerdotal en una religión.

climate / clima *s.* patrón de condiciones meteorológicas en un determinado lugar durante un largo período de tiempo.

Clovis *s.* líder de los francos, quien conquistó la provincia romana de Galia en 486 d.C. y más tarde estableció un extenso y poderoso reino franco.

codex / códice *s.* libro utilizado por las civilizaciones mesoamericanas para registrar acontecimientos históricos importantes.

Columbian Exchange / intercambio colombino *s.* intercambio de plantas, animales y otros seres vivos entre los hemisferios oriental y occidental después del viaje de Colón a América, en 1492 d.C.

Confucianism / confucionismo *s.* sistema de creencias basado en las enseñanzas de Confució, un erudito que transmitió virtudes morales y ética.

Constantine / Constantino *s.* emperador romano de 306 a 337 d.C., que terminó con la persecución de los cristianos y mudó la capital del imperio a Bizancio (más tarde conocida como Constantinopla).

continent / continente *s.* una de las siete extensas masas de tierra del planeta: América del Norte, América del Sur, Europa, Asia, África, Australia y la Antártida.

convert / convertir *v.* persuadir a alguien de adoptar una nueva religión o creencia.

Córdoba *s.* capital de al-Andalus.

Cortés, Hernán *s.* explorador español que conquistó a la civilización azteca de México en 1521 d.C.

covenant / pacto *s.* acuerdo mutuo.

Crusades / Cruzadas *s.* serie de expediciones militares desde la Europa cristiana hasta Palestina entre los siglos XI y XIII d.C.

culture / cultura *s.* forma distintiva de vida compartida por un grupo de personas.

D

daimyo *s.* señor feudal japonés que poseía grandes territorios y un ejército samurai privado, y que no pagaba impuestos al gobierno.

Daoism / daoísmo *s.* sistema de creencias originado en China alrededor del 500 a.C., que enfatizaba la armonía con la naturaleza y con los sentimientos internos.

Declaration of Independence / Declaración de la Independencia *s.* documento que declaraba la independencia de las colonias americanas de Gran Bretaña.

Declaration of the Rights of Man and of the Citizen / Declaración de los Derechos del Hombre y del Ciudadano *s.* documento adoptado por el gobierno revolucionario francés en 1789 que resume los derechos de las personas.

dissection / disección *s.* corte realizado para abrir plantas y animales para estudiar e investigar sus partes.

divan / diván *s.* consejo imperial que asesoraba al sultán en el impero otomano.

E

elevation / altitud *s.* altura de la tierra por encima del nivel del mar.

elite *s.* miembros más importantes o más ricos de una sociedad o grupo.

Elizabethan Age / Era isabelina *s.* período del reinado de la reina Elizabeth I en Inglaterra, de 1558 a 1603.

embassy / embajada *s.* oficina representante del gobierno de un país en otro país.

emperor / emperador *s.* soberano de un imperio.

empire / imperio *s.* grupo de distintas culturas o territorios liderado por un único soberano todopoderoso.

enlightened despot / déspota ilustrado *s.* soberano que tenía poder absoluto pero que también tenía en cuenta las ideas políticas de la Ilustración y procuraba gobernar de manera justa y educada.

Enlightenment / Ilustración *s.* movimiento filosófico del siglo XVIII que procuraba utilizar la razón para comprender las verdades de la naturaleza humana.

epic poem / poema épico *s.* extenso poema que relata una historia de aventuras heroicas.

excavation / excavación *s.* proceso de desenterrar objetos con significación histórica para estudiarlos.

F

faction / facción *s.* pequeño grupo cuyos intereses están en contra de los de un grupo más grande al cual pertenecen.

federalism / federalismo *s.* poder compartido entre una organización o gobierno y sus miembros.

feudalism / feudalismo *s.* sistema político y social de la Edad Media en Europa, en el cual los señores feudales otorgaban tierras a vasallos a cambio de servicio y lealtad.

Forbidden City / Ciudad prohibida *s.* grupo de palacios amurallados construidos para el emperador chino poco después del año 1400 d.C. en la ciudad capital de Beijing.

Francis of Assisi, Saint / Francisco de Asís, San *s.* italiano que fundó la orden religiosa franciscana a principios del siglo XIII d.C.

G

Genghis Khan *s.* líder mongol que unificó las tribus mongolas alrededor del año 1206 d.C. y comenzó una campaña de conquista que le permitió forjar un imperio que abarcaba el norte de china y Asia central.

geocentric theory / teoría geocéntrica *s.* teoría que postula que la Tierra es el centro del universo.

geography / geografía *s.* estudio de las características naturales de la Tierra.

Ghana *s.* región entre el Sahara y los bosques del sur de África occidental, cuna de muchas civilizaciones antiguas.

glyph / glifo *s.* dibujo que representa una palabra, sílaba o sonido.

golden age / edad de oro *s.* período en el cual una sociedad o cultura alcanza su apogeo.

Great Enclosure / Gran recinto de Zimbabwe *s.* la más grande de las tres secciones principales del asentamiento shona en el Gran Zimbabwe—probablemente una residencia real.

Great Schism / Gran Cisma *s.* división de la Iglesia Católica Romana entre 1378 y 1417 d.C., que ocurrió cuando los dos centro de poder de la Iglesia, Avignon y Roma, se separaron y eligieron distintos papas.

Great Zimbabwe / Gran Zimbabwe *s.* asentamiento central del imperio shona en África, rodeado por una gran muralla de piedra, que abarca más de 100 acres y tiene una población de 10.000 a 20.000 habitantes.

Gregory VII, Pope / Gregorio VII, Papa *s.* líder de la iglesia católica romana de 1073 a 1085, que luchó con el emperador Enrique IV por el poder.

griot *s.* narrador oficial en una civilización africana.

guild / gremio *s.* asociación de personas que comparten una profesión u oficio, creada para controlar la calidad y cantidad de su producción y proteger sus intereses.

Gutenberg, Johann *s.* inventor alemán que, a mediados de 1400, inventó la prensa de tipos móviles.

H

habeas corpus *s.* derecho de las personas a no ser encarceladas en forma ilegítima.

haiku *s.* poema japonés de 17 sílabas organizadas en tres versos de 5, 7 y 5 sílabas.

harmony / armonía *s.* combinación de elementos para formar un todo agradable.

heliocentric / heliocéntrico *adj.* que tiene al sol como centro.

hemisphere / hemisferio *s.* cualquiera de las dos mitades iguales de la Tierra, marcadas por el ecuador o el primer meridiano.

Henry IV, Emperor / Enrique IV, emperador *s.* soberano del siglo XI del Santo Imperio Romano, en continua lucha por el poder con el Papa Gregorio VII.

Hijrah *s.* migración de Mahoma y sus seguidores desde La Meca hasta la ciudad de Yathrib en el año 622 d.C.

historian / historiador *s.* persona que estudia e interpreta el pasado.

history / historia *s.* estudio de acontecimientos pasados.

humanism / humanismo *s.* movimiento en la Europa renacentista que celebraba el potencial humano y los logros, enfatizando el estudio de temas como la historia, la gramática, la literatura y la filosofía.

Hundred Years' War / Guerra de los Cien Años *s.* serie de guerras entre Inglaterra y Francia, de 1337 a 1453 d.C.

I

Iberian Peninsula / Península ibérica *s.* extremo del suroeste de Europa, donde se encuentras las naciones modernas de España y Portugal.

Ignatius of Loyola, Saint / Ignacio de Loyola, San *s.* español que fundó la orden religiosa de los jesuitas a principios de 1530.

imperial *adj.* relativo a un imperio o emperador.

indulgence / indulgencia *s.* perdón del pecado otorgado por la Iglesia Católica Romana, que permite que la persona reciba un castigo de Dios después de su muerte.

Inquisition / Inquisición *s.* tribunal establecido por la Iglesia Católica Romana en 1542 d.C. para investigar a las personas que pudieran haberse desviado de la fe católica y para reforzar el poder de la iglesia.

Islam / islam *s.* religión monoteísta basada en las enseñanzas de Mahoma.

J

janissary / jenízaro *s.* miembro de una fuerza elite de soldados del impero otomano, constituido principalmente por esclavos.

Jesuit / jesuita *s.* miembro de la Sociedad de Jesús, orden religiosa fundada a principios de 1530 d.C. por San Ignacio de Loyola.

Joan of Arc / Juana de Arco *s.* joven campesina francesa que llevó a los franceses a la victoria contra los ingleses en Orleáns, en 1429 d.C.

John, King / Juan, rey *s.* rey de Inglaterra que firmó la Carta Magna en 1215 d.C.

Justinian / Justiniano *s.* soberano del Imperio Romano de Oriente de 527 a 565 d.C., que gobernó con su esposa, Teodora, y reconquistó territorios perdidos para el imperio.

Justinian Code / Código Justiniano *s.* código legal, preparado bajo la dirección del emperador bizantino Justiniano, que reglamentaba la mayor parte de la vida bizantina.

K

Kabuki / kabuki *s.* forma de teatro japonés desarrollado en el siglo 17 y que presenta canto y danza melodramáticos, mucho maquillaje y trajes elaborados.

Khmer Empire / imperio Khmer *s.* el reino más poderoso y más duradero del sureste asiático, ubicado en lo que hoy es Camboya.

Kilwa *s.* antigua ciudad estado en la costa oriental de África, habitada por personas de Irán y de Arabia, que alcanzó su apogeo a fines del siglo XIII d.C.

kinship / parentesco *s.* vínculo entre las personas por consanguinidad, por matrimonio o por adopción.

knight / caballero *s.* guerrero montado altamente entrenado al servicio de un noble durante la Edad Media europea.

Kongo / Congo *s.* antiguo reino que abarcaba las costas occidentales de África, poblado por pueblos del Congo hablantes de bantú hacia el siglo XIV d.C.

Koryo / Koryu *s.* reino de la península coreana, establecido en 935 d.C. tras el colapso del reino de Silla.

Kublai Khan *s.* nieto de Genghis Khan que asumió el poder en China del Sur en el año 1260 d.C. y venció al ejército de los Song 1279, lo que otorgó a los mongoles el control de toda China.

L

labor specialization / especialización laboral *s.* realización de tipos específicos de trabajo por parte de trabajadores capacitados o expertos.

landform / accidente geográfico *s.* característica de la superficie de la Tierra formada naturalmente, como una isla, una montaña o una meseta.

latitude / latitud *s.* distancia norte-sur con respecto al ecuador.

Leonardo da Vinci *s.* pintor italiano del Renacimiento, nacido en 1452 d.C., autor de muchas obras maestras, como por ejemplo la Mona Lisa y La última cena, además de destacarse en la investigación científica.

longbow / arco *s.* arma que puede lanzar flechas capaces de penetrar la armadura de un caballero.

longitude / longitud *s.* distancia este-oeste a partir del primer meridiano.

lord / señor *s.* poderoso noble hacendado.

Luther, Martin / Lutero, Martín *s.* teólogo alemán, nacido en 1483 d.C., líder de la Reforma, que postulaba la salvación a través de la fe en Dios en lugar de mediante obras de bien.

M

Magna Carta / Carta Magna *s.* lista de derechos redactada por la nobleza inglesa y firmada por el rey Juan en 1215 d.C.

maize / maíz *s.* cereal cultivado por las civilizaciones nativas americanas, cuyos granos se encuentran en mazorcas.

Mali / Malí *s.* imperio de África occidental establecido por el pueblo Malinké.

Manchu / manchú *s.* perteneciente a un pueblo del noreste chino que conquistó la China en 1644 d.C. y que comenzó la última dinastía de la historia china, llamada la Dinastía Qing.

manor / señorío *s.* propiedad de un noble feudal, que solía incluir una fortificación o un castillo.

Mansa Musa *s.* emperador de Malí que realizó una famosa peregrinación a La Meca en 1324 d.C.

maritime / marítimo *adj.* relativo al mar.

Maya / mayas *s.* civilización del sur de México y el norte de América Central, que alcanzó su máximo esplendor entre 250 y 900 d.C.

Mbanza *s.* capital del antiguo reino africano del Congo.

mercantilism / mercantilismo *s.* política económica basada en la idea de que el poder de una nación depende de su riqueza.

mercenary / mercenario *s.* soldado contratado para luchar.

Meso-America / Mesoamérica *s.* región que comprende el sur de México y gran parte de América Central.

Michelangelo / Miguel Ángel *s.* artista italiano del Renacimiento, nacido en 1475 d.C., que trabajó principalmente con escultor pero también pintó otras tan famosas como el cielorraso de la Capilla Sixtina en Roma.

Middle Ages / Edad Media *s.* período de la historia europea desde la caída del Imperio Romano hasta el Renacimiento (500-1450 d.C.).

missionary / misionero *s.* persona que viaja a otro país para realizar trabajos religiosos.

monastery / monasterio *s.* lugar donde los miembros de una orden religiosa practican una vida de oración y culto.

Mongol Ascendancy / Dominio mongol *s.* período en el cual los mongoles controlaron la totalidad de Asia central, lo que garantizó la seguridad del comercio y los viajes por tierra.

monotheism / monoteísmo *s.* creencia en un único dios.

Montezuma II *s.* último emperador azteca, que gobernó desde 1502 hasta 1520 d.C. y fue derrocado por los españoles.

mosaic / mosaico *s.* cuadro realizado con muchos azulejos pequeños o trocitos de vidrio coloreados.

mosque / mezquita *s.* edificio de culto musulmán, diseñado de tal modo que quede de frente a la ciudad de La Meca.

mother culture / cultura madre *s.* cultura que modela e influye las costumbres e ideas de futuras culturas.

movable type / tipo móvil *s.* pequeño bloque de metal o de madera con un solo carácter en relieve, utilizado para imprimir textos.

Murasaki Shikibu, Lady *s.* escritora japonesa de principios del siglo XI d.C., que escribió El cuento de Genji, considerado una de las primeras novelas del mundo.

Muslim / musulmán *s.* persona que sigue la religión islámica y acepta a Alá como su único Dios.

Mutapa *s.* antiguo reino en lo que hoy es el país de Zimbabwe, fundado por un rey shona alrededor del año 1440 d.C.; también se refiere al soberano de ese reino.

N

Nam Viet *s.* reino vietnamita conquistado por los chinos en 111 a.C.

natural rights / derechos naturales *s.* derechos con los que cada persona nace, tales como el derecho a la vida, a la libertad y a la propiedad, según John Locke, filósofo del siglo XVIII.

Noh *s.* forma de teatro japonés desarrollado en 1300s d.C., que a menudo relata leyendas y cuentos populares representados por actores con máscaras de madera pintadas.

nomad / nómada *s.* persona que no tiene hogar permanente y que se muda constantemente de un lugar a otro.

O

oasis *s.* zona fértil en medio del desierto.

Olmec / olmeca *s.* la primera cultura mesoamericana conocida, que floreció entre 1200 y 400 a.C. y tenía su centro en el sureste de México.

Omar Khayyám *s.* poeta musulmán nacido en Persia que solía escribir en forma de cuartetos y que también fue un gran matemático.

oral history / historia oral *s.* relato verbal no escrito de acontecimientos, como una historia que es transmitida de generación en generación.

Orthodox / ortodoxo *adj.* relativo a la iglesia cristiana que se desarrolló en el imperio bizantino y no se encontraba bajo la autoridad del papa.

Osman / Osmán *s.* soberano turco fundador del impero otomano a principios del siglo XIV d.C.

P

Pacal II *s.* rey de la ciudad maya de Palenque durante casi 70 años (a partir de 615 d.C.), y uno de los reyes mayas más importantes.

Pachacuti *s.* último soberano inca, que subió al poder en 1438 d.C. y expandió el imperio inca.

parliament / parlamento *s.* grupo de representantes con ciertos poderes de gobierno.

patron / mecenas *s.* persona que apoya una actividad o institución, especialmente en el aspecto financiero.

Peace of Westphalia / Tratado de Westphalia *s.* acuerdo alcanzado en 1648 d.C. que reconoce la división permanente de Europa Occidental en naciones católicas y protestantes, y que terminó con muchas guerras religiosas.

perspective / perspectiva *s.* técnica de pintura, desarrollada durante el Renacimiento, que representa a los objetos en un espacio tridimensional.

philosophe / filósofo *s.* pensador del siglo XVIII que procuraba aplicar el método científico a los problemas sociales.

pilgrimage / pelegrinación *s.* viaje a un lugar sagrado o santuario.

Pizarro, Francisco *s.* explorador español que llegó a Perú en 1532 d.C. y hacia el año 1535 ya había conquistado el imperio inca.

Polo, Marco *s.* comerciante veneciano que viajó por la Ruta de la Seda y llegó a China alrededor del año 1275 d.C. Se convirtió en ayudante de Kublai Khan y más tarde publicó un popular libro que relata sus aventuras.

porcelain / porcelana *s.* tipo de cerámica dura y blanca.

predestination / predestinación *s.* doctrina que postula que Dios escoge a las personas para la salvación y la condenación antes de que nazcan, y que los individuos no tienen el poder de cambiar la voluntad de Dios.

primary source / fuente primaria *s.* documento o elemento creado durante un determinado periodo histórico.

printing press / prensa *s.* máquina para imprimir un papel mediante tipos móviles con tinta.

projection / proyección *s.* forma de representar la superficie curva de la Tierra en un mapa plano manteniendo la distorsión en forma coherente y manejable.

Protestant / protestante *s.* miembro del grupo cristiano que se separó de la Iglesia Católica Romana durante o después del siglo XVI.

Q

quipu *s.* cuerdas anudadas utilizadas para contar en la antigua civilización inca.

Qur'an / Corán *s.* libro sagrado de los musulmanes, que contiene las revelaciones de Alá recopiladas por los seguidores de Mahoma después de su muerte.

R

rationalism / racionalismo *s.* idea de que las personas deben usar la razón, o el pensamiento lógico, para comprender el mundo.

Reconquista *s.* serie de campañas, finalizadas en 1492 d.C., mediante las cuales los ejércitos cristianos expulsaron a los gobernantes musulmanes de España.

Reformation / Reforma *s.* movimiento de oposición a la Iglesia Católica Romana, que comenzó en el siglo XVI.

regent / regente *s.* persona que gobierna en nombre de un monarca ausente o menor de edad.

religious order / orden religiosa *s.* grupo de personas que viven según una norma religiosa.

Renaissance / Renacimiento *s.* período de revalorización y creatividad en el arte, la escritura y el pensamiento, desde el siglo XIV hasta el siglo XVII d.C., que comenzó en Italia y se extendió gradualmente por toda Europa.

republic / república *s.* forma de gobierno en la cual el poder está en manos de los ciudadanos, que votan para elegir a sus gobernantes.

reunify / reunificar *v.* volver a unir.

Roman Catholic / católico romano *adj.* relativo a la Iglesia Cristiana de Occidente que se encuentra bajo la autoridad del papa.

S

Sahara *s.* gran desierto en el norte de África, que se extiende desde la costa del Atlántico hasta el Valle del Nilo.

Saladin / Saladino *s.* jefe militar que unió a los musulmanes para combatir a los cristianos en Palestina durante el siglo XII d.C.

salon / salón *s.* reunión de pensadores y artistas para tratar diversos temas e intercambiar ideas durante la Ilustración.

samurai *s.* guerrero entrenado de la aristocracia japonesa.

savanna / sabana *s.* extensa llanura, con pocos árboles, en una región tropical.

schism / cisma *s.* separación oficial entre dos grupos.

scholar-official / erudito-funcionario *s.* persona instruida que ocupa un puesto gubernamental.

scientific method / método científico *s.* enfoque de la investigación científica que implica realizar observaciones cuidadosas, formular y poner a prueba una hipótesis, y sacar una conclusión que confirme o modifique la hipótesis.

Scientific Revolution / Revolución Científica *s.* período que comenzó en el siglo XVI d.C., durante el cual los eruditos europeos comenzaron a cuestionar ideas científicas clásicas y creencias cristianas.

secondary source / fuente secundaria *s.* obra escrita sobre un acontecimiento histórico por una persona que no presenció los hechos.

Seljuk Turk *s.* miembro de un pueblo turco que controló Asia central y occidental entre los siglos XI y XIII.

serf / siervo *s.* campesino agricultor en la sociedad feudal, que trabajaba para un noble a cambio de protección y de ciertos derechos.

Shakespeare, William *s.* el escritor inglés más famoso del Renacimiento, conocido por sus obras Romeo y Julieta y Hamlet.

Shi'a / shi'a *s.* grupo musulmán que se resistió al dominio de los omeyas, y que creía que el califa debería ser pariente del profeta Mahoma.

Shinto / sintoísmo *s.* religión tradicional japonesa basada en el culto y el respeto a la naturaleza y los ancestros.

shogun / shogún *s.* jefe militar japonés, perteneciente a un grupo que subió al poder en el año 1192 d.C. y que gobernaba en nombre del emperador a menudo para su propio beneficio.

Shona *s.* cultura de habla bantú que prosperó en la zona que hoy ocupan los países de Botswana, Mozambique y Zimbabwe hacia el siglo XI d.C.

Shotoku, Prince / Shotoku, Príncipe *s.* regente que gobernó Japón entre 593 y 622 d.C., e introdujo elementos de la cultura china (en especial, la religión budista) a su país.

Silk Roads / Ruta de la seda *s.* antiguas rutas comerciales que conectaban Europa con la China.

slash-and-burn agricultura / agricultura de tala y quema *s.* tipo de agricultura que consiste en talar y quemar la vegetación natural para preparar terrenos para el cultivo.

Songhai *s.* pueblo de África Occidental cuyos líderes crearon un gran imperio en los siglos XV y XVI d.C.

sponsor / patrocinador *s.* persona que da dinero para apoyar a una persona o proyecto.

standing army / ejército permanente *s.* fuerza militar que se conserva tanto en épocas de guerra como en épocas de paz.

stele / estela *s.* antiguo mojón de piedra esculpida que conmemoraba una fecha o acontecimiento importante.

Stoicism / estoicismo *s.* filosofía griega que enfatizaba la importancia de la virtud, el deber y la enmereza y que tuvo una gran influencia en la antigua Roma.

Suleyman I / Solimán I *s.* sultán del imperio otomano entre 1520 y 1566 d.C., que fomentó las artes y organizó un código legal.

Sundiata *s.* antiguo soberano del pueblo Malinké, que conquistó la capital de Ghana y expandió enormemente el imperio.

Sunnah / sunna *s.* palabra y obra de Mahoma, utilizada por los musulmanes como guía para vivir correctamente.

Sunni / sunni *s.* miembro del grupo musulmán que aceptaba el gobierno de los califas elegidos y no se resistía a los omeyas.

Swahili / suahili *s.* lengua africana que combina elementos del bantú y del árabe.

T

Tenochtitlán *s.* antigua ciudad azteca, fundada en 1325 d.C. en una pequeña isla en el Lago Texcoco.

Thomas Aquinas / Tomás de Aquino *s.* erudito italiano que realizó una síntesis de la filosofía clásica y teología cristiana.

Timbuktu / Timbuctú *s.* ciudad en Malí central, en África occidental, fundada en el siglo XIII, que fue un centro de comercio y de cultura.

Tokugawa Shogunate / shogunato Tokugawa *s.* gobierno de Tokugawa Ieyasu y sus sucesores en Japón, que comenzó en 1603 d.C. y logró un período de estabilidad en el país que duró 250 años.

Treaty of Tordesillas / Tratado de Tordesillas *s.* acuerdo entre España y Portugal, en 1494, que establecía que las tierras descubiertas al oeste de una línea imaginaria en el océano Atlántico pertenecerían a España, y las tierras al este de esa línea pertenecerían a Portugal.

triangular trade / triángulo comercial *s.*
intercambio de mercancías y esclavos a través del
Océano Atlántico entre América, Europa y África.

tribute/ tributo *s.* pago realizado por un país a otro
como signo de respeto.

U, V, W, X, Y, Z

**universal gravitation / gravitación
universal** *s.* teoría de Isaac Newton que postula que
la gravedad actúa sobre todos los objetos en el universo.

vassal / vasallo *s.* en la sociedad feudal, persona
que recibía tierras y protección de un señor feudal a
cambio de lealtad.

vegetation zone / zona de vegetación *s.*
región que, según su tipo de suelo y clima, presenta
especies característicos de plantas.

vernacular / vernáculo *s.* idioma propio de
un país.

weather / tiempo *s.* condición de la atmósfera en
un determinado momento y lugar.

**wood-block printing / impresión en
bloques de madera** *s.* sistema de impresión
desarrollado por los antiguos chinos, que utilizaba
bloques de madera tallados en relieve con los caracteres
suficientes para imprimir páginas enteras.

Yucatán Peninsula / península de Yucatán
s. zona del sureste mexicano que se extiende hacia el
mar Caribe y el golfo de México.

Zen / zen *s.* forma japonesa de budismo que se basa
en la autodisciplina, la simpleza y la meditación.

Zheng He *s.* admirante chino cuyos largos viajes
entre 1405 y 1433 d.C. expandieron enormemente el
comercio exterior y la reputación de China.

SPANISH

SPANISH

英文－中文詞彙

詞彙是將各章的關鍵性字詞按字母順序排列並附上其意義的清單。詞彙中列出的定義適用於各字詞在本教科書中的使用方式。詞彙中提供各字詞所屬的詞類。採用的縮寫如下：

adj. = 形容詞　　　**n.** = 名詞　　　**v.** = 動詞

A

Abd al-Malik / 阿不都 阿・馬力克 **n.** 一位穆斯林統治者，於公元 685 年成為哈里發，並讓阿拉伯語成為所有穆斯林領土上的政府官方語言。

Abd al-Rahman III / 阿不都 阿・拉曼三世 **n.** 阿爾・安達魯斯 (al-Andalus) 的第八任酋長，阿爾・安達魯斯在其統治期間達到其最盛期。

Afonso I / 阿爾豐索一世 **n.** 一位剛果王，其統治始於公元 1506 年。他受到葡萄牙人的影響而參與奴隸貿易。

al-Andalus / 阿爾・安達魯斯 **n.** 西班牙的一個區域，公元 700 年左右至 1492 年之間由穆斯林控制。

Allah / 阿拉 **n.** 伊斯蘭教的神。

alluvial soil / 沖積土 **n.** 一種由流水堆積的肥沃土壤。

Almoravids / 阿莫拉維德 **n.** 一個北非伊斯蘭王朝，曾經企圖強迫包括摩洛哥、西班牙和迦納等的鄰近民族改變信仰。

anatomy / 解剖學 **n.** 人體、植物和動物的外形和結構的科學研究。

Angkor Wat / 吳歌窟 **n.** 東南亞的一個寺廟群，建於公元 1100 年代，涵蓋範圍將近一平方英里，是全世界最大的宗教建築。

anthropology / 人類學 **n.** 人類和人類文化的研究。

aqueduct / 水道 **n.** 設計用來將淡水引入城鎮的建築物。

archaeology / 考古學 **n.** 對有關過去的實體證據的發掘和研究。

artifact / 人造物 **n.** 人類製造的物品。

Askia Muhammad / 阿司啟雅・默罕莫德 **n.** 公元 1493 年至 1528 年間的松海帝國統治者，他擴張了帝國的領域並組織其政府。

astrolabe / 星盤 **n.** 用來測量水平線上星星的位置，以協助航海者確定其緯度的一種儀器。

Augustus / 奧古司都 **n.** 羅馬的第一任皇帝，公元前 27 年到公元 14 年的統治期間大幅擴張了羅馬帝國的領域和影響力。

B

Baghdad / 巴格達 **n.** 一個位於現今的伊拉克的城市，曾經是阿巴息德帝國的首都。

Bantu migrations / 班圖遷徙 **n.** 從大約公元前 1000 年左右開始的一場運動，說班圖語的種族往南和往東遷徙，同時散佈其語言和文化。

bubonic plague / 淋巴腺鼠疫 **n.** 一種於 1300 年代中期襲擊歐亞大陸西部的疾病，爆發時被稱為黑死病。

Buddhism / 佛教 **n.** 一種以佛陀（西達多・喬達摩，Siddhartha Gautama）的教誨為基礎的信仰體系，其教誨強調自我要從塵世的慾望解脫出來。

bureaucracy / 官僚制度 **n.** 用來執行政府工作的部門和局處的制度。

bushido / 武士道 **n.** 武士的行為準則，要求他們寬大、勇敢而且忠誠。

Byzantine Empire / 拜占庭帝國 **n.** 從君士坦丁堡進行統治的東羅馬帝國，統治期間為第四世紀至第十五世紀。

C

cacao / 可可 **n.** 一種熱帶美洲的樹種，其種子用來生產巧克力。

caliph / 哈里發 **n.** 穆斯林社會的統治者，被視為默罕莫德的繼承者。

calligraphy / 書法 *n.* 書寫精美文字的藝術。

Calvin, John / 約翰‧卡爾文 *n.* 宗教改革的領袖，生存年代為公元 1509 年至 1564 年，強調宿命論教條。

capitalism / 資本主義 *n.* 一種經濟制度，以經濟資源私有制以及利用這些資源獲取利潤為基礎。

caravel / 輕快小帆船 *n.* 一種針對長途航行發展出來的葡萄牙帆船，有方形帆和三角帆。

cartography / 地圖學 *n.* 用來繪製地圖的技巧和方法。

celadon / 青瓷 *n.* 一種韓國陶器，通常具有灰綠色調。

Charlemagne / 查理曼 *n.* 法蘭克人的國王 (公元 768 年起)，征服了歐洲大部分地區，並將基督教傳播到所征服的地區去。

Chasqui / 印加信差 *n.* 印加帝國的長跑者，負責跨越狹長的帝國以傳遞訊息。

chivalry / 騎士精神 *n.* 中世紀歐洲武士的行為守則，其重點在於勇敢、榮譽、以及對婦女和弱者的尊重。

Christianity / 基督教 *n.* 以基督生命和教誨為基礎的一種宗教。

circumnavigate / 環航 *v.* 進行環繞世界的航行。

clan / 宗族 *n.* 有血緣或婚姻關係的一群人。

clergy / 神職人員 *n.* 在一種宗教中擁有祭師權威的人。

climate / 氣候 *n.* 一個地區長時間的天氣狀態模式。

Clovis / 克洛維斯 *n.* 法蘭克人的領袖，於公元 486 年征服羅馬的一個行省高盧，後來建立一個龐大而且強盛的法蘭克王國。

codex / 手抄本 *n.* 早期中美洲文明用來記錄重要歷史事件的那種書籍。

Columbian Exchange / 哥倫布交換 *n.* 哥倫布於公元 1492 年航行至美洲之後，東西半球之間的植物、動物和和其他生物的遷移。

Confucianism / 儒家 *n.* 一種以孔子的教誨為基礎的信仰體系，孔子是一位傳授道德和倫理學的學者。

Constantine / 君士坦丁 *n.* 公元 306 年至 337 年間的羅馬皇帝，他終止了對基督教的迫害，並將帝國首都遷移到拜占庭 (後來以君士坦丁堡為名)。

continent / 大陸 *n.* 北美洲、南美洲、歐洲、亞洲、非洲、澳洲以及南極洲等七大陸塊之一。

convert / 改變信仰 *v.* 說服某人接受新的宗教或信仰。

Córdoba / 科多巴 *n.* 阿爾‧安達魯斯的首都。

Cortés, Hernán / 荷南‧科特茲 *n.* 於公元 1521 年征服墨西哥阿茲特克文明的西班牙探險家。

covenant / 盟約 *n.* 有約束力的合約。

Crusades / 十字軍 *n.* 公元 11 和 13 世紀之間，從基督教歐洲到巴勒斯坦的一系列軍事遠征。

culture / 文化 *n.* 一群人共享的一種生活方式。

D

daimyo / 大名 *n.* 擁有大批土地和私人武士軍隊卻不用向政府繳稅的日本領主。

Daoism / 道家 *n.* 公元前 500 年左右源自中國的一種信仰體系，強調與自然和內在情感的和諧。

Declaration of Independence / 獨立宣言 *n.* 宣稱美洲殖民地從大不列顛獨立出去的文件。

Declaration of the Rights of Man and of the Citizen / 人權與公民權宣言 *n.* 法國革命政府於 1789 年採用的一份概述人民權利的文件。

dissection / 解剖 *n.* 剖開植物和動物以研究和探討其各部分。

divan / 國務會議 *n.* 奧圖曼帝國中為蘇丹提供建言的皇家顧問團。

E

elevation / 海拔 *n.* 海平面以上的土地高度。

elite / 菁英 *n.* 一個社會或團體中最優秀或最富裕的成員。

Elizabethan Age / 伊莉沙白時代 *n.* 伊莉沙白一世女皇統治英國的時期，從公元 1558 年到 1603 年。

embassy / 大使館 **n.** 一國政府在另一個國家中的辦公場所。

emperor / 皇帝 **n.** 帝國的統治者。

empire / 帝國 **n.** 由一個非常強大的統治者領導的不同文化或領土組成的團體。

enlightened despot / 開明的專制君主 **n.** 擁有絕對權力但是也注意啟蒙時代的政治思想，而試圖以公平而有教養的方式進行統治的統治者。

Enlightenment / 啟蒙主義 **n.** 18 世紀的一種哲學運動，哲學家在此運動中以理性了解關於人性的真理。

epic poem / 史詩 **n.** 述說英雄冒險事蹟的長詩。

excavation / 挖掘 **n.** 挖掘出歷史性重要物件以便加以研究的過程。

F

faction / 派系 **n.** 興趣與所屬的大團體相衝突的小團體。

federalism / 聯邦制度 **n.** 組織或政府與其成員之間分享權力。

feudalism / 封建制度 **n.** 歐洲中世紀時的一種政治和社會制度，在這種制度中，領主將土地授予臣屬，以換取服務和忠誠。

Forbidden City / 紫禁城 **n.** 公元 1400 年後不久在首都北京為中國皇帝建造的城牆圍繞的宮殿群。

Francis of Assisi, Saint / 聖方濟 **n.** 公元 1200 年代初期創立方濟會的義大利人。

G

Genghis Khan / 成吉思汗 **n.** 公元 1206 年左右統一蒙古部族的蒙古領袖，他開始了一場征服戰役，建立的帝國橫跨中國北部和中亞。

geocentric theory / 地球中心論 **n.** 認為地球是宇宙中心的理論。

geography / 地理學 **n.** 對於地球自然特徵的研究。

Ghana / 迦納 **n.** 介於撒哈拉和非洲西南部森林地帶之間的一個區域，是許多古老文化的發源地。

glyph / 字形 **n.** 用來表示一個字、音節或聲音的圖形。

golden age / 黃金時代 **n.** 一個社會或文明達到其顛峰狀態的時期。

Great Enclosure / 大圍場 **n.** 大辛巴威的索納人 (Shona) 定居地三個主要部分中最大的一個，可能是皇室居住地。

Great Schism / 大分裂 **n.** 羅馬天主教會從公元 1378 年至 1417 年間的分裂，在此次分裂中，阿威尼昂 (Avignon) 和羅馬這兩個教會的權力中心分裂而且選舉不同的教皇。

Great Zimbabwe / 大辛巴威 **n.** 索納 (Shona) 帝國在非洲建立的核心定居地，有大石牆圍繞，涵蓋面積超過 100 英畝，人口為 10000 至 20000 人。

Gregory VII, Pope / 教皇葛列哥里七世 **n.** 公元 1073 年至 1085 年間的羅馬天主教會領袖，與亨利四世皇帝爭奪權力。

griot / 葛里歐特 **n.** 非洲文化中官方的說書人。

guild / 同業公會 **n.** 由同行業的人們建立的協會，目的在控制其產品的品質和數量，並保護其利益。

Gutenberg, Johann / 約翰·顧登堡 **n.** 1400 年代發明活字印刷的德國人。

H

habeas corpus / 人身保護令 **n.** 不被非法拘禁的人權。

haiku / 俳句 **n.** 日本式的詩，由分成三行的 5, 7, 5 個音節等共 17 個音節構成。

harmony / 和諧 **n.** 將元素組合成一個令人愉悅的整體。

heliocentric / 太陽中心論的 **adj.** 以太陽為中心的。

hemisphere / 半球 **n.** 地球兩個相等的一半之一，由赤道或本初子午線劃分。

Henry IV, Emperor / 亨利四世皇帝 **n.** 11 世紀時神聖羅馬帝國的統治者，持續不停的與教皇葛列哥里七世爭奪權力。

Hijrah / 遷徙 **n.** 默罕莫德於公元 622 年從麥加遷徙至雅司律布 (Yathrib)。

historian / 歷史學家 *n.* 研究並詮釋過去的人。

history / 歷史 *n.* 有關過去事件的研究。

humanism / 人文主義 *n.* 文藝復興時期歐洲的一項運動，頌揚人類的潛能和成就，並強調歷史、文法、文學以及哲學之類學科的研究。

Hundred Years' War / 百年戰爭 *n.* 公元 1337 年至 1453 年間英法兩國之間的一系列戰爭。

I

Iberian Peninsula / 伊比利亞半島 *n.* 現代的西班牙和葡萄牙所在處的歐洲西南端。

Ignatius of Loyola, Saint / 聖羅耀拉 *n.* 公元 1530 年代初期創立耶穌會的西班牙人。

imperial / 皇帝的，帝國的 *adj.* 與帝國或皇帝有關的。

indulgence / 赦免 *n.* 羅馬教會對於罪惡的寬恕，允許人們死後不會受到上帝的懲罰。

Inquisition / 宗教裁判所 *n.* 羅馬天主教於公元 1542 年建立的法庭，目的在調查可能偏離羅馬天主教信仰的人們，以強化教會的力量。

Islam / 伊斯蘭 *n.* 以穆罕默德的教誨為基礎的一神教。

J

janissary / 蘇丹禁衛軍 *n.* 奧圖曼帝國的一支精銳部隊，主要由奴隸組成。

Jesuits / 耶穌會士 *n.* 耶穌會的成員，耶穌會是聖羅耀拉 (Ignatius of Loyola) 於公元 1530 年代初期創立的一個教派。

Joan of Arc / 聖女貞德 *n.* 一個法國的農家女，於公元 1429 年領導法國在奧良 (Orléans) 打敗英國。

John, King / 約翰王 *n.* 於公元 1215 年簽署大憲章的英國國王。

Justinian / 查士丁尼 *n.* 公元 527 年至 565 年間的東羅馬帝國統治者，與其妻子西奧朵拉 (Theodora) 一起進行統治，並且收復帝國失去的領土。

Justinian Code / 查士丁尼法典 *n.* 在拜占庭皇帝查士丁尼指導下完成的法典，約束著大部分的拜占庭生活。

K

Kabuki / 歌舞伎 *n.* 公元 1600 年代發展出來的一種日本歌劇，特色為輕歌劇似的歌唱和舞蹈、濃重的化妝以及精緻的服飾。

Khmer Empire / 高棉帝國 *n.* 東南亞大陸上最強大而且持久的一個帝國，中心位置在現在的柬埔寨。

Kilwa / 基爾瓦 *n.* 非洲東岸的古代城邦，居民來自伊朗和阿拉伯，於公元 1200 年代末期達到顛峰狀態。

kinship / 親屬關係 *n.* 因為血緣、婚姻、或領養而產生的人際關係。

knight / 騎士 *n.* 訓練有素的騎馬戰士，在歐洲的中世紀時期為貴族服務。

Kongo / 剛果 *n.* 非洲西岸的古代王國，大約公元 14 世紀前由說班圖語的剛果人定居。

Koryo / 高麗 *n.* 新羅王國崩潰之後，於公元 935 年在朝鮮半島上建立的一個王國。

Kublai Khan / 忽必烈汗 *n.* 成吉思汗的孫子，於公元 1260 年在南中國掌權，而於 1279 年打敗宋朝軍隊，讓蒙古人控制了整個中國。

L

labor specialization / 勞工專業化 *n.* 將特定類型的工作由受過訓練或有知識的工人進行的作法。

landform / 地形 *n.* 自然形成的地表特徵，例如島嶼、山岳或高原。

latitude / 緯度 *n.* 赤道以南或以北的距離衡量標準。

Leonardo da Vinci / 李奧納多‧達文西 *n.* 義大利文藝復興時期的畫家，生於公元 1452 年，繪製的傑作很多，例如蒙娜麗莎和最後的晚餐，在科學研究方面也很傑出。

longbow / 長弓 *n.* 一種能用箭射穿武士甲冑的武器。

CHINESE

latitude / 經度 *n.* 本初子伍線以東或以西的距離衡量標準。

lord / 領主 *n.* 勢力強大而且擁有土地的貴族。

Luther, Martin / 馬丁路德 *n.* 德國神學家,生於公元 1483 年,是宗教改革的領導者,其教誨為救贖要透過對上帝的信仰而非透過善行。

M

Magna Carta / 大憲章 *n.* 一份由英國貴族撰寫而由約翰王於公元 1215 年簽署的人權清單。

maize / 玉米 *n.* 一種由美洲原住民文明種植的穀物。

Mali / 馬利 *n.* 由馬林凱 (Malinke) 人建立的西非帝國。

Manchu / 滿族 *n.* 中國東北民族的一支,於公元 1644 年征服中國,開創了名為清朝的中國歷史上的最後一個王朝。

manor / 莊園 *n.* 封建貴族的領地,通常包含一座強化的建築或城堡。

Mansa Musa / 曼撒・木撒 *n.* 馬利的一個皇帝,於公元 1324 年進行前往麥加的著名朝聖。

maritime / 海上的 *adj.* 與海有關的。

Maya / 馬雅 *n.* 墨西哥南方和中美洲北方的一個文明,於公元 250 年和 900 年間達到其顛峰狀態。

Mbanza / 猛班札 *n.* 古代非洲剛果王國的首都。

mercantilism / 重商主義 *n.* 一種經濟政策,以國家力量在於其財富的觀念為其基礎。

mercenary / 傭兵 *n.* 受雇作戰的軍人。

Meso-America / 中美洲 *n.* 包括墨西哥南部和中美洲大部分的一個區域。

Michelangelo / 米開朗基羅 *n.* 義大利文藝復興時期的藝術家,生於 1475 年,主要工作身份為雕刻家,但是也畫出了諸如羅馬西斯丁教堂天花板之類的著名作品。

Middle Ages / 中世紀 *n.* 歐洲歷史中介於羅馬崩潰和文藝復興之間的時期,大約從公元 500 年至 1450 年。

missionary / 傳教士 *n.* 旅行到另一個國家去做宗教工作的人。

monastery / 修道院 *n.* 宗教派系的成員進行終身的禱告和禮拜的場所。

Mongol Ascendancy / 蒙古優勢時期 *n.* 蒙古人控制整個中亞地區,使得陸路的貿易和旅行得以安全進行的時期。

monotheism / 一神教 *n.* 對於一神的信仰。

Montezuma II / 蒙地祖馬二世 *n.* 最後一位阿茲特克皇帝,從公元 1502 年統治到 1520 年,後來被西班牙人推翻。

mosaic / 馬賽克 *n.* 由眾多彩色的小磁磚或玻璃構成的圖畫。

mosque / 清真寺 *n.* 穆斯林的禮拜場所,設計成面朝麥加的方向。

mother culture / 母文化 *n.* 塑造和影響後來文化的習俗和觀念的文化。

movable type / 活字 *n.* 具有一個凸出字元的一小塊金屬或木頭,用來印刷文字。

Murasaki Shikibu, Lady / 紫氏部 *n.* 公元 1000 年代早期的日本作家,寫下的源氏物語被認為是世界第一部小說之一。

Muslim / 穆斯林 *n.* 信仰伊斯蘭教、接受阿拉為唯一真神的人。

Mutapa / 穆塔帕 *n.* 一個位於現代辛巴威的古代王國,由索納國王於公元 1440 年建立,他也是這個王國的統治者。

N

Nam Viet / 南越 *n.* 一個於公元前 111 年被中國人征服的越南王國。

natural rights / 天賦人權 *n.* 18 世紀的哲學家約翰・洛克 (John Locke) 認為全人類生而有之的權利,例如生存、自由和財產等權利。

Noh / 能劇 *n.* 一種日本戲劇形式,發展於公元 1300 年代,通常由帶著彩色木質面具的演員複述傳奇和民間故事。

nomad / 游牧民 *n.* 遷徙各地而不永久定居的人。

O

oasis / 綠洲 *n.* 沙漠中間的一個肥沃地區。

Olmec / 歐梅克 *n.* 已知最早的中美洲文化，興盛於公元前 1200 年至 400 年間，以墨西哥東南方為中心。

Omar Khayyám / 歐瑪‧開陽 *n.* 生於波斯的回教詩人，通常以四行詩的形式寫作，也是個偉大的數學家。

oral history / 口述歷史 *n.* 口述而未筆之於書的事件，例如代代相傳的故事。

Orthodox / 東正教的 *adj.* 與天主教會有關，在拜占庭帝國發展而不受教皇的約束。

Osman / 奧斯曼 *n.* 公元 1300 年代早期創立奧圖曼帝國的土耳其領袖。

P

Pacal II / 帕卡二世 *n.* 統治馬雅城市帕仁克 (Palenque) 將近 70 年（從公元 615 年起）的一個國王，是最偉大的馬雅國王之一。

Pachacuti / 帕恰庫地 *n.* 第九位印加統治者，於公元 1438 年掌權，他擴張了印加帝國的領域。

parliament / 國會 *n.* 具有某些政府權利的一群代表。

patron / 贊助者 *n.* 提供財務後盾以支持一個活動或機構的人。

Peace of Westphalia / 西伐里亞和平 *n.* 公元 1648 年達成的和議，承認西歐永久劃分為天主教和新教國家，結束了很多進行中的宗教戰爭。

perspective / 透視法 *n.* 文藝復興時期發展出來的一種繪畫技巧，以三度空間的方式呈現物體。

philosophe / 哲學家 *n.* 18 世紀時企圖將科學方法套用到社會問題上的思想家之一。

pilgrimage / 朝聖 *n.* 前往聖地或聖殿的旅程。

Pizarro, Francisco / 法蘭西斯科‧皮薩羅 *n.* 公元 1532 年到達秘魯的西班牙探險家，於 1535 年征服印加帝國。

Polo, Marco / 馬可波羅 *n.* 一名威尼斯商人，公元 1275 年左右經由絲路旅行到達中國，他成為成吉思汗的助手，後來出版了一本有關其冒險的通俗書籍。

porcelain / 瓷器 *n.* 一種堅硬的陶瓷材料，通常稱為 china。

predestination / 宿命論 *n.* 認為上帝在人類出生前就已經選擇要拯救和詛咒的人們而且個人無力改變上帝意志的教條。

primary source / 原始來源 *n.* 在特定的歷史時期建立的文件或物品。

printing press / 印刷機 *n.* 將紙張壓印在沾了油墨的活字上的機器。

projection / 投影 *n.* 將地球曲面呈現在平面地圖上時能夠將變形維持一致而且在可控制範圍內的一種方法。

Protestant / 新教徒 *n.* 16 世紀或者 16 世紀之後與羅馬天主教會決裂的一個天主教團體的成員。

Q

quipu / 秘魯結繩文字 *n.* 古印加文明的一種計算工具，由位於各個點的繩結構成。

Qur'an / 可蘭經 *n.* 回教的聖經，由默罕莫德的追隨者在其死後收集的阿拉的啟示組成。

R

rationalism / 理性主義 *n.* 認為人類應該利用其理性或邏輯思考理解世界的觀念。

Reconquista / 重新征服 *n.* 終止於 1492 年的一系列戰役，基督徒軍隊在這些戰役中將回教徒趕出西班牙。

Reformation / 宗教改革 *n.* 反對羅馬天主教的運動，始於 16 世紀。

regent / 攝政 *n.* 代替不在其位或未成年的帝王治理的人。

religious order / 教派 *n.* 根據一種宗教規則生活的一群人。

Renaissance / 文藝復興 *n.* 公元 1300 年至 1600 年間藝術、寫作和思想再生和創造的時期，始於義大利，最後遍及整個歐洲。

republic / 共和國 *n.* 一種主權在民的政府形式，人民投票以選出領導人。

reunify / 再統一 *v.* 再度合在一起。

Roman Catholic / 羅馬天主教的 *adj.* 與教皇統治下的西方天主教會有關的。

S

Sahara / 撒哈拉 *n.* 北非的一個大沙漠，從大西洋岸延伸到尼羅河谷。

Saladin / 薩拉丁 *n.* 公元十二世紀時將回教徒團結起來對抗巴勒斯坦的基督教徒的軍事領袖。

salon / 沙龍 *n.* 啟蒙時期思想家和藝術家討論問題和交換觀念的聚會。

samurai / 日本武士 *n.* 日本貴族中受過訓練的戰士。

savanna / 稀樹草原 *n.* 熱帶地區樹木不多的平坦草地。

schism / 分裂 *n.* 兩個團體的正式分離。

scholar-official / 從政學者 *n.* 受過教育而擁有政府職位的人。

scientific method / 科學方法 *n.* 一種科學的調查研究方法，包括進行仔細的觀察、提出並測試假設、然後導出證實或修正假設的結論。

Scientific Revolution / 科學革命 *n.* 始於 1500 年代的一個時期，在此期間內，歐洲學者開始質疑古典科學觀念和天主教信仰。

secondary source / 第二手來源 *n.* 由不在場的人製造的關於歷史事件的作品。

Seljuk Turk / 塞爾柱土耳其人 *n.* 從 11 世紀到 13 世紀控制中亞和西亞的一支土耳其人。

serf / 農奴 *n.* 封建社會中的農民，他們為貴族勞動以換取保護和某些權利。

Shakespeare, William / 莎士比亞 *n.* 文藝復興時期最著名的英國作家，最有名的劇作為羅蜜歐與朱麗葉和哈姆雷特。

Shi'a / 什葉派 *n.* 一個拒絕烏麥雅德 (Umayyads) 統治的回教團體，相信哈里發應該是先知默罕莫德的親戚。

Shinto / 神道教 *n.* 日本的傳統宗教，以崇拜和尊敬自然及祖先為基礎。

shogun / 將軍 *n.* 日本的軍事領袖，是公元 1192 年首先掌權的團體之一，以天皇的名義進行統治，但是往往是以自己的利益為考量。

Shona / 素納 *n.* 公元 1000 年時興盛於現在的波札納、莫三鼻克以及辛巴威的班圖語文化。

Shotoku, Prince / 聖德太子 *n.* 公元 593 年至 622 年間統治日本的攝政王，他將中國文化的元素—尤其是佛教—帶入這個國家。

Silk Roads / 絲路 *n.* 連接歐洲和中國的古代貿易路線。

slash-and-burn agriculture / 刀耕火種農耕法 *n.* 一種農耕方法，人們砍倒並焚燒天然植被，以準備作為農耕用地。

Songhai / 松海 *n.* 一個西非民族，其領袖在公元 15 和 16 世紀建立了一個大帝國。

sponsor / 資助者 *n.* 提供金錢支持某人或某個計畫的人。

standing army / 常備軍 *n.* 承平時期和戰爭時期都要維持的一支戰鬥武力。

stele / 石柱 *n.* 紀念重要日期或偉大事件的古代石雕紀念碑。

Stoicism / 斯多葛哲學 *n.* 一種希臘哲學，強調德行、義務和堅忍的重要，在古羅馬時代特別有影響力。

Suleyman I / 蘇里曼一世 *n.* 公元 1520 年至 1566 年間的奧圖曼帝國蘇丹，他獎勵藝術並編組了一套法典。

Sundiata / 山狄雅塔 *n.* 馬林凱人的古代統治者，他攻佔了迦納首都並大幅擴張帝國的領土。

Sunnah / 遜納 *n.* 默罕莫德的言行，被回教徒當成正當生活的指引。

Sunni / 遜尼派 *n.* 回教團體的一支，接受選出來的哈里發的統治，不抗拒烏麥雅德 (Umayyads) 的統治。

Swahili / 史瓦西里語 *n.* 一種混合了班圖和阿拉伯元素的非洲語言。

T

Tenochtitlán / 提諾克提蘭 **n.** 古代的阿茲特克城市，公元 1325 年創建於德司科克 (Texcoco) 湖中的一個小島。

Thomas Aquinas / 托瑪斯‧阿圭納 **n.** 綜合了古典哲學和天主教神學的義大利學者。

Timbuktu / 廷卜土 **n.** 西非馬利中部的一個城市，建立於 13 世紀，曾經是貿易和文化的中心。

Tokugawa Shogunate / 德川幕府 **n.** 德川家康及其繼承者在日本的統治，始於公元 1603 年，為該國帶來 250 年的穩定時期。

Treaty of Tordesillas / 托德西拉條約 **n.** 西班牙和葡萄牙於 1494 年簽訂的條約，從北到南環繞地球建立一條想像的界線，讓西班牙聲稱擁有此線以西的土地，而讓葡萄牙聲稱擁有此線以東的土地。

triangular trade / 三角貿易 **n.** 美洲、歐洲和非洲之間橫越大西洋交換貨物和奴隸。

tribute / 貢品 **n.** 一國為了表示尊敬而支付給另一國的東西。

U

universal gravitation / 萬有引力 **n.** 以撒克‧牛頓的理論，認為重力會作用於宇宙萬物上。

V

vassal / 臣屬 **n.** 在封建社會中，從領主接受土地和保護而以忠誠作為交換的人。

vegetation zone / 植被地帶 **n.** 因為土壤和氣候而擁有獨特植物的一個區域。

vernacular / 本地話 **n.** 人們的母語。

W

weather / 天氣 **n.** 特定地方和時間的大氣狀況。

wood-block printing / 木刻版印刷 **n.** 古代中國人發明的一種印刷系統，這種印刷術是在一塊木板上刻上可以印刷一整頁的文字。

X, Y, Z

Yucatán Peninsula / 猶加敦半島 **n.** 墨西哥東南方延伸至加勒比海和墨西哥灣的一個區域。

Zen / 禪 **n.** 一種日本的佛教，重點在於自律、簡約以及冥想。

Zheng He / 鄭和 **n.** 一位中國的艦隊司令，他在公元 1405 年至 1433 年的廣闊航程大大的擴展了中國的海外貿易和名聲。

Thuật ngữ tiếng Việt

Phần Thuật ngữ là một danh sách theo vần ABC gồm nhiều những từ ngữ chủ chốt từ các chương, cùng với nghĩa của chúng. Các định nghĩa được liệt kê trong Phần Thuật ngữ là những định nghĩa được áp dụng cho cách sử dụng các từ trong sách này. Phần Thuật ngữ còn có phần nói cho từng từ. Các chữ viết tắt sau đây được sử dụng:

tt. = tính từ   *dt.* = danh từ   *đt.* = động từ

A

Abd al-Malik *dt.* một nhà cai trị Hồi giáo trở thành vua Hồi năm 685 sau CN và lấy tiếng A Rập làm ngôn ngữ cầm quyền chính thức tại tất cả các phần đất Hồi giáo.

Abd al-Rahman III *dt.* tiểu vương A Rập thứ tám của al-Andalus, dưới thời ông ta al-Andalus đạt đỉnh cao quyền lực của nó.

Afonso I *dt.* một vị vua xứ Kongo lên nắm quyền năm 1506 sau CN. Ông ta bị ảnh hưởng bởi người Bồ Đào Nha và tham gia vào việc buôn bán nô lệ.

al-Andalus *dt.* một vùng của Tây Ban Nha dưới quyền kiểm soát của Hồi giáo giữa những năm 700 sau CN và 1492.

Allah *dt.* Thượng Đế trong đạo Hồi.

alluvial soil / đất bồi *dt.* một loại đất rất màu mỡ được lắng đọng bởi dòng nước chảy.

Almoravids *dt.* một triều đại Hồi giáo Bắc Phi tìm cách biến đổi bằng vũ lực các dân tộc láng giềng, thuộc những nước Morocco, Tây Ban Nha và Ghana.

anatomy / giải phẫu học *dt.* ngành khoa học nghiên cứu về hình thể và cấu trúc con người, thực vật và động vật.

Angkor Wat *dt.* một quần thể các đền đài ở Đông Nam Á, được xây dựng vào những năm 1100 sau CN, chiếm diện tích gần một dặm vuông và là cấu trúc tôn giáo lớn nhất thế giới.

anthropology / nhân loại học *dt.* ngành nghiên cứu về con người và các nền văn hóa.

aqueduct / cống dẫn nước *dt.* một cấu trúc được thiết kế để đem nước ngọt vào một thành phố hay thị trấn.

archaeology / khảo cổ học *dt.* việc phục hồi và nghiên cứu các chứng tích cơ thể trong quá khứ.

artifact / đồ thủ công *dt.* một vật do con người làm.

Askia Muhammad *dt.* nhà cai trị đế quốc Songhai từ năm 1493 đến 1528 sau CN, người đã mở rộng đế chế và tổ chức chính quyền của nó.

astrolabe / thiên thể kế *dt.* một dụng cụ dùng để đo các góc của các vì sao phía trên chân trời, từ đó giúp các thủy thủ xác định vĩ độ của họ.

Augustus *dt.* hoàng đế đầu tiên của La Mã, người đã cai trị từ năm 27 trước CN đến năm 14 sau CN và bành trướng mạnh mẽ diện tích và ảnh hưởng của Đế Quốc La Mã.

B

Baghdad *dt.* một thành phố, tọa lạc tại nơi ngày nay là Iraq, trước là thủ đô của đế quốc Abbasid.

Bantu migrations / sự di cư Bantu *dt.* một sự di chuyển, bắt đầu khoảng năm 1000 trước CN, của các tộc người nói tiếng Bantu từ Tây Phi đến phía nam và đông, lan rộng các nền văn hóa và ngôn ngữ của họ.

bubonic plague / dịch hạch *dt.* một loại bệnh đã tấn công vùng tây Tiểu Á vào giữa những năm 1300, trong một đại dịch có tên là Thần Chết Đen.

Buddhism / Phật giáo *dt.* một hệ thống tín ngưỡng dựa trên sự giáo huấn của Siddhartha Gautama, đức Phật, nhấn mạnh việc giải phóng bản thân ra khỏi những ham muốn trần tục.

bureaucracy / bộ máy quan liêu *dt.* một hệ thống các bộ ngành và cơ quan thực hiện các công việc của một chính quyền.

bushido / võ sĩ đạo *dt.* những đạo lý của các chiến binh samurai, đòi hỏi họ phải khoan dung, can đảm và trung thành.

Byzantine Empire / Đế Chế Đông La Mã *dt.* được cai trị từ Constantinople và từ thế kỷ thứ 4 đến thứ 15.

C

cacao *dt.* một loại cây nhiệt đới châu Mỹ có hạt được dùng để sản xuất chocolate.

caliph / Hồi vương *dt.* một nhà cai trị cộng đồng Hồi giáo, được xem như người kế tục Muhammad.

calligraphy / thư pháp *dt.* nghệ thuật viết chữ đẹp.

Calvin, John / John Calvin *dt.* một nhà lãnh đạo Cải Cách Tin Lành, sống từ năm 1509 đến 1564 sau CN và nhấn mạnh học thuyết tiền định.

capitalism / tư bản chủ nghĩa *dt.* một hệ thống kinh tế dựa trên sự sở hữu tư nhân đối với các nguồn tài nguyên kinh tế và việc sử dụng các nguồn lực này để tạo ra lợi nhuận.

caravel / thuyền buồm Bồ *dt.* một loại thuyền buồm Bồ Đào Nha có cả buồm hình vuông và hình tam giác, được đóng cho những chuyến hành trình đường dài.

cartography / thuật bản đồ *dt.* các kỹ năng và phương pháp dùng trong việc chế tạo bản đồ.

celadon / men ngọc bích *dt.* một loại đồ gốm Triều Tiên, thường có màu xanh lá pha xanh dương.

Charlemagne *dt.* một vị vua của người Frank (từ năm 768 sau CN) người đã chinh phục phần lớn châu Âu và truyền bá đạo Cơ Đốc tại các vùng bị chinh phục.

chasqui *dt.* Một người chạy bộ ở đế chế Inca, mang thư từ lên xuống suốt chiều dài lãnh thổ đế quốc này.

chivalry / tinh thần hiệp sĩ *dt.* đạo lý của các hiệp sĩ châu Âu thời trung cổ, tập trung vào lòng can đảm, danh dự và sự tôn trọng phụ nữ và người yếu thế.

Christianity / Cơ Đốc giáo *dt.* một tôn giáo dựa trên cuộc đời và giáo huấn của Jesus.

circumnavigate / đi vòng quanh trái đất *dt.* làm một cuộc hành trình trọn vẹn vòng quanh thế giới.

clan / gia tộc *dt.* một nhóm người có quan hệ ruột thịt hoặc do hôn nhân.

clergy / tăng lữ *dt.* những người có thẩm quyền tu sĩ trong một tôn giáo.

climate / khí hậu *dt.* kiểu mẫu điều kiện thời tiết tại một địa điểm nhất định qua một khoảng thời gian dài.

Clovis *dt.* một nhà lãnh đạo của người Frank, đã chinh phục tỉnh Gaul thuộc La Mã vào năm 486 sau CN và sau đó thiết lập một vương quốc Frank rộng lớn và hùng mạnh.

codex / sách ghi tay *dt.* một cuốn sách thuộc loại được những nền văn minh Meso-American xưa dùng để ghi chép những sự kiện lịch sử quan trọng.

Columbian Exchange / Sự Trao Đổi Columbus *dt.* việc di chuyển động thực vật và các vật sống khác giữa hai bán cầu đông và tây sau cuộc hành trình của Columbus tới châu Mỹ năm 1492 sau CN.

Confucianism / Khổng Giáo *dt.* một hệ thống tín ngưỡng dựa trên những giáo huấn của Khổng Tử, một học giả dạy về những luân lý và phẩm chất đạo đức.

Constantine *dt.* hoàng đế La Mã từ năm 306 đến 337 sau CN, người đã chấm dứt sự ngược đãi những người Cơ Đốc giáo và di dời thủ đô của đế chế đến Byzantium (sau này được biết với tên Constantinople).

continent / lục địa *dt.* một trong bảy khối đất lớn của Trái Đất—Bắc Mỹ, Nam Mỹ, châu Âu, châu Á, châu Phi, Úc và Nam Cực.

convert / cải đạo *dt.* thuyết phục một người đi theo một tôn giáo hay tín ngưỡng mới.

Córdoba *dt.* thủ đô của al-Andalus.

Cortés, Hernán / Hernán Cortés *dt.* nhà thám hiểm Tây Ban Nha người đã chinh phục nền văn minh Aztec của Mexico vào năm 1521 sau CN.

covenant / giao kèo *dt.* một thỏa thuận ràng buộc.

Crusades / Thập Tự Chinh *dt.* một loạt các cuộc viễn chinh từ châu Âu Cơ Đốc giáo đến Palestine vào giữa các thế kỷ 11 và 13 sau CN.

culture / văn hóa *dt.* một lối sống chung của một nhóm người.

D

daimyo *dt.* một lãnh chúa Nhật Bản có nhiều sở hữu đất đai và một lực lượng quân đội riêng, và không nộp thuế cho chính phủ.

Daoism / Lão giáo *dt.* một hệ thống tín ngưỡng bắt nguồn từ Trung Quốc khoảng năm 500 trước CN, nhấn mạnh sự hòa hợp với thiên nhiên và với những xúc cảm bên trong.

Declaration of Independence / Tuyên Ngôn Độc Lập *dt.* một văn bản tuyên bố sự độc lập của các thuộc địa Mỹ khỏi Anh Quốc.

Declaration of the Rights of Man and of the Citizen / Tuyên Ngôn về các Quyền của Con Người và của Công Dân *dt.* một văn bản được chính quyền cách mạng Pháp thông qua năm 1789, nêu rõ các quyền của người dân.

dissection / cắt xẻ *dt.* việc mổ xẻ động thực vật ra để nghiên cứu và điều tra về các bộ phận của chúng.

divan / nội các Thổ *dt.* một hội đồng đế chế chuyên cố vấn cho vua Thổ tại Đế Quốc Ottoman.

E

elevation / cao độ *dt.* độ cao của đất so với mực nước biển.

elite / tinh hoa *dt.* các thành viên cao cấp hoặc giàu có nhất của một xã hội hay một nhóm.

Elizabethan Age / Thời Elizabeth *dt.* thời kỳ cai trị của Nữ Hoàng Elizabeth I tại Anh Quốc, từ năm 1558 đến 1603.

embassy / đại sứ quán *dt.* văn phòng của chính phủ một nước tại một nước khác.

emperor / hoàng đế *dt.* nhà cai trị một đế chế.

empire / đế chế *dt.* một nhóm các nền văn hóa hay lãnh thổ khác nhau được lãnh đạo bởi một nhà cai trị toàn quyền duy nhất.

enlightened despot / nhà chuyên quyền khai sáng *dt.* một nhà cai trị có quyền lực tuyệt đối nhưng đồng thời chú ý đến các quan niệm chính trị của Thời Đại Ánh Sáng và cố gắng cầm quyền theo một cách công bằng và có giáo dục.

Enlightenment / Thời Đại Ánh Sáng *dt.* một phong trào triết học thế kỷ 18 trong đó các triết gia dùng lý lẽ để hiểu các chân lý về bản chất con người.

epic poem / thiên sử thi *dt.* một bài thơ dài kể câu chuyện về những cuộc phiêu lưu anh hùng.

excavation / việc khai quật *dt.* quá trình đào lên các vật thể lịch sử quan trọng cho mục đích nghiên cứu chúng.

F

faction / bè phái *dt.* một nhóm nhỏ có các lợi ích đi ngược lại lợi ích của một nhóm lớn hơn mà họ là một phần trong số đó.

federalism / chế độ liên bang *dt.* sự chia sẻ quyền lực giữa một tổ chức hay chính quyền và các thành viên của nó.

feudalism / phong kiến *dt.* hệ thống chính trị xã hội của thời Trung Cổ ở châu Âu, trong đó các lãnh chúa cấp đất cho chư hầu để đổi lại sự phục vụ và lòng trung thành.

Forbidden City / Tử Cấm Thành *dt.* một nhóm các cung điện có tường bao quanh được xây dựng cho hoàng đế Trung Quốc ngay sau năm 1400 sau CN tại thủ đô Bắc Kinh.

Francis of Assisi, Saint / Thánh Francis vùng Assisi *dt.* một người Ý đã sáng lập trật tự tôn giáo Francis vào đầu những năm 1200 sau CN.

G

Genghis Khan / Thành Cát Tư Hãn *dt.* một lãnh đạo Mông Cổ đã thống nhất các bộ lạc Mông Cổ vào khoảng năm 1206 sau CN và bắt đầu một chiến dịch chinh phục, lập nên một đế quốc bao trùm vùng bắc Trung Quốc và Trung Á.

geocentric theory / thuyết địa cầu là tâm *dt.* giả thuyết rằng Trái Đất ở tại trung tâm của vũ trụ.

geography / địa lý *dt.* ngành nghiên cứu các đặc tính tự nhiên của Trái Đất.

Ghana *dt.* một vùng nằm giữa sa mạc Sahara và các khu rừng thuộc Tây Phi, vốn là xứ sở của nhiều nền văn hóa cổ đại.

glyph *dt.* một hình vẽ biểu thị cho một chữ, âm hay âm tiết.

golden age / thời vàng son *dt.* một thời kỳ trong đó một xã hội hoặc nền văn hóa ở vào đỉnh cao phát triển của nó.

Great Enclosure / Sự Sáp Nhập Lớn *dt.* phần lớn nhất trong ba phần chính của khu định cư Shona của Đại Zimbabwe—giống như một nơi cư trú hoàng tộc.

Great Schism / Sự Ly Giáo Lớn *dt.* một nhánh của Giáo Hội Thiên Chúa La Mã từ năm 1378 đến 1417 sau CN, xuất hiện khi hai trung tâm quyền lực của Giáo Hội là Avignon và La Mã, tách ra và bầu các giáo hoàng khác nhau.

Great Zimbabwe / Đại Zimbabwe *dt.* khu định cư trung tâm của đế chế Shona tại châu Phi, được bao bọc bằng một bức tường thành lớn bằng đá, trên diện tích hơn 100 mẫu Anh, và có dân số 10,000 đến 20,000 người.

Gregory VII, Pope / Giáo Hoàng Gregory Đệ Thất *dt.* người đứng đầu Giáo Hội Thiên Chúa La Mã từ năm 1073 đến 1085, người tranh giành quyền lực với Hoàng Đế Henry Đệ Tứ.

griot *dt.* một người kể chuyện chính thức của một nền văn minh châu Phi.

guild / phường hội *dt.* một hiệp hội quần chúng có chung ngành nghề, có ý định kiểm soát chất lượng và số lượng hàng sản xuất và bảo vệ lợi ích của họ.

Gutenberg, Johann / Johann Gutenberg *dt.* một người Đức, vào giữa những năm 1400, đã sáng chế ra một máy in với chữ in có thể di chuyển.

H

habeas corpus / lệnh đình quyền giam giữ *dt.* quyền của người dân không bị giam cầm một cách bất hợp lệ.

haiku / tam cú *dt.* một thể thơ Nhật Bản gồm 17 âm tiết được sắp xếp thành 3 dòng, mỗi dòng chứa 5, 7, và 5 âm tiết.

harmony / sự hòa hợp *dt.* sự kết hợp các yếu tố để hình thành một tổng thể hài hòa.

heliocentric / nhật tâm *tt.* lấy mặt trời làm trung tâm.

hemisphere / bán cầu *dt.* một trong hai nửa bằng nhau của Trái Đất, được đánh dấu bằng đường xích đạo hay kinh tuyến gốc.

Henry IV, Emperor / Hoàng Đế Henry Đệ Tứ *dt.* một nhà cai trị thế kỷ 11 của Đế Quốc La Mã Thần Thánh, người liên tục tranh giành quyền lực với Giáo Hoàng Gregory Đệ Thất.

Hijrah *dt.* cuộc di chuyển của Muhammad và các môn đồ của ông ta từ Mecca đến thành phố Yathrib vào năm 622 sau CN.

historian / sử gia *dt.* một người chuyên nghiên cứu và giải thích về quá khứ.

history / lịch sử *dt.* việc nghiên cứu về các sự kiện trong quá khứ.

humanism / chủ nghĩa nhân văn *dt.* một phong trào ở châu Âu Phục Hưng, ca ngợi tiềm năng và thành tựu của con người và nhấn mạnh việc nghiên cứu các đối tượng như lịch sử, ngữ pháp, văn học và triết học.

Hundred Years' War / Chiến Tranh Trăm Năm *dt.* một loạt các cuộc chiến giữa Anh và Pháp, từ năm 1337 đến 1453 sau CN.

I

Iberian Peninsula / Bán Đảo Iberia *dt.* mũi đất phía tây nam châu Âu, nơi ngày nay tọa lạc các quốc gia Tây Ban Nha và Bồ Đào Nha.

Ignatius of Loyola, Saint / Thánh Ignatius xứ Loyola *dt.* một người Tây Ban Nha đã sáng lập một trật tự tôn giáo là dòng Tên vào đầu những năm 1530 sau CN.

imperial / thuộc đế chế *tt.* liên quan đến một đế quốc hay hoàng đế.

indulgence / xá tội *dt.* một sự tha thứ tội lỗi do Giáo Hội Thiên Chúa La Mã ban ra, cho phép một người tránh được sự trừng phạt của Chúa trong kiếp sau.

Inquisition / Tòa Dị Giáo *dt.* một tòa án được Giáo Hội Thiên Chúa La Mã lập ra vào năm 1542 sau CN để điều tra những người bị nghi là bị lạc lối khỏi niềm tin Thiên Chúa La Mã và để củng cố thêm quyền lực của Giáo Hội.

Islam / Hồi giáo *dt.* một tôn giáo đơn thần dựa trên sự giáo huấn của Muhammad.

J

Janissary / vệ binh Thổ *dt.* thành viên của một lực lượng chiến đấu tinh nhuệ của Đế Quốc Ottoman, bao gồm chủ yếu là nô lệ.

Jesuit / dòng Tên *dt.* một thành viên của Hội Jesus, một trật tự tôn giáo được sáng lập vào đầu những năm 1530 sau CN bởi Thánh Ignatius xứ Loyola.

Joan of Arc / Joan xứ Arc *dt.* một cô gái nông dân Pháp đã dẫn dắt quân Pháp chiến thắng quân Anh tại Orléans vào năm 1429 sau CN.

John, King / Vua John *dt.* nhà vua của Anh quốc người đã ký Đại Hiến Chương vào năm 1215 sau CN.

Justinian *dt.* nhà cai trị Đế Chế Đông La Mã từ năm 527 đến 565 sau CN, đã cai trị cùng vợ là Theodora, và tái chinh phục các lãnh thổ bị mất cho đế chế.

Justinian Code / Bộ Luật Justinian *dt.* một bộ luật được soạn thảo dưới sự chỉ đạo của hoàng đế Đông La Mã Justinian, đã chỉnh đốn phần lớn cuộc sống của Đông La Mã.

K

Kabuki *dt.* một hình thức kịch nghệ Nhật Bản được phát triển vào những năm 1600 sau CN, pha trộn ca kịch và múa, trang điểm đậm và trang phục cầu kỳ.

Khmer Empire / Đế Chế Khmer *dt.* vương quốc tồn tại lâu nhất và hùng mạnh nhất của phần đất liền thuộc Đông Nam Á, tập trung tại nơi ngày nay là Campuchia.

Kilwa *dt.* một đô thị-nhà nước cổ đại nằm trên bờ duyên hải đông châu Phi, được định cư bởi người dân từ Iran và Arabia, đạt đỉnh cao vào cuối những năm 1200 sau CN.

kinship / quan hệ họ hàng *dt.* một mối quan hệ giữa những người ruột thịt, hoặc do hôn nhân hay nghĩa dưỡng.

knight / hiệp sĩ *dt.* một chiến binh cưỡi ngựa được huấn luyện cao độ để phục vụ một nhà quý tộc ở châu Âu thời Trung Cổ.

Kongo *dt.* một vương quốc cổ đại dọc theo bờ biển phía đông châu Phi, được định cư bởi người Kongo nói tiếng Bantu khoảng trước thế kỷ 14 sau CN.

Koryo / Cao Ly *dt.* một vương quốc nằm trên bán đảo Triều Tiên, được thành lập vào năm 935 sau CN sau sự sụp đổ của vương quốc Silla.

Kublai Khan / Hốt Tất Liệt *dt.* cháu nội của Thành Cát Tư Hãn, người đã lên nắm quyền tại miền nam Trung Quốc vào năm 1260 sau CN và đánh bại quân Tống năm 1279, cấp cho quân Mông Cổ quyền kiểm soát toàn bộ Trung Quốc.

L

labor specialization / chuyên môn hóa lao động *dt.* việc làm các loại công việc đặc thù của những nhân viên có kiến thức hoặc được đào tạo.

landform / địa mạo *dt.* một đặc tính được hình thành tự nhiên của bề mặt đất của Trái Đất, chẳng hạn một hòn đảo, một ngọn núi hay một cao nguyên.

latitude / vĩ độ *dt.* một sự đo lường khoảng cách về phía bắc hay nam của đường xích đạo.

Leonardo da Vinci *dt.* một họa sĩ Phục Hưng Ý, sinh năm 1452, người đã vẽ nhiều kiệt tác, chẳng hạn bức Mona Lisa và Bữa Tối Cuối Cùng, và đồng thời lỗi lạc trong nghiên cứu khoa học.

longbow / cung tên lông chim *dt.* một vũ khí có thể bắn những mũi tên có khả năng xuyên thủng áo giáp của hiệp sĩ.

longitude / kinh độ *dt.* một sự đo lường khoảng cách về phía đông hay tây của kinh tuyến gốc.

lord / lãnh chúa *dt.* một nhà quý tộc địa chủ hùng mạnh.

Luther, Martin / Martin Luther *dt.* một nhà thần học Đức, sinh năm 1483 sau CN, là lãnh đạo phong trào Cải Cách và dạy về sự cứu rỗi qua niềm tin vào Chúa hơn là qua những hành động tốt.

M

Magna Carta / Đại Hiến Chương *dt.* một danh sách các quyền lợi được giới quý tộc Anh viết ra và Vua John ký năm 1215 sau CN.

maize / bắp *dt.* một loại ngô được trồng bởi các nền văn minh Mỹ da đỏ.

Mali *dt.* một đế quốc Tây Phi được thành lập bởi người Malinke.

Manchu / Mãn Châu *dt.* thành viên của một dân tộc đông bắc Trung Quốc đã chinh phục Trung Quốc năm 1644 sau CN và khởi đầu triều đại cuối cùng trong lịch sử Trung Quốc, gọi là Triều Đại nhà Thanh.

manor / thái ấp *dt.* bất động sản của một nhà quý tộc phong kiến, thường bao gồm một tòa nhà kiên cố hoặc một lâu đài.

Mansa Musa *dt.* một hoàng đế của Mali người đã làm một cuộc hành hương nổi tiếng đến Mecca năm 1324 sau CN.

maritime / hàng hải *tt.* liên quan đến biển.

Maya *dt.* một nền văn minh thuộc miền nam Mexico và phía bắc của Trung Mỹ, đạt đỉnh cao từ năm 250 đến 900 sau CN.

Mbanza *dt.* thành phố thủ đô của vương quốc châu Phi cổ đại Kongo.

mercantilism / chủ nghĩa trọng thương *dt.* một chính sách kinh tế dựa trên quan niệm rằng sức mạnh của một quốc gia phụ thuộc vào của cải của nó.

mercenary / lê dương *dt.* một người lính được trả lương để chiến đấu.

Meso-America *dt.* một vùng bao gồm phần phía nam của Mexico và nhiều phần đất thuộc Trung Mỹ.

Michelangelo *dt.* một họa sĩ Phục Hưng Ý, sinh năm 1475 sau CN, làm việc chủ yếu như một điêu khắc gia nhưng cũng vẽ những tác phẩm nổi tiếng như trần Nhà Thờ Sistine ở Rome.

Middle Ages / Trung Cổ *dt.* giai đoạn lịch sử trong khoảng giữa sự sụp đổ của La Mã và thời Phục Hưng, kéo dài khoảng từ năm 500 đến 1450 sau CN.

missionary / nhà truyền giáo *dt.* một người đi đến một nước khác để thực hiện công việc tôn giáo.

monastery / tu viện *dt.* một nơi mà các thành viên một trật tự tôn giáo thực hành một cuộc đời cầu nguyện và tôn thờ.

Mongol Ascendancy / Uy Lực Mông Cổ *dt.* giai đoạn trong đó quân Mông Cổ kiểm soát toàn bộ Trung Á, làm cho mậu dịch và đi lại qua đất liền an toàn hơn.

monotheism / chủ nghĩa đơn thần *dt.* niềm tin vào chỉ một Thượng Đế.

Montezuma II *dt.* hoàng đế cuối cùng của Aztec, người cai trị từ năm 1502 đến 1520 và bị lật đổ bởi người Tây Ban Nha.

mosaic / tranh khảm lập thể *dt.* một bức tranh được tạo bởi nhiều mảnh đá màu nhỏ hoặc các mẩu thủy tinh.

mosque / đền thờ Hồi giáo *dt.* một tòa nhà thờ phụng của người Hồi giáo, được thiết kế hướng mặt về phía thành phố Mecca.

mother culture / văn hóa mẹ *dt.* một nền văn hóa hình thành và ảnh hưởng đến các tập quán và quan niệm của các nền văn hóa sau này.

movable type / chữ di chuyển được *dt.* một cục kim loại hay gỗ nhỏ có một ký tự nổi, dùng để in chữ.

Murasaki Shikibu, Lady / Bà Murasaki Shikibu *dt.* một tác giả Nhật Bản vào đầu những năm 1000 sau CN, người viết Truyện về Genji, được xem là một trong những tiểu thuyết đầu tiên của thế giới.

Muslim / tín đồ Hồi giáo *dt.* một người theo đạo Hồi, chấp nhận Allah là Thượng Đế duy nhất.

Mutapa *dt.* một vương quốc cổ đại tại nơi ngày nay là nước Zimbabwe, được thành lập bởi một nhà vua Shona khoảng năm 1440 sau CN; đồng thời, là một nhà cai trị vương quốc này.

N

Nam Viet / Nam Việt *dt.* một vương quốc ở Việt Nam bị người Trung Hoa chinh phục vào năm 111 trước CN.

natural rights / các quyền tự nhiên *dt.* các quyền mà mọi người đều có lúc sinh ra—chẳng hạn quyền được sống, tự do và sở hữu, theo lời triết gia thế kỷ 18 John Locke.

Noh *dt.* một dạng kịch nghệ Nhật Bản được phát triển vào những năm 1300 sau CN, thường kể lại về các truyền thuyết và chuyện dân gian được thể hiện bởi các diễn viên đeo mặt nạ gỗ có sơn vẽ.

nomad / du mục *dt.* một người chuyên di chuyển từ nơi này đến nơi khác hơn là định cư lâu dài.

O

oasis / ốc đảo *dt.* một vùng màu mỡ giữa sa mạc.

Olmec *dt.* nền văn hóa Mỹ-Mễ (Meso-America) xưa nhất được biết đến, phồn thịnh vào khoảng từ năm 1200 đến 400 trước CN và tập trung ở đông nam Mexico.

Omar Khayyám *dt.* một nhà thơ Hồi giáo sinh tại Ba Tư chuyên viết theo dạng tứ tuyệt và cũng là một nhà toán học cừ khôi.

oral history / lịch sử truyền miệng *dt.* một sự tường thuật miệng không viết ra về những sự kiện, chẳng hạn một câu chuyện được truyền từ thế hệ này sang thế hệ khác.

Orthodox / Chính Thống *tt.* liên quan đến giáo hội Thiên Chúa phát triển ở Đế Chế Đông La Mã và không dưới thẩm quyền của giáo hoàng.

Osman *dt.* một nhà lãnh đạo Thổ Nhĩ Kỳ đã sáng lập Đế Chế Ottoman vào đầu những năm 1300 sau CN.

P

Pacal II *dt.* một vị vua đã cai trị thành phố Palenque của người Maya trong gần 70 năm (từ năm 615 sau CN) một trong những vị vua Maya giỏi nhất.

Pachacuti *dt.* nhà cai trị Inca thứ chín, lên nắm quyền vào năm 1438 sau CN và mở rộng Đế Chế Inca.

parliament / nghị viện *dt.* một nhóm các đại diện có quyền lực trong chính quyền.

patron / người đỡ đầu *dt.* một người hỗ trợ một hoạt động hoặc một tổ chức bằng cách ủng hộ tài chánh.

Peace of Westphalia / nền Hòa Bình Westphalia *dt.* một thỏa ước đạt được vào năm 1648 sau CN, công nhận sự phân chia vĩnh viễn Tây Âu thành các quốc gia Thiên Chúa và Tin Lành và chấm dứt nhiều cuộc chiến tranh tôn giáo đang diễn ra.

perspective / phối cảnh *dt.* một kỹ thuật vẽ được phát triển vào thời Phục Hưng, thể hiện ngoại hình của các vật thể trong không gian ba chiều.

philosophe / triết gia *dt.* một trong những nhà tư tưởng thế kỷ 18, người tìm cách áp dụng phương pháp khoa học vào các vấn đề xã hội.

pilgrimage / cuộc hành hương *dt.* một cuộc hành trình đến một đền thờ hay nơi linh thiêng.

Pizarro, Francisco / Francisco Pizzaro *dt.* một nhà thám hiểm Tây Ban Nha đã đến Peru vào năm 1532 sau CN và chinh phụ Đế Chế Inca vào khoảng 1535.

Polo, Marco / Marco Polo *dt.* một thương nhân Venice người đã đi theo con đường tơ lụa và đến Trung Quốc vào khoảng năm 1275 sau CN. Ông đã trở thành phụ tá cho Hốt Tất Liệt và sau đó xuất bản một cuốn sách nổi tiếng về những cuộc phiêu lưu của ông.

porcelain / sứ *dt.* một chất liệu gốm trắng cứng, thường được gọi là china.

predestination / tiền định mệnh *dt.* học thuyết cho rằng Thượng Đế lựa chọn con người cho việc cứu rỗi và nguyền rủa trước khi họ sinh ra và các cá nhân không có quyền thay đổi ý Thượng Đế.

primary source / nguồn chính yếu *dt.* một tài liệu hay đồ vật chế tác được tạo ra trong một thời kỳ lịch sử riêng biệt.

printing press / máy in dập *dt.* một cái máy dùng để dập giấy vào những cục ký tự di chuyển được đã có sẵn mực.

projection / phép chiếu hình *dt.* một cách thể hiện bề mặt cong của Trái Đất lên một bản đồ phẳng trong khi vẫn giữ những sự lệch xiên một cách nhất quán và trong tầm kiểm soát.

Protestant / tín đồ Tin Lành *dt.* thành viên của một nhóm Cơ Đốc giáo đã tách khỏi Giáo Hội Thiên Chúa La Mã trong hoặc sau thế kỷ 16.

Q

quipu *dt.* một dụng cụ đếm của nền văn minh Inca cổ đại, được làm bằng dây có các nút thắt ở các điểm khác nhau.

Qur'an / kinh Côran *dt.* sách thánh của đạo Hồi, bao gồm những tiết lộ từ Allah được thu thập bởi các môn đồ của Muhammad sau khi ông ta chết.

R

rationalism / chủ nghĩa duy lý *dt.* quan niệm cho rằng con người nên dùng lý lẽ hoặc tư duy hợp lý để hiểu về thế giới.

Reconquista / Chinh Phục *dt.* hàng loạt các chiến dịch, chấm dứt vào năm 1492 sau CN, trong đó quân đội Cơ Đốc giáo đánh đuổi các nhà cai trị Hồi giáo ra khỏi Tây Ban Nha.

Reformation / Cách *dt.* một phong trào phản kháng Giáo Hội Thiên Chúa La Mã, bắt đầu vào thế kỷ 16.

regent / nhiếp chính *dt.* một người cai trị thay chỗ của một quốc vương vắng mặt hay còn nhỏ tuổi.

religious order / trật tự tôn giáo *dt.* một nhóm người sống theo luật lệ tôn giáo.

Renaissance / Phục Hưng *dt.* một giai đoạn tái sinh và sáng tạo về nghệ thuật, văn chương và tư tưởng từ khoảng năm 1300 đến 1600 sau CN, bắt đầu ở Ý và cuối cùng lan ra khắp châu Âu.

republic / cộng hòa *dt.* một hình thức chính phủ trong đó quyền lực dựa vào các công dân, những người bỏ phiếu nhằm bầu ra các nhà lãnh đạo.

reunify / tái thống nhất *dt.* gom lại một lần nữa.

Roman Catholic / Thiên Chúa La Mã *tt.* liên quan đến giáo hội Cơ Đốc ở phương Tây dưới thẩm quyền của giáo hoàng.

S

Sahara *dt.* một sa mạc lớn ở bắc Phi, trải rộng từ bờ Đại Tây Dương đến Thung Lũng sông Nile.

Saladin *dt.* một nhà lãnh đạo quân sự người đã thống nhất người Hồi giáo để đánh lại người Cơ Đốc giáo tại Palestine trong thế kỷ 12 sau CN.

salon / cuộc họp văn nghệ sĩ *dt.* một cuộc tụ họp của các nhà tư tưởng và nghệ sĩ để thảo luận các vấn đề và trao đổi ý tưởng vào Thời Đại Ánh Sáng.

samurai *dt.* một chiến binh được huấn luyện của tầng lớp quý tộc Nhật Bản.

savanna / thảo nguyên *dt.* một đồng cỏ phẳng có ít cây cối, thuộc một vùng nhiệt đới.

schism / sự phân ly *dt.* một sự chia cắt chính thức giữa hai nhóm.

scholar-official / viên chức-học giả *dt.* một người có giáo dục ở một chức vụ thuộc chính phủ.

scientific method / phương pháp khoa học *dt.* một phương pháp nghiên cứu khoa học bao gồm việc quan sát kỹ lưỡng, hình thành và thử nghiệm một giả thuyết, và rút ra một kết luận xác nhận hoặc thay đổi giả thuyết đó.

Scientific Revolution / Cách Mạng Khoa Học *dt.* một giai đoạn, bắt đầu vào những năm 1500 sau CN, trong đó các học giả châu Âu bắt đầu chất vấn về các quan niệm khoa học kinh điển và những niềm tin Cơ Đốc giáo.

secondary source / nguồn thứ yếu *dt.* một công trình được công bố về một sự kiện lịch sử của một người thật sự không có mặt ở đó.

Seljuk Turk *dt.* thành viên một dân tộc Thổ Nhĩ Kỳ đã kiểm soát trung và tây Á từ thế kỷ 11 đến 13.

serf / nông nô *dt.* một nông dân tá điền trong xã hội phong kiến, làm việc cho một nhà quý tộc để đổi lấy sự bảo vệ và các quyền nhất định.

Shakespeare, William / William Shakespeare *dt.* văn hào Anh quốc nổi tiếng nhất của thời Phục Hưng, được biết đến nhiều nhất vì các vở kịch Romeo and Juliet và Hamlet.

Shi'a *dt.* một nhóm Hồi giáo chống lại luật Umayyads, tin rằng vua Hồi có lẽ là một người thân của đấng tiên tri Muhammad.

Shinto / Thần Đạo *dt.* tôn giáo truyền thống của Nhật Bản, dựa trên sự tôn thờ và kính trọng thiên nhiên và tổ tiên.

shogun / tướng quân *dt.* một nhà lãnh đạo quân đội Nhật—một trong những nhóm lần đầu nắm quyền vào năm 1192 sau CN và cai trị thay mặt hoàng đế nhưng thường vì lợi ích riêng của họ.

Shona *dt.* một nền văn hóa nói tiếng Bantu, phát đạt tại nơi ngày nay là các nước Botswana, Mozambique, và Zimbabwe khoảng năm 1000 sau CN.

Shotoku, Prince / Thái Tử Shotoku *dt.* một vị nhiếp chính đã cai trị Nhật Bản từ năm 593 đến 622 sau CN và đem những nhân tố của văn hóa Trung Hoa—cụ thể là Phật giáo—đến nước này.

Silk Roads / Con Đường Tơ Lụa *dt.* các tuyến đường mậu dịch cổ đại nối liền châu Âu với Trung Quốc.

slash-and-burn agriculture / nền nông nghiệp chặt-và-đốt *dt.* một dạng canh nông trong đó những miếng đất được sửa soạn để gieo trồng bằng cách chặt hạ và đốt các cây cối tự nhiên.

Songhai *dt.* một dân tộc Tây Phi, lãnh đạo của họ đã tạo nên một đế chế mạnh vào các thế kỷ 15 và 16 sau CN.

sponsor / nhà tài trợ *dt.* một người cấp tiền để hỗ trợ cho một người hay một dự án.

standing army / quân đội thường trực *dt.* một lực lượng chiến đấu được duy trì trong các thời bình cũng như thời chiến.

stele / bia *dt.* một vật ghi chép bằng đá chạm cổ để tưởng nhớ một thời điểm quan trọng hay sự kiện trọng đại.

Stoicism / chủ nghĩa nghịch cảnh *dt.* một triết lý Hy Lạp nhấn mạnh tầm quan trọng của đạo đức, nghĩa vụ và sự nhẫn nại và đặc biệt có tầm ảnh hưởng lớn ở La Mã cổ đại.

Suleyman I *dt.* hoàng đế của Đế Chế Ottoman từ năm 1520 đến 1566 sau CN, người đã khuyến khích các môn nghệ thuật và thiết lập nên một bộ luật.

Sundiata *dt.* một nhà cai trị cổ đại của dân tộc Malinke, đã chiếm được thủ đô của Ghana và bành trướng mạnh mẽ đế chế này.

Sunnah *dt.* những lời lẽ và ghi chép của Muhammad, đóng vai trò chỉ đạo cho cuộc sống đúng đắn của người Hồi giáo.

Sunni *dt.* thành viên của một nhóm Hồi giáo chấp nhận luật lệ của các vua Hồi được bầu lên và không chống lại Umayyads.

Swahili *dt.* một ngôn ngữ Phi châu pha trộn các thành tố Bantu và A Rập.

T

Tenochtitlán *dt.* một đô thị Aztec cổ đại, được thành lập năm 1325 sau CN trên một hòn đảo tại Hồ Texcoco.

Thomas Aquinas *dt.* một học giả Ý người đã tạo nên một sự tổng hợp triết lý kinh điển và thần học Cơ Đốc.

Timbuktu *dt.* một đô thị thuộc trung phần Mali ở Tây Phi, được thành lập vào thế kỷ 13 và là trung tâm mậu dịch và văn hóa.

Tokugawa Shogunate / Tướng Quân Tokugawa
dt. sự cai trị của Tokugawa Ieyasu và những người
kế vị ông ta ở Nhật Bản, bắt đầu năm 1603 sau CN và
đã đem đến một thời kỳ ổn định kéo dài 250 năm cho
đất nước.

Treaty of Tordesillas / Hiệp Ước Tordesillas *dt.*
một thỏa hiệp giữa Tây Ban Nha và Bồ Đào Nha năm
1494, thiết lập một đường tưởng tượng từ bắc xuống
nam vòng quanh thế giới và cho phép Tây Ban Nha
tuyên bố chủ quyền các phần đất về phía tây của
đường này và Bồ Đào Nha tuyên bố chủ quyền những
phần đất về phía đông của nó.

triangular trade / mậu dịch hình tam giác *dt.* việc
trao đổi hàng hóa và nô lệ xuyên Đại Tây Dương giữa
châu Mỹ, châu Âu và châu Phi.

tribute / cống nạp *dt.* một sự chi trả của một nước
cho một nước khác như một biểu hiện tôn kính.

U, V, W, X, Y, Z

universal gravitation / lực hấp dẫn vạn vật *dt.*
thuyết của Isaac Newton rằng lực hấp dẫn tác động
vào mọi vật trên toàn vũ trụ.

vassal / chư hầu *dt.* trong xã hội phong kiến, một
người nhận được đất đai và sự bảo vệ từ một lãnh chúa
để đổi lại lòng trung thành.

vegetation zone / vùng thực vật *dt.* một vùng mà,
do đất đai và khí hậu của nó, có các dạng cây cối
đặc biệt.

vernacular / tiếng mẹ đẻ *dt.* ngôn ngữ bẩm sinh của
một người.

weather / thời tiết *dt.* điều kiện của không khí tại
một địa điểm và thời điểm cụ thể.

wood-block printing / in ấn cục-gỗ *dt.* một hệ
thống in ấn do người Trung Hoa cổ đại phát triển,
trong đó các cục gỗ được đục chạm với đủ các ký tự để
in toàn bộ các trang.

Yucatán Peninsula / Bán Đảo Yucatán *dt.* một
vùng thuộc đông nam Mexico vươn dài ra Biển
Caribbean và Vịnh Mexico.

Zen / Thiền *dt.* một hình thức Phật giáo của Nhật
Bản, tập trung vào sự tự kỷ luật, tính giản dị và sự trầm
ngâm suy nghĩ.

Zheng He *dt.* một đô đốc người Trung Quốc đã có
các chuyến hành trình rộng lớn giữa những năm 1405
và 1433 làm phát triển mạnh mẽ nền ngoại thương và
uy tín của Trung Quốc.

សន្ទានុក្រមភាសាអង់គ្លេស

សន្ទានុក្រមគឺជាការរាយឈ្មោះតូអក្សរតាមលំដាប់នៃពាក្យសំខាន់ៗដកស្រង់ចេញពីកថាភាគផ្សេងៗដែលមានអត្ថន័យរបស់វា ។ និយមន័យទាំងឡាយដែលបានរាយនៅក្នុងសន្ទានុក្រមគឺជាអត្ថន័យ ដែលត្រូវទៅនឹងពាក្យពេចន៍ប្រើប្រាស់នៅក្នុងអត្ថបទសៀវភៅ ។ សន្ទានុក្រមផ្ដល់នៅប្រភេទនៃពាក្យនិមួយៗ ។ ខាងក្រោមនេះជាអក្សរកាត់ទាំងឡាយដែលត្រូវបានគេប្រើ:

$គុ$ = គុណនាម $ន$ = នាម $កិ$ = កិរិយាស័ព្ទ

A

Abd al-Malik / អាប់ដ៏ អាល់ម៉ាលីក *(ន)*
អ្នកគ្រប់គ្រងជនជាតិមូស្លីមម្នាក់ ដែលក្លាយជាព្រះចៅកាលីហ្វនៅឆ្នាំ ៦៨៥ នៃគ្រិស្តសករាជ និង បានធ្វើភាសា អារ៉ាប់ទៅជាភាសាផ្លូវការ សម្រាប់រាល់ប្រទេសទាំងឡាយណាដែល កាន់សាសនាមូស្លីម ។

Abd al-Rahman III / អាប់ដ៏ អាល់ រ៉ាម៉ាន់ ទី៣ *(ន)*
អ្នកគ្រប់គ្រងទី៨ របស់ អាល់ អែនដាល្លុស ដែលមានឥទ្ធិពលអំណាចដ៏ធំធេងនៅក្នុងរយ:កាល នៃការគ្រប់គ្រង ។

Afonso I / អាហ្វនស្វ *(ន)* មហាក្សត្ររបស់ប្រទេសកុងហ្គោ ចាប់ផ្ដើមនៅឆ្នាំ ១៥០៦ នៃគ្រិស្តសករាជ ។ អង្គនេះត្រូវបានទទួលឥទ្ធិពលពីប៉ុរទុយហ្គីស និង បាន ចូលរួមក្នុងការជួញដូរទាសករ ។

al-Andalus / អាល់ អែនដាល្លុស *(ន)* តំបន់នៅប្រទេសអេស្បាញដែល ស្ថិតនៅក្រោមការគ្រប់គ្រងរបស់ សាសនា មូស្លីមនៅចន្លោះសតវត្សរ៍ឆ្នាំ ៧០០ និង ១៤៩២ នៃគ្រិស្តសករាជ ។

Allah / ព្រះអាឡ្លា *(ន)* ព្រះនៃសាសនាអ៊ីស្លាម ។

alluvial soil / ដីល្បាប់ *(ន)* ប្រភេទដីដែលមានជីជាតិច្រើនដែលបាន បន្សល់ទុកបន្ទាប់ពីការលេចធ្លើក ។

Almoravids / អាល់ម៉្វ៉រ៉ិឌស្ *(ន)*
ជារាជវង្សសាសនាអ៊ីស្លាមរបស់ប្រទេស អាហ្រ្វិកខាងជើងដែលបានលុបបាត់ចោលសាសនានារបស់ប្រជាជនជិតខាងដែ លរួមមាន ម៉្វ៉រ៉ុក អេស្ប៉ាញ និង ហ្គាណា ។

anatomy / អាណាតូមី *(ន)* វិទ្យាសាស្ត្រសិក្សាពីរចនាសម្ព័ន្ធរបស់មនុស្ស សត្វ និង រុក្ខជាតិ ។

Angkor Wat / អង្គរវត្ត *(ន)*
ប្រាសាទបុរាណដែលមានក្បាច់រចនាដ៏អស្ចារ្យ ស្ថិតនៅអាស៊ីអគ្នេយ៍ សាងសង់ឡើងនៅឆ្នាំ ១១០០ នៃគ្រិស្តសករាជ និង ជា សំណង់សាសនាដ៏ធំជាងគេបង្អស់នៅលើពិភពលោក ។

anthropology / នរវិទ្យា *(ន)* ការសិក្សាលើមនុស្ស និងវប្បធម៌របស់ មនុស្ស ។

aqueduct / ជលមាគ៌ា *(ន)*
សំណង់ដែលធ្វើឡើងដើម្បីបង្ហូរទឹកឱ្យចូលមក ក្រុង ឬ រដ្ឋធានី ។

archaeology / បុរាណវិទ្យា *(ន)* ការសិក្សាប្ររកគំហើញនៃវត្ថុតាងពី អតីតកាល ។

artifact / ស្នាដៃ *(ន)* វត្ថុដែលបង្កើតឡើងដោយមនុស្ស ។

Askiac Muhammad / អាស់គីអាក់ មូហាម៉ាត់ *(ន)*
អ្នកគ្រប់គ្រងរបស់ មធាមអំណាចសុងហៃចាប់ពី ឆ្នាំ១៤៩៣ ដល់ ឆ្នាំ១៥២៨ នៃគ្រិស្តសករាជ ហើយ បានពង្រឹកសេដ្ឋកិច្ចនិង រៀបចំរដ្ឋាភិបាលរបស់ខ្លួន ។

astrolabe / តារាមាត្រ *(ន)*
ឧបករណ៍ម្យ៉ាងប្រើសម្រាប់វាស់មុមនៃផ្កាយ ដែលស្ថិតនៅលើអ័ក្សដេក។ ការវាស់នេះគឺជួយដល់អ្នកបើកនាវ៉ាដឹងអំពីរយ: ទីម៉ង ។

Augustus / អហ្គើសធីស *(ន)* រាជាធិរាជទីមួយរបស់រ៉ូម ដែលគ្រប់គ្រង អំណាចចាប់ពីឆ្នាំ២៧មុនគ្រិស្តសករាជ ដល់ឆ្នាំ១៤នៃគ្រិស្តសករាជ និង បាន ពង្រីកអំណាច និង ទំហំនៃចក្រភពរ៉ូម៉ាំង ។

B

Baghdad / ទីក្រុងបាដាត *(ន)*
បច្ចុប្បន្នជាទីក្រុងមួយ មានទីតាំងនៅប្រទេស អ៊ីរ៉ាក់ ដែលពីមុនធ្លាប់ជារដ្ឋធានីរបស់ចក្រភពអាបាស៊ីឌ ។

Bantu migrations / ចលនាភាសខួនក្រុមបិនទូ *(ន)* ចលនាម្ចយ៉ាដែល ចាប់ផ្ដើមប្រហែលនៅឆ្នាំ១០០០ មុនគ្រិស្តសករាជ នៃប្រជាជនម្ចយ៉ាក្រុមនិយាយ ភាសាបិនទូ ដែលបានចេញពីអាហ្រ្វិកខាងលិចឆ្នោះទៅ អាហ្រ្វិកខាងត្បួង និង ខាងកើតដើម្បីផ្សព្វផ្សាយភាសា និងវប្បធម៌របស់ពួកគេ ។

bubonic plague / ជំងឺគ្រុន *(ន)*
ជំងឺដែលបានយាយីជនជាតិអ៊្វា៉រ៉ាប្រ៉ៀខាងលិច នៅពាក់កណ្ដាលសតវត្សរ៍ឆ្នាំ១៣០០ ។ ការកើតឡើងនៃជំងឺនេះត្រូវបានគេស្គាល់ ថាជាការសម្លាប់ខ្មៅ (Black Death) ។

Buddhism / សាសនាព្រះពុទ្ធ *(ន)*
ជាជំនឿសាសនាមួយដែលផ្ដែកលើការ បង្រ្កៀនរបស់ព្រះសិទ្ធត្ថ គោតម ឬព្រះពុទ្ធ ដែលរំដោះខួនចេញពីកាមកេឡេស ទាំងឡាយដែលមាននៅលើលោក ។

bureaucracy / ការិយាធិបតេយ្យ *(ន)*
ប្រព័ន្ធរបស់ក្រសួងឬផ្នាក់ងារណា មួយដែលគ្រប់គ្រងការងាររបស់រដ្ឋាភិបាល ។

bushido / ក្រមបាស់ស៊ីដូ *(ន)*
ក្រមទម្រង់នានាសម្រាប់ក្រុមអ្នកចម្បាំងសាម៉ូរ៉ៃ
ដែលតម្រូវឱ្យស្រមាជិកមានមនុស្សធម៌ ក្លាហាន និងស្មោះស័ត្រចំពោះក្រុម ។

Byzantine Empire / ចក្រភពប៊ីហ្សាន់ទីន *(ន)*
ចក្រភពរ៉ូម៉ាំងខាងកើត ដែលច្បាប់
ផ្ដើមគ្រប់គ្រងអំណាចចាប់ពីខាងស្ថេនទិណូបផល គីពីសតវត្សរ៍ទី
៤ ដល់ទី ១៥ ។

C

cacao / ដើមកាកាវ *(ន)* ប្រភេទដើមឈើម្យ៉ាងដែលដុះនៅតំបន់ ត្រូពិក
អាមេរិក ដែលគ្រាប់វ៉ាប្រើសម្រាប់ធ្វើស្ងួកូឡា ។

caliph / ព្រះចៅកាលីហ្វ *(ន)* ជាអ្នកគ្រប់គ្រងអំណាចនៃសហគមន៍
មូស្លីម ហើយដែលត្រូវគេស្គាល់ថាជាទាយាទ័ររបស់មូហាម៉ាត់ ។

calligraphy / អក្សរវិចិត្រសាស្ត្រ *(ន)*
ជាសិល្បៈក្នុងការសរសេរអក្សរផ្ដង់ ។

Calvin, John / អ្នកដឹកនាំខាងវិន ចន *(ន)* អ្នកដឹកនៃរ័របស់ចលនា
ប្រូតេស្ដង់ ដែលរស់នៅចាប់ពីឆ្នាំ ១៥០៩ ដល់ឆ្នាំ ១៥៦៤ នៃគ្រិស្តសករាជ
ដែល យកចិត្តទុកដាក់លើលទ្ធិនៃបុព្វរាសនា ។

capitalism / មូលធននិយម *(ន)*
ប្រព័ន្ធសេដ្ឋកិច្ចដែលផ្ដែកទៅលើកម្មសិទ្ធ ឯកជននៃធនធានសេដ្ឋកិច្ច
និង ប្រើប្រាស់ធនធានទាំងនោះសម្រាប់រកប្រាក់ ចំណេញ ។

caravel / សំពៅ *(ន)*
ប្រភេទសំពៅរបស់ជនជាតិព័រទុយហ្គាល់ម្យ៉ាងដែល មានក្លោងការ៉េ
និង រាងត្រីកោណ បង្កើតសម្រាប់ការធ្វើដំណើរផ្លូវវែងឆ្ងាយ ។

cartography / ក្បូនផ្ទៃផែនទី *(ន)*
ជំនាញនិងវិធីសាស្ត្រប្រើសម្រាប់ធ្វើ ផែនទី ។

celadon / ឆ្នាំងស្លន *(ន)* ប្រភេទឆ្នាំងស្លូនរបស់ជនជាតិចិនកូវ៉ែដែលជាទូទៅ
មានពណ៌បៃតងកាប់ស្តាំង ។

Charlemagne / ព្រះមហាក្សត្រ្ដឆាល់ម៉ឺកន៍ *(ន)*
ព្រះមហាក្សត្រ្ដនៃជន ជាតិប្រៃ្យង ចាប់ពីឆ្នាំ៧៦៨ នៃគ្រិស្តសករាជ
ដែលបានឤណ្ដើមយកអំណាចខេត្ត ជាច្រើន នៅភាគអឺរ៉ុប
និងផ្សព្វផ្សាយសាសនាគ្រិស្តលើអំណាចខេត្តទាំងនោះ ។

chasqui *(ន)* ជាអ្នករត់ម្នាក់នៅក្នុងអាណាចក្រអ៊ីនកា
ហើយដែលជាអ្នកនាំសារចុះឡើងនៅក្នុងរង្វង់អាណាចក្រនេះ ។

chivalry / វីរធម៌ *(ន)* ជាទ្រឹស្តីឧត្តុង្គឧត្តមវិន័យនៅក្នុងក្រុមអប្បរូទ្ធិអឺរ៉ុប
នៅយុគសម័យកណ្ដាល ដែលផ្ដោតជាសំខាន់ទៅលើសេចក្ដី ក្លាហាន ស្មោះត្រង់
និងការគោរពចំពោះស្ត្រីភេទ និងជនទន់ខ្សោយ ។

Christianity / សាសនាគ្រិស្ត *(ន)*
សាសនាដែលចេញពីជីវិតនិងការទូន្មាន បង្រៀនរបស់ព្រះយេស៊ូ ។

circumnavigate / ធ្វើនាវាចរណ៍ជុំវិញផ្ទៃ *(កិ)*
ធ្វើដំណើរជុំវិញផ្ទៃភព លោក ។

clan / ត្រកូល *(ន)*
ក្រុមមនុស្សម្យ៉ាយក្រុមដែលមានទំនាក់ទំនងតាមរយៈការជាប់ សាច់ឈាម
ឬតាមរយៈការរៀបការ ។

clergy / បព្វជិត *(ន)* អ្នកដែលមានឥទ្ធិពលខ្ពស់ជាគេនៅក្នុងសាសនា ។

climate / អាកាសធាតុ *(ន)*
លក្ខណៈរបស់អាកាសធាតុនៅក្នុងតំបន់ជាក់លាក់ ណាមួយ
ដែលស្ថិតនៅក្នុងអំឡុងពេលមួយវែង ។

Clovis / អ្នកដឹកនាំខ្លូវីស *(ន)* ជាអ្នកដឹកនាំរបស់
ជនជាតិហ្រ្វេង័រដែលដណ្ដើម យកខេត្ដរ៉ូម៉ាំងរបស់តំបន់ហ្គោល នៅឆ្នាំ៤៨៦
នៃគ្រិស្តសករាជ ហើយក្រោយមកបាន
បង្កើតរាជាណាចក្រហ្រ្វេងដែលមាននិទ្ធិអំណាចដ៏ចំធេង ។

codex / សៀវភៅកំណត់ហេតុស័ខាន់ៗ *(ន)*
សៀវភៅប្រើប្រាស់នៅដើម អរ្យធម៌ ម៉ឺស្ល-អាមេរិក
សម្រាប់កត់ត្រាព្រឹត្តិការណ៍ប្រវត្តិសាស្ត្រស័ខាន់ៗ ។

Columbian Exchange / បន្លាស់ប្ដូរទំនិញកុល្អុមប៊ី *(ន)*
ការធ្វើការ ផ្លាស់ប្ដូររុក្ខៃ សត្វ និងរបស់មានជីវិតដទៃទៀត
រវាងអង្គរគោលខាងកើតនិងខាង លិច
បន្ទាប់ពីការមកដល់របស់នាវិកកូឡុំប៊ុសលើទឹកដីអាមេរិក
នៅឆ្នាំ១៤៩២នៃ គ្រិស្តសករាជ ។

Confucianism / លទ្ធិខុងជី *(ន)*
លទ្ធិនេះមានមូលដ្ឋានសំខាន់ចេញពីទ្រឹស្ដី បង្រៀនរបស់ ខុងជី
ដែលជាអ្នកប្រាជ្ញបង្រៀនផ្ដែកគុណធម៌និងសិលធម៌ ។

Constantine / រាជាធិរាជជុំម៉ាំង *(ន)*
រាជាធិរាជរបស់ទឹកដីរ៉ូម៉ាំងដែលចាប់
ផ្ដើមគ្រប់គ្រងពីឆ្នាំ៣០៦ដល់ឆ្នាំ៣៣៧នៃគ្រិស្តសករាជ
ដែលបានបញ្ឈប់ការធ្វើ ទុក្ខបុកម្នេញលើអ្នកកាន់សាសនាគ្រិស្ត
ហើយបានស្គាល់រដ្ឋធានីនៃចក្រភព បំសហ្រ្វានធឹម (ក្រោយមក
គេបានស្គាល់ថាជាទីក្រុងឧន្ស្ថេនទិណូផល) ។

continent / ទ្វីប *(ន)* ទឹកដីមួយក្នុងចំណោមទឹកដីទាំង៧
នៃភពផែនដី ដែលរួមមានអាមេរិកខាងជើង អាមេរិកខាងត្បូង អ៊ឺរ៉ុប
អាស៊ី អាហ្រ្វិក អូស្ត្រាលី និង អង់តាកទិកា ។

convert / ផ្លាស់ប្ដូរសាសនា *(កិ)*
បញ្ចុះបញ្ចូលនរណាម្នាក់ឱ្យទទួលយកជំនឿ ឬសាសនាថ្មីឱនុសសានសាដើម ។

Córdoba / រាជធានីខរដូបា *(ន)* រាជធានីរបស់តំបន់ អាល់
អៃនដាលូស ។

Cortés, Hernán / ខរតេស ហ៊ីណាន់ *(ន)*
អ្នករកឃើញជនជាតិអេស្ប៉ាញ ដែលបានដណ្ដើមគ្រប់គ្រងអារ្យធម៌អាស់តិច
របស់ប្រទេសម៉ិចស៊ិកូនៅឆ្នាំ១៥២១ នៃគ្រិស្តសករាជ ។

covenant / កតិកាសញ្ញា *(ន)*
កិច្ចព្រមព្រៀងរវៃតបន្លឹងចំណងសាមគ្គីភាព ។

Crusades / បុជនីយកិច្ច *(ន)*
ដំណើរវាយលុកជាបន្ដបន្ទាប់ពីសាសនាគ្រិស្តនៅ អឺរ៉ុប ទៅប៉ាឡេស្ទីន
រវាងឆ្នាំ សតវត្សរ៍ទី១១ ដល់ ១៣ នៃគ្រិស្តសករាជ ។

culture / វប្បធម៌ *(ន)*
របៀបនៃការរស់នៅដែលអនុវត្តដោយមនុស្សមួយ ក្រុម ។

D

daimyo / អធិរាជ ដាវ្យូ *(១)*
អធិរាជជប៉ុនដែលមានទ្រព្យសម្បត្តិជីផ្ទីជាច្រើន និងក្រុមទាហានសាមីរ៉ៃផ្ទាល់ខ្លួន ហើយនិងមិនបង់ពន្ធឲ្យរដ្ឋាភិបាលជប៉ុន ។

Daoism / សសនាតៅ *(១)*
សាសនាមួយដែលមានដើមកំណើតពីប្រទេសចិន នៅអំឡុងឆ្នាំ៥០០ មុនគ្រឹស្តសករាជ ដែលសង្កត់ធ្ងន់លើការរស់នៅជាមួយនឹង ធម្មជាតិ និងអារម្មណ៍ខាងក្នុងរបស់មនុស្ស ។

Declaration of Independence / ការប្រកាសឯករាជ្យ *(១)*
ឯកសារ ថ្លែងអំពីសេចក្តីប្រកាសឯករាជ្យរបស់សហរដ្ឋអាមេរិក ពីអណានិគមអង់គ្លេស ។

Declaration of the Rights of Man and of the Citizen / សេចក្តីប្រកាសសិទ្ធិមនុស្ស និងប្រជាពលរដ្ឋ *(១)*
ឯកសារដែលបង្កើតឡើង ដោយរដ្ឋាភិបាលបដិវត្តន៍របស់បារាំងនៅឆ្នាំ១៧៨៩ ដើម្បីទាមទារឲ្យមានសិទ្ធិ មនុស្ស ។

dissection / ការវះកាត់សត្វ ឬ រុក្ខជាតិ *(១)* ការវះកាត់រុក្ខជាតិ ឬ សត្វដើម្បី សិក្សា និង ស្រាវជ្រាវពីផ្នែកទាំងនោះ ។

divan / ក្រុមប្រឹក្សាផ្តល់យោបល់របស់សុលតង់ *(១)* ក្រុមប្រឹក្សាយោបល់ ដល់ស្តេច សុលតង់ នៅក្នុងចក្រភពអូតូម៉ាន់ ។

E

elevation / កំពស់ *(១)* កំពស់នៃដីលើកម្រិតទឹកសមុទ្រ ។

elite / អធិបតី *(១)* សមាជិកជាន់ខ្ពស់ ឬមានទ្រព្យសម្បត្តិច្រើនបំផុតនៅក្នុង សង្គមឬក្រុម ។

Elizabathan Age / សម័យអេលីហ្សាបិត *(១)*
អំឡុងពេលនៃការគ្រប់ គ្រងរបស់ម្ចាស់ក្សត្រីអេលីហ្សាបិតទីមួយ នៃចក្រភពអង់គ្លេស ចាប់ពីឆ្នាំ១៥៥៨ ដល់ឆ្នាំ១៦០៣ ។

embassy / ស្ថានទូត *(១)*
ជាការិយាល័យតំណាងឲ្យរដ្ឋាភិបាលរបស់ប្រទេស មួយនៅក្នុងប្រទេសដទៃមួយទៀត ។

emperor / រាជាធិរាជ *(១)* ជាអ្នកគ្រប់គ្រងរបស់ចក្រភពណាមួយ ។

empire / ចក្រភព *(១)* ក្រុមមនុស្សរួមដែលមានវប្បធម៌ ឬ ទឹកដីផ្សេងៗគ្នា ប៉ុន្តែ គ្រប់គ្រងដោយរាជាធិរាជតែមួយគត់ ។

enlightened despot / អ្នកកាន់អំណាចដែលមានការយល់ដឹងខ្ពស់
(១) អ្នកគ្រប់គ្រងដែលមានអំណាចពេញលេញ ប៉ុន្តែឃយចិត្តទុកដាក់ចំពោះគំនិត នយោបាយ ដែលចេញពីការរៀនសូត្រ ការបំភ្លឺពីការពិត ហើយឃ្ញាយាម គ្រប់គ្រងប្រទេសក្នុងផ្លូវវប្បធម៌មិនឲ្យមានការអបរំ ។

Enlightenment / ការបំភ្លឺពីធាតុពិតរបស់មនុស្ស *(១)*
ចលនាមួយបង្កើត ដោយទស្សនវិទូនៅក្នុងសតវត្សរ៍ទី១៨ដែលប្រើហេតុផល ក្នុងការស្វែងរកការពិតអំពីធាតុដើមរបស់មនុស្ស ។

epic poem / កំណាព្យវីរកថា *(១)*
ប្រភេទកំណាព្យម្យ៉ាងដែលបរិយាយអំពី ការផ្សងគ្រោះថ្នាក់របស់វីរបុរស ។

excavation / ការកាស់កកាយ *(១)*
ដំណើរនៃការកាស់កកាយវត្ថុតាង ប្រវត្តិសាស្ត្រសំខាន់ផ្សេងៗ ក្នុងគោលបំណងសិក្សាអំពីវត្ថុទាំងនោះ ។

F

faction / បក្សពួក *(១)*
ក្រុមតូចមួយដែលធ្វើការប្រឆាំងនឹងក្រុមដែលធំជាង ប៉ុន្តែស្ថិតនៅក្នុងក្រុមធំតែមួយ ។

federalism / សហព័ន្ធនិយម *(១)*
ការបែងចែកអំណាចរវាងអង្គការ ឬ រដ្ឋាភិបាលជាមួយសមាជិករបស់ខ្លួន ។

feudalism / សក្តិភូមិនិយម *(១)*
ប្រព័ន្ធនយោបាយឬសង្គមនៅបែបកអឺរ៉ុប ក្នុងមធ្យមសម័យ ដែលមហាក្សត្រផ្តល់ដីធ្លីដល់បរិវារដើម្បីជាថ្នូរនឹងការបម្រើ និងភក្តីភាព ។

Forbidden City / ទីក្រុងបណ្ដោះអាសន្ន *(១)*
ក្រុមនៃវាំងដែលមាន ៩ប្រាំង សាងសង់ឡើងសម្រាប់រាជាធិរាជចិន ក្នុងរយៈពេលខ្លីបន្ទាប់ពីឆ្នាំ ១៤០០ នៃគ្រឹស្តសករាជ នៅក្នុងរាជធានីបេក៉ាំង ។

Francis of Assisi, Saint / ព្រះខ្ញុំណាស្រេត សាសនាប្រាង់ប៊ីស ន៉ែ អាស៊ីស៊ី *(១)* ជនជាតិអីតាលី ដែលបានរកឃើញឲ្យច្បាប់សាសនាប្រាង់ស៊ីសសង់ នៅដើមសតវត្សរ៍ឆ្នាំ ១២០០នៃគ្រឹស្តសករាជ ។

G

Genghis Khan / អ្នកដឹកនាំហ្គាំងស៊ី ខាន់ *(១)* អ្នកដឹកនាំជនជាតិ ម៉ុងហ្គោល នៅអំឡុងឆ្នាំ១២០៦នៃគ្រឹស្តសករាជ ដែលចាប់ផ្តើមធ្វើយុទ្ធនាការ វាយទីអំណាចតាមរយៈបង្កើតចក្រភពមួយ ដែលគ្រប់គ្រងប្រទេសចិនខាងជើង និងអាស៊ីកណ្តាល ។

geocentric theory / ទ្រឹស្តីភូគព្វនាភី *(១)*
ទ្រឹស្តីមួយបែបដែលយល់ថា ផែនដីស្ថិតនៅចំកណ្តាលនៃសកល ។

geography / ភូមិវិទ្យា *(១)*
ការសិក្សាអំពីទ្រង់ទ្រាយរបស់ផែនដី ។

Ghana / ប្រទេសហ្គាណា *(១)*
តំបន់នេះស្ថិតនៅចន្លោះរវាងខ្សាច់សាហារ៉ា និងព្រៃនៅភាគខាងត្បូងនៃអាហ្រ្វិកខាងលិច ហើយតំបន់នេះសម្បូរទៅ ដោយវប្បធម៌បុរាណជាច្រើនបែប ។

glyph / ចម្លាក់លិច *(១)* រូបភាពដែលអាចតំណាងឲ្យពាក្យសម្តី ព្យាង្គ ឬ សម្លេង ។

golden age / យុគសម័យមាស *(១)*
ជារយៈកាលដែលវប្បធម៌ឬសង្គមមាន ការរីកចម្រើនបំផុត ។

Great Enclosure / មហាកំពែង *(ន)*
ការខណ្ឌចែកទីលំនៅជាងតែក្នុង ចំណោម
ផ្នែកទាំងពសង់ខាន់នៃទីលំនៅ របស់ស្ពូណានៃប្រទេស ហ្ស៊ីមបាវេ
ដែល ទំនងជាកន្លែងសម្រាប់ស្នាក់នៅរបស់ក្រុមរាជវង្ស ។

Great Schism / ក្រេត ស៊ីសហ្ស៊ីម *(ន)*
អង្គភាពអំណាចនៃវិហារសាសនា រ៉ូម៉ាំងកាតូលិក ដែលចាប់ផ្ដើមនៅឆ្នាំ១៣៧៨
រហូតដល់ ១៤១៧នៃគ្រិស្តសករាជ ដែលបានកើតឡើងនៅពេលដែលអំណាច
ធំៗរបស់សសានាកាតូលិក គឺ អាវីក ណុន និង រ៉ូម
ត្រូវបានបំបែកនិងមានការបោះ ឆ្នោតជ្រើសសង្ឃរាជផ្សេងគ្នា ។

Great Zimbabwe / ក្រេត ហ្ស៊ីមបាវេ *(ន)*
ការតាំងលំនៅមជ្ឈមរបស់ ចក្រពាស្ពូណា នៅអាហ្វ្រិក
ដែលហ៊ុមព័ទ្ធដោយជញ្ជាំងថ្មៗ ដែលគ្រប់ដណ្ដប់ ផ្ទៃដីជាង ១០០អារ
ហើយមានប្រជាពលរដ្ឋចន្លោះមួយម៉ឺនទៅពីរម៉ឺននាក់ ។

Gregory VII, Pope / ស្ដេចប៉ាប ហ្គ្រិកថ្វរីទី៧ *(ន)* សង្ឃរាជរបស់
សាសនាកាតូលិកពីឆ្នាំ១០៧៣ ដល់ឆ្នាំ១០៨៥ ដែលបានធ្វើការតស៊ូប្រឆាំង
ដណ្ដើមអំណាចជាមួយនឹងអធិរាជហ្វ៊នីទីប៊ូន ។

griot / អ្នកនិទានរឿង *(ន)*
ជាអ្នកនិទានរឿងផ្លូវការរបស់អារ្យធមិអាហ្វ្រិក ។

guild / អជីវសង្គម *(ន)*
ជាសមាគមន៍នៃមនុស្សមួយក្រុមដែលមានពាណិជ្ជកម្ម និងសិប្បកម្មដូចគ្នា
មានគោលបំណងចម្បត់ត្រួតពិនិត្យគុណភាព និងចំនួនរបស់ទំនិញ
ក៏ដូចជាការពារផលប្រយោជន៍របស់ពួកគេ ។

Guteberg, Johann / យ៉ូសបឺ៊ក ធូហាន់ *(ន)* ជនជាតិ
អាល្លឺម៉ង់ម្នាក់ ដែលនៅពាក់កណ្ដាលសតវត្សរ៍ឆ្នាំ១៤០០ នៃគ្រិស្តសករាជ
បានបង្កើតម៉ាស៊ីន បោះពុម្ពមួយប្រភេទដែលមានដុំអក្សរផ្លិតអាចប្ដើរបាន ។

H

habeas corpus / សិទ្ធិមិនជាប់ទោស *(ន)*
សិទ្ធិរបស់មនុស្សរំដែលមិនត្រូវ បានទទួលទោស
ក្នុងករណីការដាក់ទោសខុសច្បាប់ ។

haiku / ក្យូនកំណាព្យ៉ៃហគុ *(ន)* ក្យូនកំណាព្យជប៉ុនមួយប្រភេទដែលមាន
១៧ ព្យាង្គ រៀបជាបីបន្ទាត់គឺ ៥ . ៧ . និង ៥ព្យាង្គ ។

harmony / សុខដុមរម្យនា *(ន)*
ការបូកបញ្ចូលធាតុផ្សេងៗដើម្បីបង្កើតការ ពេញចិត្តមួយ ។

heliocentric / សុរិយានាគី *(គុ)* ដែលយកព្រះអាទិត្យជាទីមជ្ឈឹម ។

hemisphere / អឌ្ឍគោល *(ន)* ផ្នែកពាក់កណ្ដាលពីស្វ៊ីគ្តានៃផែនដី
ដែលខណ្ឌដោយខ្សែអេក្វាទ័រ ឬ ខ្សែវ៉ាណ៌ធំបង ។

Henry IV, Emperor / រាជាធិរាជហ៊ីនរីទី៤ *(ន)*
អ្នកគ្រប់គ្រងអំណាច របស់អាណាចក្រហ្សូលីរ៉ូម៉ាំង នាសតវត្សទី១១
ដែលបន្តធ្វើការតស៊ូដើម្បីអំណាច ជាមួយសង្ឃរាជ ហ្គ្រិកថ្វរីទី៧ ។

Hijrah / ហ៊ីជរាហ *(ន)* ការផ្លាស់ទីតាំងរបស់ម្ពូហាម៉ាត់ និង កូនចៅ ពី
មេកា ទៅទីក្រុងយ៉ាស្រ៊ីកក្នុងឆ្នាំ៦២២ នៃគ្រិស្តសករាជ ។

historian / ប្រវត្តិវិទូ *(ន)* អ្នកសិក្សា និង បកស្រាយប្រវត្តិសាស្ត្រ ។

history / ប្រវត្តិសាស្ត្រ *(ន)* ការសិក្សាលើព្រឹត្តិការណ៍ពីអតីតកាល ។

humanism / បុរាណភាសានិយម *(ន)*
ចលនាវិទ្យាសាស្ត្រសិល្បៈរបស់អឺរ៉ុប ប្រារព្ធឡើង
សម្រាប់បង្ហាញពីសារសំខាន់របស់មនុស្ស និង ស្នាដែលម្របរបស់ មនុស្ស
ក៏ដូចជាសង្កត់ធ្ងន់ទៅលើការសិក្សាមុខវិជ្ជាមួយចំនួនដូចជាប្រវត្តិសាស្ត្រ
វេយ្យាករណ៍ អក្សរសាស្ត្រ និង ទស្សនៈវិជ្ជា ។

Hundred Years' War / សង្គ្រាមរយឆ្នាំ *(ន)*
សង្គ្រាមជាបន្តបន្ទាប់ រវាងប្រទេសអង់គ្លេស និង បារាំងចាប់ពីឆ្នាំ
១៣៣៧ ដល់ឆ្នាំ ១៤៥៣ នៃគ្រិស្តសករាជ ។

I

Iberian Peninsula / ជ្រោយអីប៊ីរ៉េន *(ន)*
ជ្រោយនៅទិសនិរតីបែកអឺរ៉ុប ដែលជាទីតាំងរបស់ជនជាតិទំនើបអេស្បាញ
និង ប៊ុរទុយហ្គាល់ ។

**Ignatius of Loyola, Saint /
ព្រះខ្លឹណាស្រា សាសនា អ៊ីគណាធីអីស នៃ ឡូយ៉ូឡា** *(ន)*
ជនជាតិអេស្ប៉ាញដែលបានរកឃើញច្បាប់សាស័នា យេស៊ីត នៅដើមឆ្នាំ
១៥៣០ នៃគ្រិស្តសករាជ ។

imperial / នៃរាជាធិរាជ *(គុ)* ដែលទាក់ទងនឹងអាណាចក្រ ឬ
រាជាធិរាជ ។

indulgence / ការមិនប្រកាន់ទោស *(ន)*
ការមិនប្រកាន់ទោសដែលផ្ដល់ដោយ
សាសនាកាតូលិកចំពោះជនណាម្នាក់ដើម្បីឲ្យចេញសុ្ខពីការទទួលទារុណកម្មដោយ
ព្រះនៅជាតិខាងមុខ ។

Inquisition / សាលាក្ដី *(ន)* សាលាក្ដីបង្កើតឡើងដោយព្រះវិហាររ៉ូម៉ាំង
កាតូលិក នៅ ឆ្នាំ ១៥៤២ នៃគ្រិស្តសករាជ ដើម្បីតាមដានអ្នកដែលឃ្លាតចាក
ពីភាពស្មោះត្រង់ ចំពោះព្រះវិហារកាតូលិក និង ព្ម្រឹងអំណាចសម្រាប់
ព្រះវិហារ ។

Islam / សាសនាអ៊ីស្លាម *(ន)* ជាសាសនាឯកទេវនិយមដែលផ្ដែកលើ
ការបង្រៀនរបស់ម្ពូហាម៉ាត់ ។

J

janissary / ទាហានជេទីសារី *(ន)* សមាជិកមួយនៃវិវេរជនប្រយុទ្ធចក្រភព
អ៊ូតូម៉ាន់ ដែលបង្កើតឡើងដោយពីរស់ផ្នែកលើកម្លាំងទាសករជាច្រើន ។

Jesuit / យេស៊ីត *(ន)* អង្គនៃសង្ឃមសាសនាយេស៊ី ដែលជាច្បាប់សាសនា
ត្រូវបានរកឃើញព្រៃនៅដើមឆ្នាំ ១៥៣០ នៃគ្រិស្តសករាជ ដោយ ព្រះខ្លឹណាស្រា
អ៊ីគណាធីអីស នៃ ឡូយ៉ូឡា ។

Joan of Arc / ធូអាន់ នៃ អាក *(ន)*
ក្មេងស្រីវវិសករបារាំងដែលបានដឹកនាំ
ប្រទេសបារាំងទៅទល់ជ័យជនៈលើប្រទេសអង់គ្លេស នៅ
អូលីន នៅឆ្នាំ ១៤២៩ នៃ គ្រិស្តសករាជ ។

John, King / ព្រះមហាក្សត្រ ចន *(ន)* ព្រះមហាក្សត្រដែលបានចុះព្រះ
ហស្ថលេខាលើបញ្ជីច្បាប់ស្តីពីសិទ្ធិអភិជន ម៉ាកណា សាកតា នៅឆ្នាំ ១២១៥ នៃ
គ្រិស្តសករាជ ។

Justinian / រាជាធិរាជ ចាស្ទីនៀន *(ន)* អ្នកគ្រប់គ្រង
នៅចក្រភពពុំរ៉ាំងខាង កើត ចាប់ពីឆ្នាំ ៥២៧ ដល់ ៥៦៥ នៃគ្រិស្តសករាជ
ដែលបានគ្រប់គ្រងជាមួយ មហេសី ណ្យោះធេអូដូរ៉ា និង
បានដណ្តើមយកទឹកដីដែលបាត់បង់ទៅមកវិញ ។

Justinaian Code / ច្បាប់ ចាស្ទីនៀន
(ន) ក្រមច្បាប់ដែលបង្កើតឡើង
ក្រោមការដឹកនាំរបស់រាជាធិរាជចាស្ទិនៀននៃប្រទេសបីសង់ទីន ដែលទ្រឹស្ដី
ច្បាប់នេះត្រូវបានអនុវត្តន៍ជាច្រើននៅក្នុងជីវភាពរបស់ បីសង់ទីន ។

K

Kabuki / ល្ខោនកាប៊ូគី *(ន)* ល្ខោនជប៉ុនដែលបង្កើតនៅឆ្នាំ១៦០០
មុនគ្រិស្ត សករាជ ដែលសម្តែងពីរឿងកំសត់តាមរយៈការច្រៀង រាំ និង
មានតូអង្គលាបមុខ ក្រាស់ៗ ហើយស្ដើកសំលៀកបំពាក់ច្រាំ ។

Khmer Empire / អាណាចក្រខ្មែរ *(ន)*
ជាអាណាចក្រដែលមានអំណាច ចំចេង និង
មានរយៈពេលវែងជាគេបង្កស់នៅអាស៊ីអាគ្នេយ៍ ដែលមណ្ឌល
កណ្តាលនៃអាណាចក្រនោះសព្វថ្ងៃគឺ ប្រទេសកម្ពុជា ។

Kilwa / ទីក្រុងចាស់គីលវ៉ា *(ន)*
ជាទីក្រុងចំណោតមួយស្ថិតនៅឆ្នេរភាគខាង កើតនៃអាហ្វ្រិកដែលមានប្រជាជន
អ៊ីស្លាំ និង អារ៉ាប់មករស់នៅ ។ នៅចុង ឆ្នាំ ១២០០ នៃគ្រិស្តសករាជ
ការចូលមកនៅឆ្នេរនេះមានចំនួនច្រើនបំផុត ។

kinship / សាច់សាឡោហិត *(ន)*
ទំនាក់ទំនងកើតចេញពីការជាប់សាច់ឈាម រៀបការ និង
ការទទួលចូលជាសាច់ញាតិ ។

knight / អប្បរ៉ូទ្ធិ *(ន)* អ្នកប្រហារដែលមានការហ្វឹកហ្វឺនខ្ពស់
សម្រាប់បម្រើ ដល់ពួកអភិជន នៅអ៊ីរ៉ុប នាមស្មីមសម័យ ។

Kongo / រាជាណាចក្រកុងហ្គោ *(ន)*
រាជាណាចក្របុរាណមួយដែលស្ថិតនៅឆ្នេរ ខាងលិចនៃអាហ្វ្រិក
ដែលជាផ្នែករស់រ៉ាស់របស់ប្រជាជនកុងហ្គោនិយាយភាសា ប៉ិនទូ
នៅអំឡុងមួយមុនសតវត្សទី១៤ នៃគ្រិស្តសករាជ ។

Koryo / រាជាណាចក្រកូរ៉ូ *(ន)*
ជារាជាណាចក្រនៅឧបទ្វីបកូរ៉េ បង្កើតឡើង នៅឆ្នាំ ៩៣៥
នៃគ្រិស្តសករាជបន្ទាប់ពីការដួលរលំរបស់រាជាណាចក្រស៊ីល្លា ។

Kublai Khan / គូបឡៃ ខាន់ *(ន)* ជាចៅប្រុសរបស់
ហ្សាំងស៊ី ខាន់ ដែល កាន់អំណាចនៅភាគខាងត្បូងនៃប្រទេសចិន
ក្នុងឆ្នាំ១២៦០ នៃគ្រិស្តសករាជ
ហើយក៏ជាអ្នករ៉ាយឈ្នះសង្គ្រាមជាមួយទាហានសុងនៅឆ្នាំ១២៧៩
ដែលធ្វើឱ្យ ម៉ុងហ្គោលអាចគ្រប់គ្រងប្រទេសចិនទាំងមូល ។

L

labor specialization / ជំនាញការងារ *(ន)*
ការធ្វើការងារជាក់លាក់ ដោយបុគ្គលិកដែលបានទទួលការហ្វឹកហ្វឺន និង
មានជំនាញប្រចំណោះដឹង ។

landform / សណ្ឋានដី *(ន)* ជាទ្រង់ទ្រាយនៃផ្ទៃផែនដី ដែលមានមកពី
ធម្មជាតិ ដូចជា ដី ភ្នំ ឬ ខ្លង់រាប ជាដើម ។

latitude / រយៈទឹង *(ន)* ជារង្វាស់ចម្ងាយនៃភាគខាងជើង ឬ ត្បូង
នៃខ្សែ អេក្វាទ័រ ។

Leonardo da Vinci / ឡេអូណាដូ ដា វិនស៊ី *(ន)* ជាងសិល្បៈគំនូរ
ជនជាតិអ៊ីតាលីម្នាក់ មានកំណើតនៅឆ្នាំ ១៤៥២ នៃគ្រិស្តសករាជ ដែលបានគូរ
គំនូរជាស្នាដៃកជាច្រើន រួមមាន ម៉ូណា លីសា និង ឌីឡ្លាស់ ស៊ុបជ៍ហើយគាត់
ក៏ពូកែខាងផ្នែកវិស្សាស្ត្រវិទ្យាវិទ្យាសាស្ត្រដែរ ។

longbow / ធ្នូវែង *(ន)*
ប្រភេទធ្នូវែងម្យ៉ាងដែលអាចបាញ់ទម្លុះខែលរបស់ ទាហានជិះសេះបាន ។

longitude / រយៈបណ្ដោយ *(ន)* ជារង្វាស់ចម្ងាយនៃភាគខាងកើត
ឬ ខាងលិច នៃអក្ស្សគោល ។

lord / ខុនណាង *(ន)*
អភិជនដែលកាប់កាប់ដីធ្លីជាច្រើន និង មានអំណាច ។

Luther, Martin / ទេវិទូ លូថ័រ ម៉ាទីន *(ន)*
ទេវិទូជនជាតិអាល្លឺម៉ង់ កើតនៅឆ្នាំ ១៤៨៣ នៃគ្រិស្តសករាជ
ដែលជាអ្នកដឹកនាំការកែសាសនា និង បង្រៀនពីការជួយស្រោចស្រង់ពីព្រះ
ដោយសារការមានភក្តីភាពជាមុខព្រះ
មិនមែនដោយសារការប្រព្រឹត្តូអំពើល្អនោះទេ ។

M

Magna Carta / បញ្ជីរសិទ្ធិមៃកណា ខាត *(ន)*
ជាបញ្ជីរាយអំពីសិទ្ធិដែល សរសេរឡើងដោយពួកអភិជន
របស់ប្រទេសអង់គ្លេស ហើយត្រូវបានចុះ ព្រះហស្ថលេខាខាងដោយ
ព្រះមហាក្សត្រ ចន នៅឆ្នាំ ១២១៥ នៃគ្រិស្តសករាជ ។

maize / ពោត ម៉ៃ *(ន)*
ជាប្រភេទពោតមួយប្រភេទដែលដាំដោយអារ្យធម៌ ជនជាតិដើមអាមេរិក ។

Mali / ចក្រភពម៉ាលី *(ន)* ជាចក្រភពមួយរបស់អាហ្វ្រិកខាងលិច
ហើយដែល បង្កើតឡើងដោយក្រុមមនុស្សឈ្មោះម៉ាលីងកេ ។

Manchu / រាជវង្សម៉ាន់ជូ *(ន)*
ជាក្រុមសមាជិករបស់ប្រទេសចិនភាគឥសាន
ដែលបានគ្រប់គ្រងអំណាចនៅប្រទេសចិន នៅឆ្នាំ ១៦៤៤ នៃគ្រិស្តសករាជ
ហើយ បានបង្កើត រាជវង្សចុងក្រោយគេបង្កស់នៅក្នុងប្រវត្តិសាស្ត្រចិន
ដែលហៅថា រាជវង្សឈេង ។

manor / ភូមិគ្រឹះ *(ន)* សម្បត្តិដីធ្លីសក្តិភូមិរបស់ពួកអភិជន
ដែលជាទូទៅរួម មានអគារវិងម៉ា ឬ ប្រាសាទ ។

Mansa Musa / រាជាធិរាជ ម៉ាន់សា ម៉ូសា
(ន.) ជារាជាធិរាជជាអាណាចក្រ ម៉ាលី
ដែលបានធ្វើធម្មយាត្រាដ៏ល្បីល្បាញមួយទៅកាន់
មេកា នៅឆ្នាំ ១៣២៤ នៃគ្រិស្តសករាជ ។

maritime / នៃសមុទ្រ *(គុ.)* ដែលទាក់ទង ឬ នៅជិតសមុទ្រ ។

Maya / អារ្យធម៌ម៉ាយ៉ា *(ន.)*
ជាអារ្យធម៌មួយនៃប្រទេសមិកស៊ិកកូខាងត្បូង និង
នៅចំណុចនៃភាគខាងត្បូងអាមេរិក ដែលមានការវិវត្តច្រើនខ្លះបំផុត
នៅ ចន្លោះឆ្នាំ ២៥០ ទៅ ៩០០ នៃគ្រិស្តសករាជ ។

Mbanza / ទីក្រុងម៉ាបែនហ្សា *(ន.)*
ជារដ្ឋធានីរបស់រាជាណាចក្រកុងហ្គោ បុរាណ នៅអាហ្រ្វិក ។

mercantilism / ពាណិជ្ជវិស័យនិយម
(ន.) នយោបាយសេដ្ឋកិច្ចដែលផ្តែកលើ
គំនិតដែលថាអំណាចរបស់រដ្ឋអាស្រ័យទៅនឹងធនធានហិរញ្ញវត្ថុរបស់រដ្ឋ ។

mercenary / ភតិការី *(ន.)* ទាហានដែលគេជួលឱ្យទៅវាយ ។

Meso-America / ម៉ីស្ទ-អាមេរិក *(ន.)*
តំបន់ដែលរួមមានភាគខាងត្បូង នៃប្រទេសមិកស៊ិកកូ
និងភាគច្រើននៃតំបន់អាមេរិកកណ្តាល ។

Michelangelo / សិល្បករម៉ៃឃើលលេងហ្គីលឡូ *(ន.)*
សិល្បករជនជាតិ អ៊ីតាលីមួយរូប កើតនៅឆ្នាំ ១៤៧៥
នៃគ្រិស្តសករាជ ដែលមានជនាញចំបង ជាជាងម្នាក់
បំផ្នៃតក៏បានគូររូបដែលមានភាពល្បីល្បាញមួយទៀតដែរ
គឺនៅលើពិដានដំបូលវិហារ ស៊ីសស្ទីន នៅទីក្រុងរ៉ូម ប្រទេសអ៊ីតាលី ។

Middle Ages / មជ្ឈិមសម័យ *(ន.)*
ជាសម័យកាលមួយនៃប្រវត្តិសាស្រ្តរបស់ អ៊ឺរ៉ុប
ដែលរាប់ចាប់ពីការដួលរលំរបស់រ៉ូម និង រ៉ែណេសាន់ គឺពីឆ្នាំ
៥០០ ដល់ឆ្នាំ ១៤៥០ នៃគ្រិស្តសករាជ ។

missionary / សាសនទូត *(ន.)*
អ្នកធ្វើដំណើរទៅប្រទេសផ្សេងៗដើម្បី ផ្សព្វផ្សាយសាសនា ។

monastery / វត្ត ឬ វិហារ *(ន.)*
ទីកន្លែងសម្រាប់សមាជិកនៃសាសនាណា មួយមកប្រតិបត្តិជីវិតជាអ្នកឧទ្ទិស
និង ការគោរព ។

Mongol Ascendancy / ការគ្រប់គ្រារបស់ម៉ុងហ្គោល *(ន.)*
ជារយៈពេល មួយដែលម៉ុងហ្គោលគ្រប់គ្រងភូមិភាគកណ្តាលនៃអាស៊ី
ហើយធ្វើឱ្យភូមិភាគ ទាំងនេះជាកន្លែងធ្វើពាណិជ្ជកម្មផ្លូវគោក និង
មានសុវត្ថិភាពសម្រាប់ធ្វើដំណើរ ឆ្លងកាត់ ។

monotheism / ឯកាទិទេវនិយម *(ន.)* ជំនឿចំពោះតែព្រះមួយ ។

Montezuma II / រាជាធិរាជម៉ុងតេហ្ស៊ូម៉ា ២ *(ន.)*
រាជាធិរាជចុងក្រោយគេ បង្អស់នៃអាណាចក្រអាស់ធិក
ដែលគ្រប់គ្រងអំណាចចាប់ពីឆ្នាំ ១៥០២ ដល់ ឆ្នាំ ១៥២០ នៃគ្រិស្តសករាជ
ហើយក្រោយមកត្រូវបានមន្ត្រាក់ពីតំណែងដោយពួក អេស្ប៉ាញ ។

mosaic / រូបគំនូរផ្តិតម៉ូសាអ៊ិក *(ន.)*
គំនូរដែលផ្តិតឡើងដោយថ្មក្បៀ្រសពណ៌តូចៗ ឬ ដោយកំទេចកញ្ចក់ជាច្រើន ។

mosque / វិហារម៉ូស្លីម *(ន.)*
ព្រះវិហារសម្រាប់អ្នកកាន់សាសនាម៉ូស្លីមមក គោរព
ដែលសាងសង់បែរទៅរកទីក្រុងមេកា ។

mother culture / វប្បធម៌មេ *(ន.)* ជាវប្បធម៌ដែលផ្តល់ទម្រង់ និង
មាន ឥទ្ធិពលទៅលើប្រពៃណី និង គំនិតនៃវប្បធម៌ដែលកើតក្រោយៗឡើត ។

movable type / ប្រភេទម៉ាស៊ីនបោះពុម្ពអាចលេងនាបាន
(ន.) ដុំដែលកប្បឈើ មានអក្សរតែមួយដែលសើបម្ងើង
ដែលគេប្រើប្រាស់សម្រាប់បោះពុម្ពអក្សរ ។

Murasaki Shikibu, Lady / អ្នកនិពន្ធ ម៉ូរ៉ាសាតិ ស៊ីគីបុ
(ន.) អ្នកនិពន្ធ ជប៉ុនមួយរូបនៅដើមសតវត្សរ៍ឆ្នាំ ១០០០
នៃគ្រិស្តសករាជ ដែលបានសរសេរ *រឿងនិទាន របស់ ហ្គិនហ្ស៊ី*
ដែលត្រូវបានទទួលស្គាល់ជាប្រឡោមលោកទី១ របស់ ពិភពលោក ។

Muslim / អ្នកកាន់សាសនាម៉ូស្លីម *(ន.)* អ្នកកាន់សាសនាអ៊ីស្លាម
ហើយទទួល យកព្រះអល្លោះ ជាព្រះតែមួយគត់ ។

Mutapa / រាជាណាចក្រមុីតាប៉ា *(ន.)*
រាជាណចក្រក៏ណ៏ណ៍មួយបង្កើតនិង
ជាគ្រប់គ្រងអំណាចដោយមហាក្សត្រស្ទ្សៀ នៅឆ្នាំប្រហែល ១៤៥០
នៃគ្រិស្ត សករាជ បច្ចុប្បន្នតំបន់នេះជាប្រទេសហ្ស៊ីមបាវេ ។

N

Nam Viet / រាជាណាចក្រណាមវៀត *(ន.)*
ជារាជាណាចក្ររបស់វៀតណាម
ដែលស្ថិតនៅក្រោមការគ្រប់គ្រងរបស់ប្រទេសចិនឆ្នាំ ១១១
មុនគ្រិស្តសករាជ ។

natural rights / សិទ្ធិធម្មជាតិ *(ន.)* សិទ្ធិដែលមនុស្សមានតាំងពីកំនើត
ដូចជា សិទ្ធិរស់រានមានជីវិត សេរីភាព និង កម្មសិទ្ធ
បើយោងទៅតាមទស្សនវិទូ ឈ្មោះ ចន ឡុក នៅសតវត្សរ៍ទី១៨ ។

Noh / ឈោណ *(ន.)*
ប្រភេទឈោនជប៉ុនម្យ៉ាងដែលមានដើមកំនើតសតវត្សរ៍ឆ្នាំ ១៣០០
នៃគ្រិស្តសករាជ ដែលជាម្ងួតា បង្ហាញឱ្យឃើញពីរឿងព្រេងនិទាន ផ្សេងៗ
តាមរយៈតួសម្ដែងដែលមានពាក់មុខលើលាបាណាំ ។

nomad / ចរកជន *(ន.)* មនុស្សដែលផ្លាស់ទីពីកន្លែងមួយទៅកន្លែងមួយ
ជាជាង រស់នៅទីកន្លែងណាមួយជាប់លាប់ ។

O

oasis / តំបន់អូអាស៊ីស *(ន.)*
ទីកន្លែងដែលមានជីជាតិមួយស្ថិតនៅកណ្តាល វាលខ្សាច់ ។

Olmec / វប្បធម៌អូលមិក *(ន.)* ជាវប្បធម៌មុនដ៏បូរបង្កស់របស់
ម៉ីស្ត-អាមេរិក ដែលរីករាំចំនើនចាប់ ពីឆ្នាំ ១២០០ ដល់ ៤០០
មុនគ្រិស្តសករាជ ដែលមណ្ឌល កណ្តាលនៃវប្បធម៌នេះស្ថិតនៅភាគ
អាគ្នេយ៍នៃប្រទេសមិកស៊ិកកូ ។

Omar Khayyám / អ្នកនិពន្ធកំណាព្យអូម៉ា ខាយយ៉ាំ (១)
អ្នកនិពន្ធ កំណាព្យមូស្លីម ជនជាតិអារ្សេរ្យ៉ន ដែលធម្មតា
គាត់សរសេរកំណាព្យ៧អក្សរ៤ ហើយគាត់ក៏ជាគណិតវិទ្យូដ៏អស្ចារ្យមួយរូបដែរ ។

oral history / ប្រវត្តិសាស្ត្រចេញពីការនិយាយ (១) ប្រវត្តិដែលចេញពី
ការនិយាយពីជំនាន់មួយទៅជំនាន់មួយទៀត ដោយមិនតាមរយៈការសរសេរ ។

Orthodox / គន្ថឬដ៏ិបន្ថ (គុ)
ដែលទាក់ទងនឹងវិហារសាសនាគ្រឹស្តដែលវិវត្តន៍ នៅក្នុងចក្រភពបីហ្សាន់ទីន
ហើយមិនស្ថិតនៅក្រោមឥទ្ធិពលរបស់សង្ឃរាជណា មួយទេ ។

Osman / អ្នកដឹកនាំ អូស្មេន (១)
ជាអ្នកដឹកនាំជនជាតិមូយរូបដែលបាន បង្កើតចក្រភពអូតូម៉ាន់នៅឆ្នាំ
១៣០០ នៃគ្រឹស្តសករាជ ។

P

Pacal II / មហាក្សត្រប៉ាកាល់ទី២ (១) ព្រះមហាក្សត្រអស្ចារ្យជាងគេមួយ
ដែលគ្រប់គ្រងទីក្រុងម៉ាយ៉ាន់នៃប្រទេសជាលីនហ្សេ
ប្រហែលរយៈពេល៧០ឆ្នាំ (ពី ឆ្នាំ ៦១៥ នៃគ្រឹស្តសករាជ) ។

Pachacuti / អ្នកគ្រប់គ្រងប៉ាកាយុទី (១) អ្នកគ្រប់គ្រងទី៩ នៃចក្រភព
អ៊ីនកា នៅក្នុងឆ្នាំ ១៤៣៨ នៃគ្រឹស្តសករាជ ហើយបានពង្រីកឥទ្ធិពលអំណាច
របស់ចក្រភព អ៊ីនកា ។

parliament / តំណាងរាស្ត្រ (១) ក្រុមនៃអ្នកតំណាង
ដែលមានអំណាចខ្លះ នៅក្នុងរដ្ឋាភិបាល ។

patron / បរិបាល (១) អ្នកគាំទ្រសកម្មភាព ឬ
ស្ថាប័នណាមួយដោយផ្ដល់នូវ ការគាំទ្រខាងហិរញ្ញវត្ថុ ។

Peace of Westphalia / កិច្ចព្រមព្រៀងសិទ្ធិភាពវេស្តផាលៀ
(១) កិច្ច ព្រម ព្រៀងដែលធ្វើឡើងនៅឆ្នាំ១៦៤៨ នៃគ្រឹស្តសករាជ
ដែលទទួលស្គាល់ ការបំបែករបស់អឺរ៉ុបបែកខាងលិចទៅជាជាតិកាន់
សាសនាកាតូលិក និង ប្រុតេសតង់ ហើយបានបញ្ចប់សង្គ្រាមសាស
នាវាំរៃជាច្រើន ។

perspective / កំឡុរបើមៃពីទិដ្ឋភាព (១) វិធីសាស្ត្រនៃកំឡុរមួយបែប
កើតនៅក្នុង សម័យរ៉េណែសាន់ ដែលបង្ហាញអំពីរវាងវត្ថុជាបីលំហារ ។

philosophe / ទស្សនវិទូ (១)
អ្នកគិតអស្ចារ្យមួយរូបនៅក្នុងសតវត្សទី១៨
ដែលចង់បញ្ចូលវិធីសាស្ត្រវិទ្យាសាស្ត្រទៅក្នុងបញ្ហាសង្គម ។

pilgrimage / ធម្មយាត្រា (១)
ការធ្វើដំណើរជាក្រុមទៅកាន់កន្លែងសាសនា ឬ ចេតិយ ។

Pizzaro, Francisco / ភីហ្សារ៉ូ
ហ្វ្រង់ស៊ីស្កូ (១) ជាអ្នកផ្សងព្រេង ជនជាតិ
អេស្ប៉ាញមួយរូបដែលធ្វើដំណើរមកដល់ប្រទេសប៉េរូនៅឆ្នាំ ១៥៣២
នៃគ្រឹស្តសករាជ ហើយបានដណ្ដើមអំណាចគ្រប់គ្រងលើចក្រភព អ៊ីនកា
នៅឆ្នាំ ១៥៣៣ នៃគ្រឹស្តសករាជ ។

Polo, Marco / ពាណិជ្ជករ ប៉ូឡូ ម៉ាកូ (១) អ្នកធ្វើពាណិជ្ជកម្មជនជាតិ
វីណីទ្យេន ដែលបានធ្វើដំណើរឆ្លងកាត់ ផ្លូវស្ងួត មកដល់ប្រទេសចិននៅឆ្នាំ
១២៧៥ នៃគ្រឹស្តសករាជ ។ គាត់បានក្លាយជាអ្នកជំនិតរបស់មហាក្សត្រ គូបឡៃ
ខាន ហើយក្រោយមកបានបោះពុម្ពសៀវភៅដ៏មានប្រជាប្រិយភាពអំពីការផ្សង
ព្រេងរបស់គាត់ ។

porcelain / ព័រស៊ីឡេន (១) សារធាតុរឹងពណ៌សម្រាំង
ដែលជាទឹកទៅហៅថា ថ្ម គែរ ព័រស៊ីឡេន ។

predestination / ព្រហ្មលិខិត (១)
ការផ្ដល់ឱ្យពីព្រះដល់មនុស្សនូវការ ស្រោចស្រង់ និង ការផ្ដន្ទា
នៅមុនពេលមនុស្សចាប់កំណើត ដែលមនុស្សមិនអាច ប្រឆាំងបាន ។

primary source / ប្រភពដើម (១) ឯកសារ ឬ
វត្ថុមួយបង្កើត ឡើងនៅក្នុងអំឡុងព្រឹត្តការប្រវត្តិសាស្ត្រណាមួយ ។

printing press / ម៉ាស៊ីនបោះពុម្ព (១)
ជាប្រភេទម៉ាស៊ីនប្រើសម្រាប់ថ្លើមឱ្យ ក្រដាស់ប៉ះនឹងទឹកខ្មៅរបស់ម៉ាស៊ី
នពុម្ពតាមរយៈដុំអក្សរដែលធើ្វចុះឡើង ។

projection / ការបញ្ចាំងបង្ហាញ (១)
ការបង្ហាញសណ្ឋានដីតាមរយៈរូបផែន ទីរាបស្មើ និង
រក្សាបន្ថាស់បូរនេះឱ្យមានភាពដូច១គ្នា និងមានរូបរេបៀបរយ ។

Protestant / ប្រូតេស្តង់ (១) ជាក្រុមសាសនាយេស៊ូ
មួយដែលបែក ចេញពីរ៉ុមាុំងកាតូលិក នៅក្នុង ឬ បន្ទាប់ពីសតវត្សទី១៦ ។

Q

quipu / ប្រដាប់រាប់ (១) ឧបករណ៍រាប់ម្យ៉ាងរបស់អារ្យធមិបុរាណអ៊ីនកា
ដែលធ្វើឡើងដោយចំណាងលើខ្សែមួយ និង ចំណាងជាច្រើនកន្លែង ។

Qur'an / គម្ពីគោរ៉ាន់ (១)
ជាសៀវភៅគម្ពីរនៅក្នុងសាសនាម៉ុស្លីម មានថ្លៃង បង្ហាញពីព្រះអល្ឡា
ហើយសៀវភៅនេះបានរៀបធ្វើឡើងដោយអ្នកគោរព មួយមា៉ត់
បន្ទាប់ការសុគតរបស់គាត់ ។

R

rationalism / សនិទាននិយម (១)
គំនិតមួយដែលថាមនុស្សគួរប្រើហេតុ ផល និង
ការគិតតាមតក្កក្នុងការស្វែងយល់អំពីពិភពលោក ។

Reconquista / ការយោសនាបណ្ដេញមូស្លីមចេញពីរៀម (១)
យុទ្ធនាការ ជាបន្លួបន្ទាប់ដែលបានបញ្ចប់នៅ ឆ្នាំ ១៤៩២
នៃគ្រឹស្តសករាជ យោសនា ដោយ ទ័ពរបស់សាសនាគ្រឹស្តដើម្បី
ដែលបានបណ្ដេញអ្នកគ្រប់ គ្រងមូស្លីមចេញពីប្រទេស អេស្ប៉ាញ ។

Reformation / ការកែទម្រង់ (១)
ចលនាមួយដែលកើតឡើងនៅក្នុង សតវត្សរ៍ ទី១៦
ដើម្បីប្រឆាំងនឹងរ៉ុមាុំងកាតូលិក ។

regent / រាជានុសិទ្ធ (១)
អ្នកដែលគ្រប់គ្រងនៅពេលអវត្តមានព្រះមហាក្សត្រ ឬ
ព្រះមហាក្សត្រមិនទាន់គ្រប់អាយុគ្រងរាជ្យ ។

religious order / គណៈសាសនា (១)
ក្រុមមនុស្សមួយក្រុមដែលរស់នៅ តាម ច្បាប់របស់សាសនា ។

Renaissance / រីណែសាង់ *(ន)* ជាសម័យកាលដែលសិល្បៈ អក្សរសាស្ត្រ គំនិត ចាប់ផ្តើមមានកំនើតឡើងវិញ នៅឆ្នាំប្រហែល ១៣០០ ដល់ ១៦០០ នៃ គ្រិស្តសករាជ ។ ការរស់ឡើងវិញនេះគឺចាប់ផ្តើមមុនគេនៅប្រទេស អ៊ីតាលី ហើយបានសាយភាយទូទាំងទ្វីបអឺរ៉ុប ។

republic / សាធារណរដ្ឋ *(ន)* ទំរង់របស់រដ្ឋាភិបាលមួយប្រភេទដែលអំណាច ស្ថិតនៅលើប្រជាជន ដែលមានសិទ្ធិបោះឆ្នោតរើសអ្នកដឹកនាំដោយខ្លួនឯង ។

reunify / ការរួបរួម *(កិ)* ការរួបរួមឡើងវិញម្តងទៀត ។

Roman Catholic / នៃសាសនារ៉ូម៉ាំង កាតូលិក *(គុ)* ដែលទាក់ទងនឹង វិហារសាសនាយេស៊ូនៅលោកខាងលិច ដែលស្ថិតនៅក្រោមអំណាចរបស់ សង្ឃរាជបាប ។

S

Sahara / វាលខ្សាច់សាហារ៉ា *(ន)* វាលខ្សាច់ដ៏ធំមហិមានៅក្នុងអាហ្រ្វិកខាង ជើង ដែលលាតសន្ធឹងពីឆ្នេរអាត្លង់ទិក ដល់ទន្លេនីល ។

Saladin / មេទ័ពសាឡាឌីន *(ន)* មេទ័ពដែលកែនអ្នកកាន់សាសនាមូស្លីម ធ្វើសង្គ្រាមប្រឆាំងនឹងពួកសាសនាយេស៊ូ នៅចុងឆ្នាំស្ទីន ក្នុងអំឡុងសតវត្សរ៍ទី ១២ នៃគ្រិស្តសករាជ ។

salon / ការប្រមូលផ្តុំអ្នកគិត និង សិល្បករ *(ន)* ការប្រមូលផ្តុំទស្សនវិទូ និង សិល្បករដើម្បីពិភាក្សាពូករយោបល់ក្នុងពេលធ្វើការសិក្សាពីធាតុពិតរ បស់មនុស្ស ។

samurai / ក្រុមសាំមីរ៉ៃ *(ន)* អ្នកធ្វើសង្គ្រាមដែលទទួលការហ្វឹកហ្វឺនរបស់ ពួកអភិជនជប៉ុន ។

savanna / វាលស្មៅសាវ៉ាណា *(ន)* វាលស្មៅរាបស្មើរមួយដែលមានដើមឈើ បន្តិចបន្តួច ស្ថិតនៅក្នុងតំបន់ត្រូពិច ។

schism / ការបំបែកក្រុមជាផ្លូវការ *(ន)* ការបំបែកជាផ្លូវការរវាងក្រុមពីរ ។

scholar-official / មន្ត្រីដែលមានចំណេះដឹង *(ន)* អ្នកដែលមានចំណេះដឹង ខ្ពស់ហើយមានតំណែងក្នុងជួររដ្ឋាភិបាល ។

scientific method / ក្បួនវិទ្យាសាស្ត្រស្រាវជ្រាវ *(ន)* វិធីសាស្ត្រស្រាវជ្រាវ មួយដែលមានការធ្វើរួមក្នុងការកត់សម្គាល់យ៉ាង ប្រុងប្រយ័ត្ន បង្កើត និងធ្វើការ សាកល្បងសម្មតិកម្ម និង បង្កើតជាសេចក្តីសន្និដ្ឋានមួយដែលអាចបញ្ជាក់ឲ្យបាន តែផ្អែកលើអ្វីសម្មតិកម្ម ។

Scientific Revolution / បដិវត្តន៍វិទ្យាសាស្ត្រ *(ន)* រយៈពេលមួយចាប់ ផ្តើមនៅក្នុងឆ្នាំ ១៥០០ នៃគ្រិស្តសករាជ ដែលពួកអ្នកប្រាជ្ញអឺរ៉ុបចាប់ផ្តើមសួរ ទៅលើគំនិតវិទ្យាសាស្ត្របុរាណ និង ជំនឿចំពោះសាសនាយេស៊ូ ។

secondary source / ប្រភពទីពីរ *(ន)* ការងារដែលធ្វើចេញពីព្រឹត្តិការណ៍ ប្រវត្តិសាស្ត្រដោយនរណាម្នាក់ដែលមិនបានស្ថិតនៅក្នុងព្រឹត្តិការណ៍នោះ ។

Seljuk Turk / អ្នកដឹកនាំសែលជឹក ទឹក *(ន)* អ្នកកាន់កាប់អំណាចជនជាតិ ទួរគី មួយរូបដែលគ្រប់គ្រងលើអាស៊ីកណ្តាល និង អាស៊ីខាងលិច ចាប់ពីសតវត្សរ៍ ទី ១១ ដល់សតវត្សរ៍ទី១៣ ។

serf / អ្នកស្រែចម្ការ *(ន)* ក្រុមអ្នកស្រែចម្ការនៅក្នុងសម័យសក្តិភូមិ ដែលធ្វើ ការឲ្យពួកភិជនដើម្បីជាថ្នូរនឹងការការពារ និង ទទួលបានសិទ្ធិជាកាប់លោកម៉ូយ ចំនួន ។

Shakespeare, William / អ្នកកវីនិពន្ធ វីល្លៀម សេកស្ពៀរ *(ន)* អ្នក និពន្ធជនជាតិអង់គ្លេសដ៏ល្បីល្បាញនៅសម័យរីណែសាង ដែល ស្គាល់ល្បោម របស់ គាត់ដែលល្បីល្បោះជាងគេនោះគឺ *រ៉ូមីអូ និង ជូលៀត* និង *ហែម៉លែត* ។

Shi'a / ក្រុមសាសនាស៊ីអា *(ន)* ក្រុមសាសនាមូស្លីមមួយក្រុមដែលប្រឆាំងនឹង ច្បាប់ អ៊ីម៉ែយ៉ាត់ ដោយជឿថាព្រះចៅកាលីហ្ឌជាសាត់ញាតិរបស់ព្យាការី ម៉ូហាម៉ាត់ ។

Shinto / សាសនាស៊ីនតូ *(ន)* សាសនារបស់ជប៉ុនមួយដែលជឿលើការបន់ស្រន់ និង ការគោរពចំពោះធម្មជាតិ និង បុព្វជន ។

shogun / មេទ័ពស្ថូហ្គុន *(ន)* មេទ័ពជប៉ុនដែលជាក្រុមមួយឡើងកាន់អំណាច ដ៏ប្លូងគេនៅឆ្នាំ១១៩២ នៃគ្រិស្តសករាជ ហើយបានគ្រប់គ្រងក្នុងនាមជាការ៉ាជិរ៉ាជ ប៉ុន្តែជាធម្មតាគឺបម្រើប្រយោជន៍ផ្ទាល់ខ្លួនរបស់ពួកគេ ។

Shona / វប្បធមិស្ហូណា *(ន)* វប្បធមិដែលបង្រើភាសាបែនទូ ហើយបង្កប់ប្បន្ត ជាប្រទេសបូព៌ាណ មួយហ្វាប៊ីក និងហ្ស៊ីមបារវ៉េ នៅឆ្នាំ១០០០នៃគ្រិស្តសករាជ ។

Shotoku, Prince / ព្រះអង្គម្ចាស់ ស្ថូតូកុ *(ន)* រាជាមួយរូបដែលគ្រប់គ្រង ប្រទេសជប៉ុនពីឆ្នាំ ៥៩៣ ដល់ ៦២២ នៃគ្រិស្តសករាជ ហើយបាននាយកវប្បធមិ ចិន ជាពិសេសគឺសាសនាព្រះពុទ្ធ មកក្នុងប្រទេសជប៉ុន ។

Silk Roads / ផ្លូវសូត្រ *(ន)* ជាច្រកពាណិជ្ជកម្មបុរាណមួយដែលភ្ជាប់ទ្វីប អឺរ៉ុប និង ប្រទេសចិន ។

slash-and-burn agriculture / កសិកម្មឆ្ការរដុត *(ន)* ការដាំដុះដំណាំ មួយប្រភេទ ដែលគេកាប់ឆ្ការ និង ដុតដើមឈើរាស់ចោលដើម្បីដាំដុំណាំថ្មី ។

Songhai / សុងហៃ *(ន)* ជនជាតិអាហ្រ្វិកខាងលិច ដែលអ្នកដឹកនាំរបស់ខ្លួន បានបង្កើត ចក្រភពមួយនៅក្នុងសតវត្សរ៍ទី១៥ និង១៦ នៃគ្រិះសករាជ ។

sponsor / អ្នកផ្តល់ជំនួយ *(ន)* អ្នកផ្តល់លុយជាជំនួយដល់ជនណាម្នាក់ ឬ គម្រោងការអ្វីមួយ ។

standing army / ទាហានឈរជើង *(ន)* កងកម្លាំងទាហានដែលបម្រុកចុក ទាំងនៅក្នុងពេលប្រទេសមានសន្តិភាព និង សង្គ្រាម ។

stele / សិលាចារិក *(ន)* សិលាចារិកសម្រាប់ផ្ទុកពីការបរិច្ចេទ និង ព្រឹត្តការណ៍ សំខាន់ៗ ។

Stoicism / អកម្មភាពនិយម *(ន)*
ទស្សនវិជ្ជារបស់ក្រិចដែលសង្កត់ធ្ងន់លើ សារសំខាន់នៃការមានគុណធម៌ កាតព្វកិច្ច និង ការអត់ធ្មត់ ដែលទស្សនៈនេះ មានឥទ្ធិពលខ្លាំងនៅក្នុងចក្រភពរ៉ូមបុរាណ ។

Suleyman I / ស្តេចស៊ុយលីយម៉ាន់ទី១ *(ន)*
អ្នកគ្រប់គ្រងមូស្លីមនៃទ្រូកភាគ អូតូម៉ាន់ ចាប់ពីឆ្នាំ ១៥២០ ដល់ឆ្នាំ ១៥៦៦ នៃគ្រិស្តសករាជ ហើយគេជាអ្នកមាន ការគាំទ្រខ្លាំងចំពោះសិល្បៈ និង បានបង្កើតទ្រឹស្តីច្បាប់ទ្បើតឡើង ។

Sundiata / រាជាទិរាជសាន់ឌីអាតា *(ន)*
អ្នកគ្រប់គ្រងបុរាណរបស់ប្រជាជន ម៉ាលីងគេ ហើយក្រោយមកបានដណ្តើមយករដ្ឋធានីរបស់ហ្គាណា និង បង្កើន ឥទ្ធិពលចក្រភព របស់ខ្លួនយ៉ាងខ្លាំងក្លា ។

Sunnah / ទ្រឹស្តីសាន់ណា *(ន)* ពាក្យសម្តី និង អំពើរបស់មូហាម៉ាត់ដែល បង្រៀនមូស្លីមជាសាសនាមូស្លីម ជាអ្នកនាំផ្លូវទៅដល់ការរស់នៅដែលមានលក្ខណៈ ត្រឹមត្រូវ ។

Sunni / ក្រុមសាសនាសាន់នី *(ន)*
ក្រុមមូស្លីមរបស់សាសនាមូស្លីមដែលគោរព តាមច្បាប់ដែលបង្កើតទ្បើងដោយព្រះចៅកាលីហ្ស និង មិនប្រឆាំងនឹងច្បាប់ អ៊ីម៉ែយ៉ាត់ ។

Swahili / ភាសាស្វាហ៊ីលី *(ន)*
ភាសារបស់អាហ្វ្រិកដែលកើតចេញពីការបូក បញ្ចូលធាតុជាច្រើនរវាងភាសាបិនទូ និង ភាសាអារ៉ាប់ ។

T

Tenochtitlán / ទីក្រុងតេណុចទិតឡាន *(ន)*
ទីក្រុងបុរាណរបស់អាស់តិច ដែលបានរកឃើញ នៅឆ្នាំ ១៣២៥ នៃគ្រិស្តសករាជ លើកោះតូចមួយក្នុងបឹង តិតក្លូក្លូ ។

Thomas Aquinas / អ្នកប្រាជ្ញថូម៉ាស់ អាក្វីណាស់ *(ន)* អ្នកប្រាជ្ញ ជនជាតិ អ៊ីតាលីម្នាក់ដែលបានធ្វើការរួមបញ្ចូលគ្នារវាងទស្សនវិជ្ជាបុរាណ និង ទ្រឹស្តីសាសនាយេស៊ូ ។

Timbuktu / ទីក្រុងធីមបុកទុ *(ន)* ទីក្រុងមួយនៃម៉ាលីកណ្តាល នៅអាហ្វ្រិក ខាងលិច ដែលបានបង្កើតទ្បើងនៅសតវត្សរ៍ទី ១៣ ហើយទីក្រុងនេះ ជា មជ្ឈមណ្ឌលពាណិជ្ជកម្ម និង វប្បធម៌ ។

Tokugawa Shogunate / ច្បាប់ តូតូហ្គាវ៉ា ស៊ូហ្គាន់ណេត *(ន)*
ច្បាប់បង្កើតទ្បើងដោយ មហាក្សត្រតូតូហ្គាវ៉ា អ៊ីយ៉ាស៊ូ និង អ្នកស្នងតំណែង របស់គាត់ ដែលបានចាប់ផ្តើម នៅក្នុងឆ្នាំ ១៦០៣ នៃគ្រិស្តសករាជ ហើយបាននាំ សុខភាពរយៈពេល ២៥០ឆ្នាំ ដល់ប្រទេសជប៉ុន ។

Treaty of Tordesillas / កិច្ចព្រមព្រៀង ថតដេស៊ីលឡាស *(ន)*
សេចក្តី ព្រមព្រៀងរវាងប្រទេសអេស្ប៉ាញ និង ព័រទុយហ្គាល់ក្នុងឆ្នាំ ១៤៩៤ ដើម្បីបង្កើត ព្រំដែនខបកិច្ចមួយចាប់ពីភាគខាងត្បូងទៅខាងជើងពិភពលោក ។ ការបង្កើតខ្សែ ព្រំដែននេះ អាចឱ្យប្រទេសអេស្ប៉ាញទាមទារយកដីនៅភាគខាងលិចនៃខ្សែ ព្រំដែន និង ភាគខាងកើតសម្រាប់ព័រទុយហ្គាល់ ។

triangular trade / ពាណិជ្ជកម្មត្រីកោណ *(ន)*
ការផ្លាស់ប្តូរទំនិញ និង ទាសករតាមច្រកមហាសមុទ្រប៉ាស៊ីហ្វិក គឺ ទ្វីបអាមេរិក អ៊ីរ៉ុប និង អាហ្វ្រិក ។

tribute / សួយសារអាករ *(ន)* ការផ្លាស់អ្វីមួយពីសំណាក់ប្រទេសមួយ ដល់ ប្រទេសមួយទៀតក្នុងនាមជាការគោរព ។

U, V, W, X, Y, Z

universal gravitatin / ទំនាញសកល *(ន)* ទ្រឹស្តីរបស់អ៊ីសាអាក់ ញ៉ូតុន ដែលថាទំនាញមានចំពោះវាល់វត្ថុទាំងឡាយនៅក្នុងសកល ។

vassal / បរិវា *(ន)* អ្នកដែលទទួលយកដីផ្ទី និង ការការពារពីពួកអភិជន ដើម្បីជាថ្នូរនឹងការស្មោះស្ម័គ្រ នៅក្នុងប្រទេសកាន់របបក្តិភូមិ ។

vegetation zone / តំបន់ព្រៃឈើ *(ន)*
តំបន់ដែលសំបូរទៅដោយព្រៃឈើ ជាច្រើនប្រភេទ ដោយសារអាកាសធាតុ និង លក្ខណៈដី ។

vernacular / គ្រាបភាសា *(ន)* ភាសាដើមរបស់ជនណាម្នាក់ ។

weather / អាកាសធាតុ *(ន)* លក្ខណៈរបស់ខ្យល់អាកាស នៅទីកន្លែងណា មួយ ក្នុងពេលជាក់លាក់ ។

wood-block printing / ការបោះពុម្ពអក្សរប្រើឈើ *(ន)*
ប្រព័ន្ធបោះពុម្ព អក្សរមួយដែលរកឃើញដោយជនជាតិចិនបុរាណ ក្នុងនោះគឺគេយកឈើមកឆ្លាក់ ជាពុម្ពអក្សរគ្រប់គ្រាន់សម្រាប់បោះ អក្សរពេញមួយទំព័រៗ ។

Yucatán Peninsular / ជ្រោយយូកាតាន់ *(ន)*
ជាតំបន់មួយនៅភាគ អាគ្នេយ៍ នៃប្រទេសម៉ិកស៊ិចកូ ដែលបន្លាយដល់សមុទ្រការីបៀន និង ឈូង សមុទ្រម៉ិកស៊ិចកូ ។

Zen / ហ្សិន *(ន)* បែបបទសាសនាព្រះពុទ្ធរបស់ប្រទេសជប៉ុន ដែលសង្កត់ធ្ងន់ លើការជាក់វិន័យលើខ្លួនឯង ការសម្ងួម និង ការភាវនាធម៌ ។

Zheng He / មេទ័ពជើងទឹក ជីង ហេ *(ន)*
ជាមេទ័ពជើងទឹកចិនម្នាក់ដែល ការធ្វើដំណើររបស់គាត់ពីឆ្នាំ ១៤០៥ ដល់ ១៤៣៣ នៃគ្រិស្តសករាជ បាននាំមកនូវ ពាណិជ្ជកម្មក្រៅប្រទេស និង កិត្តិយសដ៏ថ្លៃថ្លាដល់ប្រទេសចិន ។

ຜາກອະທິບາຍຄຳສັບ ພາສາລາວ

ຜາກອະທິບາຍຄຳສັບ ໄດ້ລຽງເປັນລຳດັບ ຕາມຕົວອັກສອນ ຂອງຄຳສັບທີ່ສຳຄັນຫລາຍໆຄຳ ຈາກຫລາຍບົດ, ຮວມທັງ ຄວາມໝາຍ ຂອງມັນ. ຄຳຈຳກັດຄວາມ ທີ່ຢູ່ໃນຜາກອະທິບາຍຄຳສັບ ແມ່ນຄຳທີ່ໃຊ້ ຢູ່ໃນໜັງສືຮຽນຫົວນີ້ ຜາກອະທິບາຍຄຳສັບ ໃຊ້ໜ້າຕ່າງທີ່ ບັນຍາຍຄຳ ແຕ່ລະຄຳ. ຄຳຫຍໍ້ຕ່າງໆ ທີ່ໄດ້ນຳມາໃຊ້ ແມ່ນ ຕໍ່ລົງໄປນີ້ :

adj. = adjective (ຄຳຄຸນສັບ)　　**n. = noun** (ຄຳນາມ)　　**v. = verb** (ຄຳກິຣິຍາ)

A

Abd al-Malik / ອັບ ອັລມາລິກ *n.* ຜູ້ປົກຄອງຊາວມຸດສະລິມ ຜູ້ທີ່ໄດ້ ກາຍເປັນຜູ້ສືບຕຳແໜ່ງຜະມະຫະໝັດ ໃນປີ ຄ.ສ. 685 ແລະ ຍົກພາສາ ອາຫລັບ ເປັນພາສາລັດຖະການ ຂອງບັນດາປະເທດມຸດສະລິມ.

Abd al-Rahman III / ອັບ ອັລຣາມານ ທີ III *n.* ຜູ້ປົກຄອງ ອັລ ອັນດາລັສ (al-Andalus) ອົງທີ 8 ໃນຊ່ວງທີ ອັລ ອັນດາລັສ ເຮືອງອຳນາດທີສຸດ.

Afonso I / ກະສັດອາຟອນໂຊ ທີ I *n.* ກະສັດ ແຫ່ງຂອງໂກ ອົງທີ່ໄດ້ຂຶ້ນຄອງລາດໃນປີ ຄ.ສ. 1506. ພະອົງໄດ້ປລີກທີ່ເພີ່ມຄວາມ ຄິດຈາກຊາວໂປຕຸເກດ ແລະ ການຮ່ວມຂະບວນການຄ້າຫາດ.

al-Andalus / ອັລ ອັນດາລັສ *n.* ອານາເຂດຂອງສະເປນ ທີ່ຢູ່ພາຍໃຕ້ການປົກຄອງຂອງຊາວມຸດສະລິມ ໃນລະຫວ່າງ ປີ ຄ.ສ. 700 ແລະ 1492.

Allah / ພະອັນລະຮະ *n.* ພະເຈົ້າໃນສາດສະໜາອິດສະລາມ.

alluvial soil / ດອນຊາຍ *n.* ດອນ ຫຼື ຫາດຊາຍທີ່ນ້ຳພັດມາ ແລະ ມີຄວາມອຸດົມສົມບູນ.

Almoravids / ລາດຊະວົງ ອັລໂມຣາວິດສ໌ *n.* ລາດຊະວົງອິດສະ ລາມຂອງຊາວອຟຣິກາເໜືອ ທີ່ບັງຄັບໃຫ້ປັນບຈານາເຂດເພື່ອນບ້ານ ໃຫ້ ປຽບຕາມສາດສະໜາ ລວມທັງ ຊາວໂມຣອກໂຂ, ສະເປນ ແລະ ການາ.

anatomy / ວິຊາກາຍຍະວິພາກ *n.* ວິທະຍາສາດຄະແໜງໜຶ່ງ ທີ່ສຶກສາກ່ຽວກັບ ຮຽວຣ່າງໆ ແລະ ໂຄງສ້າງຂອງມະນຸດ, ພືດ ແລະ ສັດ.

Angkor Wat / ອົງວັດ *n.* ວັດທີ່ມີຄວາມສະຫັບຊັບຊ້ອນໃນອາຊີ ຕາວັນອອກສ່ຽງໃຕ້ ຊຶ່ງໄດ້ຮັບການກໍ່ສ້າງ ໃນ ຄ.ສ. ທີ 1100 ທີ່ ມີອານາເຂດຄອບຄມ ເກືອບ ໜຶ່ງ ຕາລາງໄມ ແລະ ຊຶ່ງເປັນສິ່ງກໍ່ສ້າງ ທາງສາດສະໜາທີ່ໃຫຍ່ທີ່ສຸດໃນໂລກ.

anthropology / ມະນຸດວິທະຍາ *n.* ວິຊາທີ່ສຶກສາ ກ່ຽວກັບ ມະນຸດ ແລະ ວັດທະນະທຳ.

aqueduct / ລະບົບສົ່ງນ້ຳ *n.* ລະບົບທີ່ໄດ້ຮັບການອອກແບບ ເພື່ອ ສົ່ງນ້ຳຈືດ ເຂົ້າສູ່ຕົວເມືອງ.

archaeology / ບູຮານມະລະຄະດີ *n.* ການຂຸດຄົ້ນ ແລະ ສຶກສາ ກ່ຽວກັບ ຫຼັກຖານທາງກາຍຍະພາບຂອງສິ່ງຕ່າງໆໃນອະດີດ.

artifact / ສິ່ງທີ່ມະນຸດເຮັດຂຶ້ນ *n.*

Askia Muhammad / ຈັກກະພັດ ອັດສະກາຍ ມະຫະໝັດ *n.* ຜູ້ປົກຄອງຈັກກະຫວັດ ຊົງໄຮ (Songhai) ແຕ່ ຄ.ສ. 1493 ຫາ 1528 ຊຶ່ງເປັນຜູ້ແຜ່ອະຫນາຍ ແລະ ສ້າງຕັ້ງລັດຖະບານປົກຄອງ ຈັກກະຫວັດ ຄັ້ງກ່າວ.

astrolabe / ເຄື່ອງວັດແຫກດາລາສາດ *n.* ເຄື່ອງມືທີ່ໃຊ້ວັດແຫກ ມຸມ ຂອງດວງດາວໃນທ້ອງຟ້າ ເພື່ອຊ່ວຍໃຫ້ນັກເດີນເຮືອ ສາມາດ ກຳນົດຕຳແໜງຂອງຕົວເອງໄດ້.

Augustus / ຈັກກະພັດອໍກຸດສະຕຸດສ໌ *n.* ຈັກກະພັດອົງທຳອິດ ຂອງມະລອມໂຣມ ມັນແຕ່ 27 ປີ ກ່ອນ ຄ.ສ. ເຖິງ ຄ.ສ. 14 ແລະ ໄດ້ແຜ່ອະຫນາຍອານາເຂດ ແລະ ອິດທິພົນຂອງຈັກກະຫວັດໂຣມ ອອກໄປຢ່າງກວ້າງໄກ.

B

Baghdad / ມະຄອນແບກແດດ *n.* ມະຄອນທີ່ຕັ້ງຢູ່ອິຣັກ ໃນປະຈຸບັນ ຊຶ່ງໃນເມືອກ່ອນແມ່ນເມືອງຫຼວງ ຂອງຈັກກະຫວັດ ອັບບາຊິດ (Abbasid).

Bantu migrations / ການອົບພະຍົກຂອງຊາວບັນທຸ *n.* ການຍ້າຍຖິ່ນຖານຂອງໄພ່ພົນທີ່ເວົ້າພາສາບັນທຸ ຈາກທາງຟຣິກກາຕາ ເວັນຕົກ ໄປທາງຫິດໃຕ້ ແລະ ທິດຕາເວັນອອກ ເພື່ອເຜີຍແຜ່ອະຫນາຍ ພາສາ ແລະ ວັດທະມະທຳຂອງເຂົ້າເຈົ້າ ໃນປະມານ 1000 ປີກ່ອນ ຄ.ສ.

bubonic plague / ກາລະໂຄ *n.* ໂຣກລະບາດທີ່ແຜ່ລະບາດ ທົ່ວ ຢໂຣເຊຍ (Eurasia) ຕາເວັນຕົກ ໃນຕາງວັດຕະວັດທີ 1300 ເປັນທີ່ຮູ້ຈັກໃນຊື່ ຍຸກມໍລະນະສີດຳ (Black Death).

Buddhism / ສາດສະໜາພຸດ *n.* ຫຼັກຄວາມເຊື່ອ ຕາມຄຳສອນຂອງ ເຈົ້າຊາຍສິດທັດຖະກຸມານ ຫຼື ພະພຸດທະເຈົ້າ ທີ່ໄດ້ສັ່ງສອນກ່ຽວກັບ ການປ່ອຍວາງຈາກຄວາມຕ້ອງການຕ່າງໆ ທາງໂລກ.

bureaucracy / ລະບົບລັດຖະການ *n.* ລະບົບກົມກອງ ແລະ ໜ່ວຍງານ ທີ່ດຳເນີນອງກງານຂອງລັດຖະບານ.

bushido / ຄວາມເຊື້ອເຜື້ອ, ກ້າຫານ ແລະ ຈົງຮັກພັກດີ *n.* ຫຼັກປະຕິບັດຂອງນັກຣົບຊາມຸໄຣ ທີ່ກຳນົດໃຫ້ພວກເຂົາເຈົ້າ ມີຄວາມ ເຊື້ອເຜື້ອເຜື່ອແຜ່, ອົງອາດກ້າຫານ ແລະ ຈົງຮັກພັກດີ.

Byzantine Empire / ຈັກກະຫວັດໄບແຊນທິນ *n.* ຈັກກະຫວັດໂຣມັນຕາເວັນອອກ ທີ່ມີການປົກຄອງຕັ້ງແຕ່ສະໄໝຄອນ ສະແຕນຕິນໂນເບີນ ມີອາຍຸ ຕັ້ງແຕ່ ສັດຕະວັດ ທີ 4 ເຖິງ 15.

C

cacao / ຕົ້ນໂກໂກ້ *n.* ຕົ້ນໄມ້ຂອງຮ້ອນຊຸ່ມໃນອາເມລິກາ ທີ່ເຮົາ
ແກ່ນມາຜະລິດເປັນ ຊ໊ອກໂກແລັດ.

caliph / ຜູ້ສືບຕຳແໜ່ງຂອງພະມະຫະໝັດ *n.* ຜູ້ປົກຄອງຊຸ່ມຊົນ
ມຸດສະລີມ ທີ່ຖືວ່າເປັນຜູ້ສືບທອດຂອງພະມະຫະໝັດ.

calligraphy / ສິນລະປະໃນການຂຽນງ່າມ *n.*

Calvin, John / ທ່ານ ຈອນ ແຄລວິນ *n.* ຜູ້ນຳໃນຍຸກປະຕິຮູບ
ບົກຄານ ໂປຣເຕສະແຕນຕ໌ (Protestant Reformation) ທີ່ມີ
ອາຍຸ ແຕ່ປີ ຄ.ສ. 1509 ຫາ 1564 ແລະ ເປັນຜູ້ທີ່ສັ້ງສອນລັດທິໂປຣ
ເຕສະແຕນຕ໌.

capitalism / ລະບອບທືນນິຍົມ *n.* ລະບົບເສດຖະກິດ ທີ່ຊິງໃສ່
ກຳມະສິດເອກະຊົນ ໃນອັນຜະຍຸງການທາງເສດຖະກິດ ແລະ
ການໝູນໃຊ້ອັນຜະຍຸງ ກອນ ຕັ້ງກ່າວ ເພື່ອສ້າງຜົນກຳໄລ.

caravel / ເຮືອໃບ *n.* ເຮືອເດີນທະເລ ປະເພດໜຶ່ງຂອງຊາວ
ປ໊ອກຕຸຍການ ທີ່ມີຜ້າໃບ ສີ່ ແລະ ສາມ ຫຼ່ຽມ ເພື່ອໃຊ້ໃນການເດີນເຮືອ
ໄລຍະໄກ.

cartography / ວິຊາແຕ້ມແຜນທີ່ *n.* ຄວາມຊຳນານ ແລະ
ວິທີໃນການແຕ້ມແຜນທີ່.

celadon / ເຄື່ອງປັ້ນດິນເຜີງເກົ້າທີ່ *n.* ເຄື່ອງປັ້ນດິນ
ເຜີງຂະບົດໜຶ່ງ ຂອງ ເກົ້າທີ່ ຊຶ່ງສ່ວນໃຫຍ່ ແມ່ນມີສີຂຽວອ່ອນຟ້າ.

Charlemagne / ກະສັດຊາເລະແມນ *n.* ກະສັດ ແຫ່ງ ແຟຼ້ງຣ໌
(ນັບແຕ່ ຄ.ສ. 768) ຜູ້ທີ່ຄອບຄອງດິນແດນສ່ວນໃຫຍ່ຂອງຢູໂຣບ
ແລະ ເຜີຍແຜ່ສາດສະໝາ ຄຣິສຕ໌ ທ່ອອານາເຂດດັ່ງກ່າວ.

chasqui *n.* ຈັສທີເປັນນັກແລ່ນຄົນໜຶ່ງຜູ້ໃນຈັກກະພັບ
ອິນກາເຊິ່ງເປັນຜູ້ນຳເອົາຂ່າວສິ່ງໄປສົ່ງຕາມອານາເຂດອັນ
ກ້ວາງໄກຂອງຈັກກະພັບ.

chivalry / ຄວາມກ້າຫານ, ຮັກກຽດ ແລະ ມັບຕິ *n.*
ກົດປະຕິບັດ ຂອງ ອັດສະວິນ ໃນຢູໂຣບຍຸກກາງໆ ທີ່ສອນໃຫ້ມີຄວາມກ້າ
ຫານ, ຮັກກຽດ, ແລະ ມັບຕິ ຜຕຍັ່ງ ແລະ ຜູ້ອ່ອນແຍ.

Christianity / ສາດສະໝາຄຣິສຕ໌ ຫຼື ຄຣິສຕະສາດສະໝາ *n.*
ສາດສະໝາ ທີ່ຊິງໃສ່ການຄຳລົ້ງຊີວິດ ແລະ ກົດຄຳສອນຂອງພະເຍຊູ.

circumnavigate / ເດີນເຮືອໄປຮອບໂລກ *v.*

clan / ຕະກຸນ *n.* ກຸ່ມຄົນທີ່ກ່ຽວພັນກັບທາງສາຍເລືອດ ຫຼື
ການແຕ່ງໆ.

clergy / ພະ (ສົງ) *n.* ຜູ້ທີ່ມີອຳນາດທາງສາດສະໝາ
ໃນສາດສະໝາໆໃດໜຶ່ງ.

climate / ພູມອາກາດ *n.* ຮູບແບບຂອງສະພາບອາກາດ
ຢູ່ທ້ອງຖິ່ນໃດໜຶ່ງ ໃນໄລຍະເວລາທີ່ດົນນານລະດັບໜຶ່ງ.

Clovis / ກະສັດໂຄຼວິດສ໌ *n.* ຜູ້ປົກຄອງ ແຫ່ງ ອານາຈັກ
ແຟຼງຣ໌ ທີ່ຕີຊະນະແຄ່ມລັບ ໂຄຼ (Gaul) ຂອງໂຣມັນ ໃນປີ ຄ.ສ.
486 ແລະ ຫຼັງຈາກນັ້ນ ໄດ້ສັ້ງຕັ້ງອານາຈັກແຟຼງຣ໌ສີທີ່ຍິ່ງ
ໃຫຍ່ແລະເຮືອງຳນາດ.

codex / ຜິວສາວະດານ *n.* ປຶ້ມອະບິດໆຊຶ່ງທີ່ໃຊ້ໃນສະໄໝຕັ້ນໆ
ຂອງ ເມໂສ ອານາລິກາ ຍຸກຕັ້ນໆ ເພື່ອບັນທຶກເຫດການທີ່ສຳຄັນທາງໆ
ປະຫວັດສາດ.

Columbian Exchange / ການເຄື່ອນຍ້າຍຖຶ່ນຖານ *n.*
ການເຄື່ອນຍ້າຍຜິດຄົນ, ສັດ, ແລະ ສິ່ງມີຊີວິດອື່ນໆ ລະຫວ່າງ
ຊິກໂລກ ຕາອັນອອກ ແລະ ຕາອັນຕົກ ຜາຍຫຼັງ ການຄົ້ນພົບ
ທະວີບອາເມລິກາຂອງ ທ່ານ ໂຄລຳບັດຊ໌ ໃນ ຄ.ສ. 1492

Confucianism / ລັດທິຂົງຈື່ *n.* ຫຼັກຄວາມເຊື່ອ ທີ່ຊິງໃສ່ການ
ສິກສອນຂອງຂົງຈື່, ຊຶ່ງເປັນບັນດິດ ຜູ້ທີ່ສຶກສອນ ກ່ຽວກັບສີນທຳ ຄຸນ
ງາມຄວາມດີ ແລະ ຈັນຍາທຳ.

Constantine / ຈັກກະພັດຄອນສະແຕນໄທ *n.* ຈັກກະພັດໂຣມັນ
ນັບແຕ່ປີ ຄ.ສ. 306 ຖຶງ 337 ຜູ້ທີ່ຍຶກຄກຳກັດຂື່ງຍຸດຕິຄຂອງຄຣິສຕ໌
ແລະ ຍ້າຍນະຄອນຫຼວງຂອງຈັກກະພະທ່ອັດໄປຍັງ ໄບແຊນທຽມ
(Byzantium) (ຕໍ່ມາຮູ້ຈັກກັບໃນຊື່ ຄອນສະແຕນຕິນໂນເບິລ).

continent / ທະວີບ *n.* ຜຶ່ງໃນບັນດາ ເຈັດມະຫາແຜ່ນດິນຂອງ
ໂລກ —ທະວີບອາເມລິກາເໜືອ, ອາເມລິກາໃຕ້, ຢູໂຣບ, ເອເຊຍ,
ອາຟຣິກາ, ອົດສະຕຼເລຍ ແລະ ອັງຕາກຕິກ.

convert / ຊັກຈູງໃຫ້ເຊື່ອຖື *n.* ຊັກຈູງໃຫ້ຄົນ ປຽນສາດສະໝາ
ຫຼື ຄວາມເຊື່ອຖືຂອງຕົນ.

Córdoba / ນະຄອນຫຼວງຂອງ ອັລ ອັນດາລັດສ໌ *n.*

Cortés, Hernán / ທ່ານ ເຮີນານ ຄໍເຕ໌ *n.* ນັກສຳຫຼວດຊາວສະ
ປປນ ມີໄຊຊະນະເໜີອອ່ານະຍະທຳ ແອັດສະເຫຼັກ (Aztec) ຂອງ
ແມັກຊິໂກ ໃນ ຄ.ສ. 1521.

covenant / ຂໍ້ຕົກລົງ *n.* ຂໍ້ຕົກລົງທີ່ມີພັນທະຜູກພັນທາງໆກົດໝາຍ.

Crusades / ສົງຄາມຄຣູເສດສ໌ *n.* ການເຄື່ອນພົບທະຫານຂອງ
ຄຣິສຕ໌ໃນຢູໂຣບ ໄປຮົບໃນ ປ່າເລດສະຕາຍ ລະຫວ່າງ ສັດຕະວັດທີ
11 ແລະ 13.

culture / ອັດຕະນະທຳ *n.* ແບບແຜນການດຳລົ້ງຊີວິດ ທີ່
ມີລັກສະນະຮ່ວມ ຂອງກຸ່ມຄົນໃດໜຶ່ງ.

D

daimyo / ເຈົ້າຂອງທີ່ດິນ *n.* ເຈົ້າຂອງທີ່ດິນຂອງຍີ່ປຸ່ນ ທີ່ຖືຂອງທີ່
ດິນທັງກວ້າງໃຫຍ່ ແລະ ມີກອງທັບຊຸນໄຮ່ສ່ວນຕົວ ໂດຍບໍ່ຕ້ອງເສ
ຍພາສີແກ່ລັດຖະບານ.

Daoism / ລັດທິເຕົ໋າ *n.* ລະບົບຄວາມເຊື່ອທີ່ເກີດຂື້ນກຳເນີດໃນຈີນ
ໃນປະມານ 500 ປີ ກ່ອນ ຄ.ສ. ທີ່ສອນໃຫ້ດຳລົ້ງຊີວິດຢ່າງກົມກຽວກັບ
ທຳມະຊາດ ແລະ ຄວາມຮູ້ສຶກພາຍໃນ.

Declaration of Independence /
ຄຳແຖງການເອກະລາດ *n.* ເອກະສານທາງກົດໝາຍ ທີ່ປະກາດ
ຄວາມເປັນເອກະລາດ ຂອງ ອານານິຄົມອາເມລິກາ ອອກຈາກອັງກິດ.

Declaration of the Rights of Man and of the Citizen / ຄຳແຖງການ ວ່າດ້ວຍ ສິດທິມະນຸດ ແລະ ພົນລະເມືອງ
n. ເອກະສານທາງກົດໝາຍທີ່ຖືກຮັບຮອງ ໂດຍລັດຖະນາມປະຕິວັດ
ຂອງຝຣັ່ງ ໃນປີ 1789 ກ່ຽວກັບສິດທິຂອງປວງຊົນ.

dissection / ການອຶພາຍ ຫຼື ການຜ່າໆ *n.* ການຜ່າ (ຕັດ) ຊຶດ
ແລະ ສັດ ເພື່ອສຶກສາ ແລະ ສຳຫຼວດອົງປະກອບຕ່າງໆ.

divan / ສະພາທີ່ປຶກສາ *n.* ສະພາທີ່ໃຫ້ຄຳປຶກສາແກ່ສຸລະຕ່ານ ໃນ
ຈັກກະຫວັດອອດໂຕມັນ.

E

elevation / ຄວາມສູງຈາກທະເລ *n.* ລະດັບຄວາມສູງຂອງດິນ
ຈາກລະດັບໜ້ານ້ຳທະເລ.

elite / ຊົນຊັ້ນສູງ *n.* ກຸ່ມຄົນ ທີ່ມີອຳນາດສູງກວ່າໝູ່ ຫຼື ມັ່ງຄັ່ງທີ່ສຸດ
ໃນສັງຄົມໃດໜຶ່ງ.

Elizabethan Age / ສະໄໝພະນາງເອລິຊະເບດ *n.*
ຍຸກພາຍໃຕ້ ການປົກຄອງຂອງລາຊິນີ ເອລິຊະເບດ ທີ I (Queen
Elizabeth I) ຂອງອັງກິດ ມັຍແຕ່ປີ 1558 ເຖິງ 1603.

embassy / ສະຖານທຸດ *n.* ສຳນັກງານທາງໜ້າ ຂອງ
ລັດຖະນາປະເທດໜຶ່ງ ທີ່ຕັ້ງຢູ່ໃນປະເທດອື່ນ.

emperor / ຈັກກະພັດ *n.* ຜູ້ປົກຄອງຈັກກະຫວັດ.

empire / ຈັກກະຫວັດ ຫຼື ອານາຈັກ *n.* ບັນດາວັດທະນະທຳ
ແລະ ອານາເຂດ ຕ່າງໆ ທີ່ຖືກຕັ້ງ ໂຮມໄວ້ຢູ່ພາຍໃຕ້ການປົກຄອງ
ຂອງບຸກຄົນໃດໜຶ່ງ ທີ່ມີອຳນາດສູງສຸດ.

enlightened despot / ຜູ້ປົກຄອງແບບນັບຄົດ *n.*
ຜູ້ປົກຄອງທີ່ມີອຳນາດ ເບັດສັດໃນການປົກຄອງ ແຕ່ກໍຍັງເອົາໃຈໃສ່
ຕໍ່ແບບອລາມຄິດທາງການເມືອງຂອງຜູ້ທີ່ມີຄວາມສະຫຼາດຊ່ອງໃສ
ແລະ ພະຍາຍາມປົກຄອງ ດ້ວຍຄວາມຍຸຕິທຳ ແລະ ແບບຜູ້ມີການ
ສຶກສາ.

Enlightenment / ຍຸກແຫ່ງຄວາມສະຫຼາດຊ່ອງໃສ *n.*
ການຄຶກຄຶງ ທາງປັດຂະຍາ ໃນສັດຕະວັດທີ 18 ທີ່ບັນດານັກປັດ
ຂະຍາຕ່າງໆ ໂດຍ ພະຍາຍາມໃຊ້ເຫດຜົນ ເພື່ອສັ່ງຄວາມເຊື່ອໃຈໃນ
ຄວາມຈິງ ກ່ຽວກັບ ທຳມະຊາດຂອງມະນຸດ.

epic poem / ກອນສັນເສີນວິລະບຸລຸດ *n.* ກອນຍາວທີ່ເລົ່າໆ
ກ່ຽວກັບການຜະຈົນໄພຂອງວິລະບຸລຸດ.

excavation / ການຂຸດເພື່ອສຶກສາວັດຖຸທາງປະຫວັດສາດ *n.*
ຂັ້ນຕອນໃນການຂຸດວັດຖຸສິ່ງຂອງ ທີ່ມີຄວາມໝາຍສຳຄັນທາງ
ປະຫວັດສາດ ຂຶ້ນມາເສິກສາໆ.

F

faction / ກຸ່ມກ້ອນ *n.* ກຸ່ມຄົນນ້ອຍໆ ທີ່ເປັນສ່ວນໜຶ່ງຂອງກຸ່ມໃຫຍ່
ແຕ່ມີຜົນປະໂຫຍດຄັດກັບ ຂອງກຸ່ມໃຫຍ່.

federalism / ລະບອບການປົກຄອງແບບສະຫະພັນ *n.*
ລະບົບການປົກຄອງ ທີ່ມີການແບ່ງປັນອຳນາດ ລະຫວ່າງໆ
ອົງການຈັດຕັ້ງ ຫຼື ລັດຖະບານກາງ ແລະ ລັດສະມາຊິກ.

feudalism / ລະບອບສັກດິນາ *n.* ລະບົບການເມືອງ ແລະ
ສັງຄົມ ຂອງ ຍຸກກາງໆໃນຢູໂລບ ທີ່ສັກດິນາ (ເຈົ້າຂອງທີ່ດິນ)
ໃຫ້ຂ້າທາດ ອົມໃຊ້ທີ່ດິນ ເພື່ອແລກປ່ຽນກັບ ການຮັບໃຊ້ ແລະ
ຄວາມຈົງຮັກພັກດີ.

Forbidden City / ນະຄອນຕ້ອງຫ້າມ *n.* ບັນດາພະລາດຊຸວັງ
ທີ່ອ້ອມຮອບດ້ວຍກຳແພງໝາແໜ້ນ ກໍ່ສ້າງຂຶ້ນບັນດາການແກ່ຈັກກະ
ພັດຈີນ ໃນໄລຍະປະມານ ຄ.ສ. 1400 ຊຶ່ງຕັ້ງຢູ່ນະຄອນຫຼວງປັກກິ່ງ.

Francis of Assisi, Saint / ມັກບຸນ ເຊັ້ນທ໌ ແຟຣນຊິດສ໌
ແຫ່ງ ແອດຊີຊི *n.* ຊາວອິຕາລີ ຜູ້ທີ່ສ້າງລະບົບຕາງສາດສະໜາ
ແບບແຟຣນຊິດສ໌ ໃນໄລຍະຕົ້ນຂອງ ຄຸນປີ ຄ.ສ. 1200.

G

Genghis Khan / ເຈັງກິດສ໌ ຂ່ານ *n.* ຜູ້ນຳຂອງມົງໂກນ
ຜູ້ທີ່ເຕົ້າໂຮມບັນດາເຜົ່າຕ່າງໆ ຂອງມົງໂກນ ໃນປະມານ ປີ ຄ.ສ.
1206 ແລະ ເລີ້ມ ຕັ້ນຕໍ່ສູ້ຂະຫຍາຍຍອານາເຂດໄປຍັງຈັກກະຫວັດຕ່າງໆ
ແຖນ ທີ່ກວມເອົາທາງຕອນເໜືອຂອງຈີນ ແລະ ເອເຊຍກາງ.

geocentric theory /
ທິດສະດີທີ່ວ່າໆໂລກເປັນສູນກາງຈັກກະວານ *n.*

geography / ພູມສາດ *n.* ວິຊາທີ່ສຶກສາກ່ຽວກັບ
ລັກສະນະທາງທຳມະຊາດຂອງ ໂລກ.

Ghana / ປະເທດການາ *n.* ອານາເຂດ ລະຫວ່າງໆ ທະເລຊາຍຊຸ
ຮາຣາ ແລະ ເຂດປ່າຕຶບທາງຕອນໃຕ້ຂອງຟຣິກາຕາເວັນຕົກ ທີ່
ເປັນແຫ່ງວັດທະນະທຳບູຮານທຽບກາຍສະໄໝ.

glyph / ພາບສັນຍາລັກ *ນ.* ຮູບພາບໃຊ້ສະແດງ ຄຳເວົ້າ ພະຍາງ
ຫຼື ສຽງ ໃດໜຶ່ງ.

golden age / ຍຸກຈະເລີນຮຸ່ງເຮືອງ *n.* ຊ່ວງໄລຍະທີ່ ສັງຄົມ
ຫຼື ວັດທະນະທຳໃດໜຶ່ງ ມີຄວາມຈະເລີນຮຸ່ງເຮືອງທີ່ສຸດ.

Great Enclosure / ບໍດບັນຍັດຂ້ອມທ້າຍ *n.*
ຜາກໃຫຍ່ທີ່ສຸດ ໃນ ສາມຜາກຂອງຊີໄກ່ເກ່ຍໂຊນາ (Shona)
ແຫ່ງ ມະຫານະຄອນ ຊິມບັບເວ—ຮັ້ນ ກ່ຽວກັບ ຄວາມຈົງຮັກພັກດີ
ຂອງປະຊາຊົນ.

Great Schism / ການແບ່ງແຍກ ໃນບົກາຍໂຮມັນຄາທໍລິກ *n.*
ການແບ່ງແຍກທີ່ເກີດຂຶ້ນ ໃນບົກາຍໂຮມັນຄາທໍລິກ ມັຍແຕ່ປີ ຄ.ສ
1378 ຈົນເຖິງ 1417 ເມື່ອຂ້ອອຳນາດທັງສອງ (ອາວິຍອງ
ແລະ ໂຮມ) ແຍກອອກຈາກກັນ ແລະ ມີການເລືອກພະສັນຕະປາປາ
ຂອງໃຫມັນ.

Great Zimbabwe / ມະຫາມະຄອນຊິມບັບເວ *n.*
ການຕັ້ງຖິ່ນຖານ ຂອງ ຈັກກະຫວັດ ໂຊນາ ໃນອາຟຣິກາກາ
ທີ່ລ້ອມຮອບດ້ວຍກຳແພງຫີນ ໂດຍກວມເອົາເນື້ອທີ່ຫຼາຍກວ່າ 100
ເອເຄີ ແລະ ມີປະຊາກອນ ປະມານ 10,000 ຫາ 20,000 ຄົນ.

Gregory VII, Pope / ພະສັນຕະປະປາ ເກຣໂກຣີ ທີ VII *n.*
ຫົວໜ້າ ນິກາຍໂຣມັນຄາທໍລິກ ໃນລະຫວ່າງປີ 1073 to 1085 ທີ່ຕໍ
ສູ້ເພື່ອແຍ່ງອຳນາດກັບ ຈັກກະພັດ ເອັນຣີ ທີ IV.

griot / ນັກລ່ຳນິທານ *n.* ນັກລ່ຳນິທານທາງການ ຂອງສະໄໝ
ອາລະຍະທຳອາຟຣິກາບູຮານ..

guild / ສະມາຄົມ *n.* ສະມາຄົມທີ່ຕັ້ງຂຶ້ນ ເພື່ອ ແລກປ່ຽນສິນຄ້າ
ທີ່ ທ່າຍທອດດງານສີມື ໂດຍມີຈດປະສົງ ເພື່ອຄວບຄຸມຄຸນນະພາບ ແລະ
ປະລິມານ ການຜະລິດ ແລະ ປົກປ້ອງຜົນປະໂຫຍດຂອງກຸ່ມ.

Gutenberg, Johann / ທ່ານໂຈຣານ ກູເຕັນເບິກ *n.*
ນັກປະດິດ ຊາວເຍຍລະມັນ ໃນກາງຍຸມປີ 1400
ທີ່ປະດິດສ້າງເຄື່ອງພິມຊະນິດ ທີ່ມີແມ່ພິມແບບມີຝາປິດ.

H

habeas corpus / ໝາຍຣຽກຂອງສານ *n.* ສິດທິຂອງບຸກຄົນ
ໃນການທີ່ຈະບໍ່ຖືກຈຳຄຸກໂດຍບໍ່ໄດ້ຖືກຕ້ອງຕາມກົດໝາຍ.

haiku / ກອນຍີ່ປຸ່ນ *n.* ກອນປະເພດໜຶ່ງ ຂອງຍີ່ປຸ່ນ ທີ່ປະກອບມີ
17 ພະຍາງ ໂດຍມີການຈັດລຽງເປັນ 3 ແຖວ ທີ່ມີ 5, 7, ແລະ
5 ພະຍາງ.

harmony / ຄວາມກົມກ່ຽວ *n.* ການປະກອບ ສ່ວນຕ່າງໆ
ໃຫ້ມີຄວາມປະສົມກົມກ່ຽວກັນ.

heliocentric / ມີດວງຕາເວັນເປັນສູນກາງຂອງຈັກກະວານ
adj.

hemisphere / ເຄິ່ງໂລກ *n.* ເຄິ່ງ ຫຼື ຊີກໜຶ່ງ ຂອງພື້ນຜິວໂລກ
ທີ່ແບ່ງ ໂດຍເສັ້ນສູນສູດ ຫຼື ເສັ້ນຜ່ານອ້ຽ ໂລກ.

Henry IV, Emperor / ຈັກກະພັດ ເອັນຣີ ທີ IV *n.* ຜູ້ປົກຄອງ
ຈັກກະຫວັດໂຣມັນສັກສິດ (Holy Roman) ໃນສັດຕະວັດທີ 11
ທີ່ຕໍສູ້ຢ່າງຍືດເຍື້ອງາບການເພື່ອແຍ່ງອຳນາດກັບ ພະສັນຕະປະປາ
ເກຣໂກຣີ ທີ VII.

Hijrah / ການຍົກຍ້າຍສູ່ເມືອງຢາທຣິບ *n.* ການຍົກຍ້າຍຂອງພະ
ມະຫະໝັດ ແລະ ສາວົກ ຈາກເມືອງເມັກກະ ໄປຍັງ ເມືອງຢາທຣິບ
(Yathrib) ໃນປີ ຄ.ສ. 622.

historian / ນັກປະຫວັດສາດ *n.* ຜູ້ທີ່ສຶກສາ ແລະ ຕີຄວາມໝາຍ
ເຫດການໃນອະດີດ.

history / ປະຫວັດສາດ *n.* ວິຊາທີ່ສຶກສາກ່ຽວກັບເຫດການໃນ
ອະດີດ.

humanism / ມະນຸດສາດ *n.* ການຟື້ນຟູສິນລະປະວິທະຍາໃນຢຸ
ໂຣບ ທີ່ສະເໜີສະທ້ອງທ່າແຮງ ແລະ ຄວາມສຳເລັດຂອງມະນຸດ ພ້ອມ
ກັນນັ້ນ ກໍໄດ້ເອົາໃຈໃສ່ການສຶກສາ ອຸ້ນ ວິຊາ ປະຫວັດສາດ, ໄວຍະ
ກອນ, ວັນນະຄະຕີ ແລະ ປັດຊະຍາ.

Hundred Years' War / ສົງຄາມຮ້ອຍປີ *n.* ການຣົບ
ສົງຄາມລະຫວ່າງ ອັງກິດ ແລະ ຝຣັ່ງ ຈາກປີ ຄ.ສ. 1337 ເຖິງ
1453.

I

Iberian Peninsula / ແຫຼມໄອບີເຣຍ *n.*
ແຫຼມທາງດ້ານຕາເວັນຕົກສ່ຽງໃຕ້ຂອງໂຮບ ທີ່ປະຈຸບັນ
ແມ່ນທີ່ຕັ້ງຂອງ ສະເປນ ແລະ ປ໊ອກຕຸການ.

Ignatius of Loyola, Saint /
ນັກບຸນ ອຸ້ນທ໌ ອິກນາຕຽດສ໌ ແຫ່ງ ໂລໂຢລາ *n.*
ຊາວສະເປນຜູ້ທີ່ສ້າງລະບົບທາງສາດສະໜາຂອງພະເຍຊູອິດ
(ນິກາຍໜຶ່ງຂອງສາດສະໜາໂຣມັນຄາທໍລິກ) ໃນຍຸກຕົ້ນຂອງ
ຊຸມປີ ຄ.ສ. 1530.

imperial / ກ່ຽວກັບ ຈັກກະຫວັດ ຫຼື ຈັກກະພັດ *adj.*

indulgence / ການໄຖ່ບາບ *n.* ການໄຖ່ບາບໃນນິກາຍ
ໂຣມັນຄາທໍລິກ ເພື່ອປົດປ່ອຍມະນຸດໃຫ້ຫຼຸດພົ້ນຈາກການຖືກລົງ
ໂທດຂອງພະຜູ້ເປັນເຈົ້າພາຍຫຼັງເສຍຊີວິດໄປແລ້ວ.

Inquisition / ສານສາດສະໜາ *n.* ສານທີ່ໄດ້ຮັບການສ້າງຕັ້ງ
ໂດຍສາດສະໜາຄລິດສ໌ ນິກາຍໂຣມັນຄາທໍລິກ ໃນປີ ຄ.ສ. 1542
ເພື່ອສອບສວນຄົນທີ່ຍັງຍາດສັດທາຕໍ ນິກາຍໂຣມັນຄາທໍລິກ ແລະ
ເພື່ອສ້າງອຳນາດຂອງນິກາຍດັ່ງກ່າວ ໃຫ້ມີຄວາມເຂັ້ມແຂງ.

Islam / ສາດສະໜາອິດສະລາມ *n.* ສາດສະໜາທີ່ເຊື່ອຖືໃນການ
ບູຊາພະເຈົ້າອົງດຽວ ໂດຍອີງຕາມຫຼັກຄຳສອນຂອງ ພະມະຫະໝັດ.

J

janissary / ທະຫານຮັບ *n.* ສະມາຊິກໃນກອງກຳລັງທະຫານ
ຂອງອຸ່ນຊັ້ນສູງ ແຫ່ງ ຈັກກະຫວັດອົຶດໂຕມັນ ທີ່ສ່ວນໃຫຍ່ແມ່ນ
ຜູ້ທີ່ເສຍເປັນຂ້າທາດ.

Jesuit / ເຍຊູອິດ *n.* ສະມາຊິກຂອງສະມາຄົມ ແຫ່ງພະເຍຊູ
(Society of Jesus) ຊຶ່ງເປັນລັດທິທາງສາດສະໜາ ທີ່ຖືກສ້າງ
ຕັ້ງໂດຍ ນັກບຸນ ອຸ້ນທ໌ ອິກນາຕຽດສ໌ ແຫ່ງ ໂລໂຢລາ ໃນຕົ້ນໆ ຊຸມປີ
ຄ.ສ. 1530.

Joan of Arc / ທ່ານນາງ ໂຈນ ແຫ່ງ ອາກ *n.* ວິລະສະຕີຊາວ
ບຮ. ຂອງຝຣັ່ງ ຜູ້ທີ່ນຳພາອະບວມການຕໍສູ້ຈົນເອົາຊະນະຝ່າຍອັງກິດ
ທີ່ ອອກແລນ (Orléans) ໃນປີ ຄ.ສ. 1429.

John, King / ກະສັດຈອນ *n.* ກະສັດອັງກິດ ຜູ້ທີ່ລົງນາມໃນ
ບັນຍັດ ກ່ຽວກັບສິດທິ ແມັກນາ ກາຕາ (Magna Carta)
ໃນ ຄ.ສ. 1215.

Justinian / ຈັກກະພັດຈັດສະຕີນຽນ *n.* ຈັກກະພັດແຫ່ງຈັກກະ
ຫວັດໂຣມັນຕາເວັນອອກ ນັບແຕ່ ປີ ຄ.ສ. 527 ເຖິງ 565 ເປັນຜູ້ທີ່
ຄອງລາດຮ່ວມກັບພະມະເຫສີ ທິໂອດໍຣາ (Theodora) ແລະ ຂຶ້ນ
ຄອງລາດຍິ່ງໃຫຍ່ ພາຍຫຼັງທີ່ເຄີຍສູງເສຍງານຖວຂວດຂອງງານຈັກ.

Justinian Code / ປະມວນກົດໝາຍຈັດສະຕີນຽນ ***n.*** ປະມວນກົດໝາຍ ທີ່ລວບລວມຕາມຄຳສັ່ງຂອງ ຈັກກະພັດຈັດສະຕີນຽນ ແຕ່ງ ຈັກກະຫວັດໄປແຮນທົມ ຜູ້ທີ່ປົກຄອງເປັນໄລຍະເວລາເກືອ ບທັງໝົດຂອງອາຍຸຈັກກະຫວັດຕັ້ງກ່າວ.

K

Kabuki / ລະຄອນເອທີ່ຍີ່ປຸ່ນ ***n.*** ລະຄອນເອທີ່ປະເພດໜຶ່ງຂອງຍີ່ປຸ່ນ ທີ່ໄດ້ຮັບການພັດທະນາ ໃນຊຸມປີ ຄ.ສ. 1600 ຊຶ່ງມີລັກສະນະດັ່ງ ທີ່ມີ ການຮ້ອງເພງ ແລະ ການເຕັ້ນ ປະກອບລະຄອນ, ແຕ່ງໜ້າເຂັ້ມໆ, ແລະ ນຸ່ງຊຸດສີ້ນເຜື່ອງ.

Khmer Empire / ອານາຈັກຂອມ ***n.*** ອານາຈັກທີ່ເຮືອງ ອຳນາດ ແລະ ຍືນນານທີ່ສຸດ ໃນອິງຊະເວດອາຊີຕາເວັນອອກສ່ຽງໃຕ້ ຊຶ່ງຕັ້ງຢູ່ ປະເທດກຳປູເຈຍ ໃນປະຈຸບັນ.

Kilwa / ມະຄອນ ກິລທ່ວ່າ ***n.*** ມະຄອນບູຮານທີ່ຕັ້ງຢູ່ຝັ່ງຕາເວັນ ອອກຂອງອາຟຣິກາ ຊຶ່ງມີຊາວອິທ່ານ ແລະ ອາຣາເບຍ ຕັ້ງຖິ່ນຖານຢູ່ ແລະ ເຮືອງອຳນາດທີ່ສຸດໃນຊຸມປີ ຄ.ສ. 1200.

kinship / ເຊື້ອສາຍ ຫຼື ຕະກຸນ ***n.*** ສາຍໃຍພັນໃນຄອບຄົວ ໂດຍສາຍເລືອດ, ການແຕ່ງງານ ຫຼື ການເອົາມາລ້ຽງ.

knight / ອັດສະວິນ ***n.*** ນັກຮົບຂີ່ມ້າທີ່ໄດ້ຮັບການຝຶກຝົນ ເພື່ອຮັບໃຊ້ຊຸ້ນຊຸ້ນສູງ ໃນຢູໂຣບສະໄໝກາງ.

Kongo / ອານາຈັກ ຄອງໂກ ***n.*** ອານາຈັກບູຮານ ທີ່ຕັ້ງຢູ່ແຄມຝັ່ງ ຕາເວັນຕົກຂອງອາຟຣິກາ ໂດຍຊາວຄອງໂກທີ່ປາກພາສາບັນທູ (Bantu) ຕັ້ງຖິ່ນຖານຢູ່ ໃນປະມານ ສັດຕະວັດທີ 14.

Koryo / ອານາຈັກ ຄໍໂຍ ***n.*** ອານາຈັກທີ່ຕັ້ງຢູ່ແຫມເກົ້າຫຼີ ໄດ້ຮັບ ການສັງງຕັ້ງ ໃນປີ ຄ.ສ. 935 ພາຍຫຼັງການຫຼົ້ມສະຫຼາຍຂອງ ອານາຈັກຊິລາ (Silla kingdom).

Kublai Khan / ກຸບໄລ ຂ່ານ ***n.*** ຫຼານຊາຍຂອງ ເຈັງກິດສ໌ ຂ່ານ (Genghis Khan) ຊຶ່ງເປັນຜູ້ທີ່ຄອບຄອງພາກໃຕ້ຂອງຈີນ ໃນປີ ຄ.ສ. 1260 ແລະ ປາກຄອງທະຫາງຊົ່ງ (Song) ໃນປີ 1279 ໂດຍທີ່ ມີ່ງ ໂຄມສາມາດຄອບຄອງຈີນທັງໝົດໄດ້.

L

labor specialization / ຄວາມຊຳນານທາງສີມື ***n.*** ການເຮັດວຽກດ້ານໃດໜຶ່ງ ຂອງພະນັກງານ ທີ່ໄດ້ຮັບການຝຶກຝົນ ຫຼື ມີຄວາມຮູ້ ໃນດ້ານຕັ້ງກ່າວ.

landform / ຊັ້ນດິນ ***n.*** ການກໍ່ຕົວຂອງຊັ້ນພັດດິນ ໂດຍທຳມະ ຊາດ ເຊັ່ນ ເປັນເກາະ, ພູເຂົາ, ຫຼື ພູພຽງ.

latitude / ເສັ້ນຮຸ້ງ ***n.*** ການວັດແທກໄລຍະທາງ ຈາກເໜືອ ຫາ ໃຕ້ ຂອງເສັ້ນສູນສູດ.

Leonardo da Vinci / ລີໂອນາໂດ ດາ ວິນຊີ ***n.*** ນັກແຕ້ມຮູບ ສະໄໝພື້ນຟູສິນລະປະວິທະຍາຈາກການ ຂອງອິຕາຕຸລີ ທີ່ເກີດໃນປີ ຄ.ສ. 1452 ແລະ ໄດ້ແຕ້ມຮູບຊຸ້ນເອກກາຫຍາຍຮູບ ເຊັ່ນ ຮູບ ໂມນາ ລີຊາ (Mona Lisa) ແລະ ຮູບ ການສະເຫວີຍອາຫານຄາບສຸດທ້າຍຂອງ ພະເຍຊູກ່ອນຖືກຈັບ (The Last Supper). ນອກຈາກນີ້, ລາວຍັງມີຄວາມຊຳຮອງຊານ ໃນດ້ານການຄົ້ນຄວ້າທາງວິທະຍາ ສາດນຳ.

longbow / ທະນູ ***n.*** ອາວຸດທີ່ໃຊ້ຍິງລູກທະນູ ໂດຍສາມາດຈະາະ ເຫຼັກກັນອາວຸດຂອງອັດສະວິນໄດ້.

longitude / ເສັ້ນແວງ ***n.*** ການວັດແທກໄລຍະທາງ ຈາກທາງ ຕາເວັນອອກ ທາງທາງຕາເວັນຕົກຂອງ ເສັ້ນຜ່ານອ້ວໂລກ.

lord / ເຈົ້າຄອງທີ່ດິນ ***n.*** ຊຸ້ນຊຸ້ນສູງ ຜູ້ຄອບຄອງທີ່ດິນທີ່ມີອຳນາດ.

Luther, Martin / ທ່ານ ມາຕິນ ລູເທີ ***n.*** ນັກເຜີຍແຜ່ ສາດສະໝາຊາວ ເຢຍລະມັນ ເກີດໃນປີ ຄ.ສ. 1483 ໂດຍໄດ້ເປັນຜູ້ ນຳໃນການປະຕິຮູບ (Reformation) ແລະ ສອນກ່ຽວກັບການ ເຮັດໃຫ້ອົນນານຢ໌ລິສຸດ ໂດຍຄວາມມີສັດທາຕໍ່ພະຜູ້ປັນເຈົ້າ ຫຼາຍກວ່າ ຈະເປັນການສັງງອານກີ.

M

Magna Carta / ບັນຍັດ ແມັກນາ ກາຕາ ***n.*** ບັນດາສິທທີທີ່ ບັນຍັດ ໂດຍຊຸ້ນຊຸ້ນສູງຊາວອັງກິດ ແລະ ລົງນາມ ໂດຍກະສັດຈອນ ໃນປີ ຄ.ສ. 1215.

Maize / ເຂົ້າໂພດ ***n.*** ສາລີປະເພດໜຶ່ງ ທີ່ປູກໂດຍເຜົ່າອາເມລິກາ ພື້ນເມືອງ.

Mali / ຈັກກະຫວັດມາລີ ***n.*** ຈັກກະຫວັດໃນອາຟຣິກາທາງຕາເວັນຕົກ ສັງງຕັ້ງ ໂດຍຊາວມາລີ.

Manchu / ລາດຊະວົງແມນຈູ ***n.*** ລາດຊະວົງຊາວຈີນ ທາງຕາເວັນອອກສ່ຽງເໜືອ ໃນປີ ຄ.ສ. 1644 ແລະ ເປັນການເລີ່ ຕົ້ນລາດຊະວົງສຸດທ້າຍໃນປະຫວັດສາດຂອງຈີນ ທີ່ຮຽກວ່າ ລາດຊະ ວົງ ຊິງ (Qing Dynasty).

manor / ທີ່ດິນຂອງສັກດິນາໆ ***n.*** ທີ່ດິນຂອງສັກດິນາໆ ຊຶ່ງປັກກະຕິ ຈະລວມທັງ ອາຄານ ຫຼື ທີ່ປະສາດ ນຳ.

Mansa Musa / ຈັກກະພັດ ແມນຊາ ມູຊາ ***n.*** ຈັກກະພັດ ແຕ່ງ ມາລີ ຜູ້ທີ່ເດີນທາງໄປສະແຫວງບຸນທີ່ເມືອງມັກກະ ໃນປີ ຄ.ສ. 1324.

maritime / ກ່ຽວກັບ ທະເລ ***adj.***

Maya / ອາລະຍະທຳມາຢາ ***n.*** ອາລະຍະທຳຂອງແມັກຊິໂກຕອນ ໃຕ້ ແລະ ອະເມລິກາກາງຕອນເໜືອ ທີ່ມີຄວາມຮຸ່ງເຮືອງສູງສຸດ ນັບແຕ່ປີ ຄ.ສ. 250 ເຖິງ 900.

Mbanza / ມະບັນຊາ ***n.*** ມະຄອນຫຼວງຂອງອານາຈັກຄອງ ໂກບູຮານ ໃນອາຟຣິກາ.

mercantilism / ລັດທິພຣ຺ມິດນິຍົມ *n.* ນະໂຍບາຍເສດຖະກິດ ທີ່ຊີງໃສ່ ແນວຄວາມຄິດທີ່ວ່າ ອຳນາດຂອງຊາດໃດໜຶ່ງ ແມ່ນຂຶ້ນກັບ ຄວາມມັ່ງຄັ່ງທີ່ມີ.

mercenary / ທະຫານຮັບຈ້າງໆ *n.*

Meso-America / ເມໂສອາເມລິກາ ຫຼື ອາເມລິກາກາງ *n.* ອານາເຂດທີ່ກວມເອົາບໍລິເວນທີ່ຕາມໃຕ້ຂອງແມັກຊິໂກ ແລະ ສ່ວນໃຫຍ່ ຂອງທະວີບອາເມລິກາ.

Michelangelo / ໄມເຄິລ ແອງເຈີໂລ *n.* ນັກສິນລະປະສະ ໄໝ້ນິ້ນຝຣັ່ງສິນລະປະວິທະຍາກາງຂອງອິຕາລີ ເກີດໃນປີ ຄ.ສ. 1475 ຜູ້ທີ່ສ່ວນໃຫຍ່ສ້າງຜົນງານປະຕິມາກຳ ແລະ ຍັງສ້າງອັນນະກຳ ຮບແຕ້ມ ທີ່ມີຊື່ສຽງຫຼາຍຢ່າງ ເຊັ່ນ ແຕ້ມເພດານຂອງໂບດ ຊິດສະຕິນ (Sistine) ໃນນະຄອນໂຣມ.

Middle Ages / ຍຸກກາງໆ *n.* ຊ່ວງເວລາໃນປະຫວັດສາດຂອງຢູ ໂຣບ (ປີ ຄ.ສ. 500 ທາ 1450) ໃນລະຫວ່າງ ໄລຍະ ຕົ້ນສະຫຍາຍຂອງຈັກກະຫວັດໂຣມ ແລະ ຍຸກຟື້ນຝູສິນລະປະວິທະຍາການ (Renaissance).

missionary / ຜູ້ເຜີຍແຜ່ສາດສະໜາ *n.* ຜູ້ທີ່ເດີນທາງໄປຕ່າງໆ ແຄບ ເພື່ອເຜີຍແຜ່ຄວາມເຊື່ອທາງສາດສະໜາຂອງຕົນ.

monastery / ວັດອາຮາມ *n.* ສະຖານທີ່ທີ່ຜູ້ນັບຖືສາດສະໜາ ໃດໜຶ່ງ ທຳການພາອະບາ ແລະ ສັກກາລະບູຊາ.

Mongol Ascendancy / ຍຸກການປົກຄອງຂອງຊາວມົງໂກນ *n.* ໄລຍະທີ່ຊາວມົງໂກນປົກຄອງເອເຊຍກາງທັງໝົດ ແລະ ເຮັດໃຫ້ການ ຄ້າຂາຍ ແລະ ການເດີນທາງທາງບົກ ມີຄວາມປອດໄພ.

monotheism / ລັດທິບູຊາພະເຈົ້າອົງດຽວ *n.* ລັດທິຄວາມເຊື່ອທີ່ວ່າມີພະເຈົ້າພຽງແຕ່ອົງດຽວ.

Montezuma II / ຈັກກະພັດມອນເຕຊູມາ ທີ II *n.* ຈັກກະພັດອົງສຸດທ້າຍຂອງ ແອັດສະເຕັກ (Aztec) ຜູ້ທີ່ປົກຄອງ ແຕ່ປີ ຄ.ສ. 1502 ເຖິງ 1520 ແລະ ຖືກຂັບອອກຈາກບັນລັງ ໂດຍ ຊາວສະເປນ.

mosaic / ລວດລາຍໂມເສກ *n.* ລວດລາຍ ທີ່ເຮັດຈາກເສດກະ ເບື້ອງ ຫຼື ເສດແກ້ວ ທີ່ມີສີສັນ ຕ່າງໆ.

mosque / ສຸເຫຼົ່າ ຫຼື ມັດສະຍິດ *n.* ບ່ອນທີ່ຊາວມຸດສະລີມ ໃຊ້ສັກກາລະ ບູຊາ ໂດຍອອກແບບໃຫ້ຫັນໜ້າໄປທາງນະຄອນເມັກກະ.

mother culture / ວັດທະນະທຳແມ່ ຫຼື ຕົ້ນໆ *n.* ວັດທະນະທຳ ທີ່ ອາງຈາກຖານ ຫຼື ມີຊີດທີ່ຝັງ ຕໍ່ກັບປະໜົບປະຕິບັດ ແລະ ແນວຄວາມຄິດຂອງວັດທະນະທຳອື່ນໆ ໃນພາກພື້ນ.

movable type / ເຄື່ອງພິມຕົວໜັງສີ *n.* ແຜ່ນໂລຫະ ຫຼື ແຜ່ນໄມ້ ນ້ອຍໆ ທີ່ເບີດຂຶ້ນໄດ້ ເພື່ອໃຊ້ພິມຕົວໜັງສີ.

Murasaki Shikibu, Lady / ທ່ານນາງໆ ມຸຣະຊະກິ ຊິກິບຸ *n.* ນັກປະພັນຍິງຂອງຍີ່ປຸ່ນ ໃນກ່ອນປີ ຄ.ສ 1000 ຜູ້ທີ່ຂຽນ ນິທານ ແຕ່ງ ເຈ້ງຈີ (The Tale of Genji) ທີ່ຖືວ່າເປັນຜົນໜຶ່ງໃນ ບັນດານິທານ ຫຼືເລື້ມທຳຊີດ ຂອງໂລກ.

Muslim / ສາດສະໜານຸດສະລີມ *n.* ຜູ້ທີ່ປະຕິບັດຕາມ ຫຼັກສາດສະໜາ ອິດສະລາມ ໂດຍມີພະອັນລະຊະ ເປັນພະຜູ້ເປັນເຈົ້າ ພຽງອົງດຽວ.

Mutapa / ອານາຈັກ ມຸຕະປາ *n.* ອານາຈັກບູຮານ ທີ່ສ້າງຕັ້ງ ແລະ ປົກຄອງ ໂດຍກະສັດ ໂຊນາ ໃນປະມານ ຄ.ສ. 1440; ປະຈຸບັນ ແມ່ນ ປະເທດຊິມບັບເວ.

N

Nam Viet / ອານາຈັກນາມຫວຽດ *n.* ອານາຈັກຫວຽດນາມ ທີ່ລອບຄອງ ໂດຍຊາວຈີນໃນ 111 ປີກ່ອນ ຄ.ສ.

natural rights / ສິດທິທີ່ທຸກຄົນໄດ້ຮັບມາແຕ່ກຳເນີດ *n.* ເຊັ່ນ ສິດທິໃນການດຳລົງຊີວິດ, ເສລີພາບ ແລະ ກຳມະສິດ ຕາມ ບັນຍັດຂອງນັກປັດຊະຍາ ຈອນ ລ໊ອກ (John Locke) ໃນສັດຕະວັດທີ 18.

Noh / ລະຄອນໂນ *n.* ລະຄອນປະເພດໜຶ່ງຂອງຍີ່ປຸ່ນ ທີ່ໄດ້ຮັບການ ພັດທະນາໃນຊຸມປີ ຄ.ສ. 1300 ມີລັກສະນະເດັ່ນ ທີ່ເປັນການສະທ້ອນ ກ່ຽວກັບ ຕຳນານ ແລະ ເລື່ອງພື້ນບ້ານ ແລະ ບຳສະແດງໂດຍນັກສະ ແດງທີ່ໃສ່ໜ້າກາກໄມ້ ສີສັນຕ່າງໆ.

nomad / ຄົນລ່ອນເລ່ *n.* ສະມາຊິກຂອງຜົ່ງ ທີ່ບໍ່ມັກຕັ້ງຖິ່ນ ຖານຄົງທີ່ ແລະ ເລື້ອຍຍ້າຍຈາກບ່ອນໜຶ່ງ ໄປຍັງບ່ອນອື່ນ.

O

oasis / ບ່ອນທີ່ມີຄວາມອຸດົມສົມບູນກາງທະເລຊາຍ *n.*

Olmec / ວັດທະນະທຳ ໂອລເມັກ *n.* ວັດທະນະທຳໃນອາເມລິກາ ກາງ ທີ່ເກົ່າແກ່ທີ່ສຸດ ຊຶ່ງມີຄວາມຣຸ່ງເຮືອງ ນັບແຕ່ 1200 ເຖິງ 400 ປີ ກ່ອນ ຄ.ສ. ແລະ ເປັນສູນກາງຄວາມຈະເລີນຕາມແຄມຝັ່ງ ຂອງ ອ່າວ ແມັກຊິໂກ ຕາເວັນອອກສ່ຽງໃຕ້.

Omar Khayyám / ທ່ານ ໂອມາ ໄຄຢຳ *n.* ນັກກະວີຊາວມຸດ ສະລີມ ຜູ້ທີ່ມັກຂຽນກະວີ ປະເພດຄວັດເຣັນ (quatrain) ແລະ ຍັງເປັນນັກກະນິດສາດຜູ້ຍິ່ງໃຫຍ່.

oral history / ປະຫວັດສາດຕາມການເລົ່າໆຕໍ່ໆກາກ *n.* ເຫດການທາງ ປະຫວັດສາດທີ່ເລົ່າແບບປາກຕໍ່ປາກ ເຊັ່ນ ເລື້ອງເລົ່າໆຈາກລຸ້ນໜຶ່ງ ສູ່ອີກລຸ້ນໜຶ່ງ.

Orthodox / ກ່ຽວກັບ ນິກາຍອໍໂທດອກ *adj.* ກ່ຽວກັບນິກາຍຂອງສາດສະໜາຄຣິດສ໌ ທີ່ໄດ້ຮັບການພັດທະນາໃນ ຈັກກະຫວັດ ໄບແຊນທິນ ແລະ ບໍ່ຢູ່ພາຍໃຕ້ອານາດຂອງ ພະສັນຕະປາໆ.

Osman / ອອຕສະນານ *n.* ຜູ້ນຳກົ໊ອກກິ ຊຶ່ງເປັນຜູ້ກໍຕັ້ງ ຈັກກະຫວັດອໍອດໂຕມັນ ໃນຍຸກຕົ້ນ ປີ ຄ.ສ. 1300.

P

Pacal II / ກະສັດປາກາລ ທີ II *n.* ກະສັດຜູ້ທີ່ປົກຄອງນະຄອນມາ ຢາ ແຫ່ງ ພາເລັ່ງ (Palenque) ເປັນເວລາເກືອບ 70 ປີ (ນັບແຕ່ ຄ.ສ 615)—ໜຶ່ງໃນກະສັດທີ່ຍິ່ງໃຫຍ່ຂອງຊາວມາຢາ.

Pachacuti / ພາຊາກຸຕີ *n.* ຜູ້ປົກຄອງຜໍ່າຊົນຊາດອິນທີ່ເຊິ້າ ທີ່ອົງຄອງອຳນາດ ໃນປີ ຄ.ສ. 1438 ແລະ ແຜ່ອະຫຍາຍຈັກກະຫວັດ ອິນຄາ.

parliament / ສະພາແຫ່ງຊາດ ຫຼື ລັດຖະສະພາ *n.* ຄະນະຜູ້ແທນທີ່ຊົດທີ່ຍັນ ຕຳໜ່າງປົກຄອງຂອງລັດຖະບານ.

patron / ຜູ້ອຸປະຖຳ *n.* ຜູ້ທີ່ໃຫ້ການສະໜັບສະໜຸນທາງການເງິນ ແກ່ການເຄື່ອນໄຫວ ຫຼື ສະຖາບັນ ໃດໜຶ່ງ.

Peace of Westphalia / ສັນຕິພາບເວັດສະຟາເລຍ *n.* ຂໍ້ຕົກລົງທີ່ບັນລຸໃນ ຄ.ສ. 1648 ເພື່ອແບ່ງແຍກຍຸໂຣບຕາເວັນຕົກ ອອກເປັນ ຊາດຂອງຊາດທີ່ລີກ ແລະ ໂປຣເຕັດສະແຕນ ຢ່າງ ຖຶຖອນ ແລະ ຍຸຕິສົ້ງຄວາມທາງສາດສະໜາທີ່ຍຶດເຍື້ອຍາວນານ.

perspective / ສິນລະປະແບບໄດ້ສັດສ່ວນ *n.* ຕໍ້ນບົກໃນການ ແຕ້ນຮູບປະພວດໜຶ່ງ ທີ່ໄດ້ຮັບການນັດທະນາໃນຍຸກຟື້ນຟູສິນລະປະວິທະ ຍາການ ຊຶ່ງສະແດງພາບຂອງວັດຖຸສົ່ງຕ່າງໆ ແບບ 3 ມິຕິ.

philosophe / ທ່ານ ພີໂລໂຊບ *ມ.* ຊຶ່ງໃນບັນດານັກຄິດ ໃນສັດຕະວັດທີ 18 ຊຶ່ງເປັນຜູ້ທີ່ພະຍາຍານນຳໃຊ້ວິທີການທາງວິທະຍາ ສາດ ເຂົ້າໃນການແກ້ໄຂບັນຫາສັງຄົມ.

pilgrimage / ການສະແຫວງບຸນ *n.* ການເດີນທາງໄປຍັງ ສະຖານທີ່ ຫຼື ບ່ອນສັກກາລະບູຊາ ອັນສັກສິດ.

Pizarro, Francisco / ທ່ານ ຟຣານຊິດສະໂກ ປີຊາໂຣ *n.* ນັກສຳຫຼວດຊາວສະເປນ ຜູ້ທີ່ເດີນທາງເຖິງຝັ່ງເປຣູ ໃນປີ ຄ.ສ. 1532 ແລະ ຕີອະນະຈັກກະຫວັດອິນຄາ ໃນປີ 1535.

Polo, Marco / ທ່ານ ມາໂຄ ໂປໂລ *n.* ພໍ່ຄ້າຊາວເວນິດສ໌ ຜູ້ທີ່ ເດີນທາງຕາມເສັ້ນທາງສາຍໄໝ ແລະ ໄປເຖິງຈີນ ໃນປະມານ ຄ.ສ. 1275. ລາວໄດ້ເປັນຜູ້ອຸ່ວຍຂອງ ຄຸບໄລ ຂ່ານ (Kublai Khan) ແລະ ຕໍ່ມາໄດ້ຈັດພິມນັ້ນອັນລືຊື່ສຽງ ກ່ຽວກັບການເດີນທາງຂອງຕົນ.

porcelain / ເຄື່ອງກະເບື້ອງ *n.* ວັດສະດຸເຊຣານິກແຂງ ມີສີຂາວ.

predestination / ລັດທິເຊື່ອໃນເຄື່ອງການໄຕ່ບານ *n.* ລັດທິທີ່ເຊື່ອວ່າ ພະຜູ້ເປັນເຈົ້າ ເປັນຜູ້ລັດເລືອກຜູ້ຄົນ ໃຫ້ຫຼຸດພົ້ນຈາກ ການຕົກນະລົກ ແລະ ຖືກສາບແຊ່ງ ກ່ອນຈະໄປເກີດ ໂດຍທີ່ຕົນບໍ່ມີ ຜະລັງທີ່ຈະປ່ຽນແປງ ພະປະສົ້ງຂອງພະຜູ້ເປັນເຈົ້າ.

primary source / ແຫຼ່ງຂໍ້ມູນຂັ້ນຕົ້ນ *n.* ເອກະສານ ຫຼື ສິ່ງທີ່ສ້າງຂຶ້ນ ໃນລະຫວ່າງເຫດການທາງປະຫວັດສາດໃດໜຶ່ງ.

printing press / ແມ່ພິມ *n.* ເຄື່ອງມືທີ່ໃຊ້ພິມນ້ຳມຶກລົງເຈ້ຍ.

projection / ການສະແດງແຜນທີ່ *n.* ວິທີໃນການສະແດງພື້ນ ໜ້າໂລກ ໃນແຜ່ນທີ່ຮາບພຽງ ໂດຍການບັນວັດຕາສ່ວນ.

Protestant / ບິກາຍໂປຣເຕັດສະແຕນ *n.* ບິກາຍ ໜຶ່ງຂອງຊາດຄິດ ຕະສາດສະໜາ ທີ່ແຍກຕ່າງໆຈາກ ບິກາຍໂຣມັນຄາທໍລີກ ໃນປະມານ ສັດຕະວັດທີ 16.

Q

quipu / ເຄື່ອງນັບເລກ *n.* ເຄື່ອງນັບເລກໃນອາລະຍະທຳອິນຄາ ທີ່ເຮັດດ້ວຍ ເຊືອກ (ດ້າຍ) ແລະ ຂອດ ຕ່າງໆ.

Qur'an / ພະຄຳພີກຸຣ່ານ *n.* ຄຳພີສັກສິດຂອງຊາວມຸດສະລິມ ທີ່ແສດງໃຫ້ເຫັນເຖິງວະຈີບົຫານຂອງພະອັນລອະ ຊຶ່ງຖວຍທວນ ໂດຍສາວົກທ້ອງ ພະມະຫະນັດ.

R

rationalism / ລັດທິເຫດຜົນນິຍົມ *n.* ຫຼັກຄວາມຄິດທີ່ວ່າ ມະນຸດຄວນໃຊ້ເຫດຜົນ ຫຼື ການຄິດທາງຕັກກະ ເພື່ອທຳຄວາມເຂົ້າ ໃຈກ່ຽວກັບໂລກ.

Reconquista / ຍຸກຂອງການກູ້ເອກະຣາດ *n.* ຍຸກສົ້ງຄາມທີ່ກອງກຳລັ້ງຂອງຊາວຄຣິສຕ໌ ຂັບໄລ່ບັນດາຜູ້ປົກຄອງ ຊາວມຸດສະລິມອອກຈາກສະເປນ (ສິ້ນສຸດ ໃນ ຄ.ສ. 1492).

Reformation / ຍຸກປະຕິຮູບ *n.* ການປັບປຸງກຸ່ມທີ່ຕໍ່ຕ້ານບິກາຍ ໂຣມັນຄາທໍລີກ ຊຶ່ງເລີ່ມຕົ້ນ ໃນສັດຕະວັດທີ 16.

regent / ຜູ້ສຳເລັດຣາຊການຊະການ *n.* ຜູ້ປົກຄອງອານາຂອດໃດໜຶ່ງ ທີ່ຍັ່ມ ກະສັດ ຫຼື ມີເຊື້ອສາຍລາດຂຸ່ວໄວ້ ທີ່ມີອາຍຸໜ້ອຍ.

religious order / ຜູ້ນັບຖືສາດສະໜາ *n.* ກຸ່ມຄົນໃດໜຶ່ງ ທີ່ດຳລົງຊີວິດຕາມຫຼັກສາດສະໜາໃດໜຶ່ງ.

Renaissance / ຍຸກຟື້ນຟູສິນລະປະວິທະຍາການ *n.* ຊ່ວງໄລຍະແຫ່ງຄວາມຟື້ນຟູ ແລະ ສັ່ງສົມ ສິນລະປະ, ການຂິດຄຽນ, ແລະ ຄວາມຄິດ (ປີ ຄ.ສ. 1300 ຫາ 1600) ຊຶ່ງມີຈຸດເລີ່ມຕົ້ນໃນອິ ຕາລີ ແລະ ໃນທີ່ສຸດໄດ້ແຜ່ອະຫຍາຍໄປທົ່ວ ຍຸໂຣບ.

republic / ສາທາລະນະລັດ *n.* ຮຸບແບບໜຶ່ງຂອງລັດຖະບານ ໂດຍທີ່ປະຊາຊົນມີອຳນາດໃນການເລືອກຕັ້ງເອົາຜູ້ນຳມັ້ງຄັ້ງຫານປະເທດ.

reunify / ລວມກັນອີກໃໝ່ *v.*

Roman Catholic / ກ່ຽວກັບ ບິກາຍໂຣມັນຄາທໍລີກ *adj.* ກ່ຽວກັບບິກາຍ ໂຣມັນຄາທໍລີກຂອງຊາວຕາເວັນຕົກ ອັນຢູ່ພາຍໃຕ້ອາ ນັດຂອງພະສັນຕະປາ.

S

Sahara / ທະເລຊາຍ ຊາຮາຣາ *n.* ທະເລຊາຍອັນກວ້າງໃຫຍ່ ໄພສານໃນວ່າຟຣິກາເໜືອ ຊຶ່ງກວມເອົາ ແຕ່ຟັ່ງແອັດລັງຕິກ ເຖິງ ຣ່ອມພູໄນ (Nile Valley).

Saladin / ທ່ານ ສະລາດິນ *n.* ຜູ້ນຳທາງການທະຫານຜູ້ທີ່ເຕົ້າ ໂຮມຊາວມຸດສະລິມ ເພື່ອຕໍ່ສູ້ກັບຊາວຄຣິສຕ໌ ໃນປາງລັດສະຕາຍ ໃນສັດຕະວັດ ທີ 12.

salon / ການປະຊຸມ *n.* ການລວບລວມບັນດານັກຄິດ ແລະ ນັກສິລະປະ ເພື່ອປຶກສາຫາລື ແລະ ແລກປ່ຽນແນວຄວາມຄິດກັບ ໃນຍຸກແຫ່ງຄວາມຮູ້ແຈ້ງເຫັນຈິງ (the Enlightenment).

samurai / ຊາມູໄຣ *n.* ນັກຮົບທີ່ໄດ້ຮັບການຝຶກຝົນ ເພື່ອຮັບໃຊ້ຊັ້ນສູງໆໃນຍີ່ປຸ່ນ.

savanna / ທົ່ງຫຍ້າ *n.* ທົ່ງຫຍ້າ ທີ່ບໍ່ຄ່ອຍມີຕົ້ນໄມ້ ໃນອ້ຽເຂດທີ່ມີອາກາດຮ້ອນ.

schism / ການແຍກຈາກກັນຂອງ 2 ກຸ່ມ (ໃນນິກາຍໂຮມັນຄາທໍລິກ) ຢ່າງເປັນທາງການ *n.*

scholar-official / ຜູ້ມີການສຶກສາ ທີ່ມີຕຳແໜ່ງໃນລັດຖະບານ *n.*

scientific method / ວິທີການທາງວິທະຍາສາດ *n.* ຂັ້ນຕອນໃນການທົດສອບທາງວິທະຍາສາດ ທີ່ກ່ຽວຂ້ອງກັບການສັງ ເກດ, ການສ້າງ ແລະ ທົດສອບສົມມຸດຕິຖານ, ແລະ ການທາຂໍ້ສະຫຼຸບ ເພື່ອຢັ້ງຢືນ ຫຼື ປັບປຸງ ສົມມຸດຕິຖານຄັ້ງກ່ອນ.

Scientific Revolution / ການປະຕິວັດທາງວິທະຍາສາດ *n.* ຊ່ວງເວລາ (ເລີ່ມຕົ້ນ ແຕ່ ຄ.ສ 1500) ທີ່ບັນດານັກຄິດຢູ່ໂດຍ ເລີ່ມຕົ້ນຕັ້ງຄຳຖາມ ຕໍ່ໄພແບບຄວາມຄິດ ແລະ ຫຼັກຄວາມເຊື່ອຂອງ ອະດີດຕະ ສາດສະໜາ.

secondary source / ແຫຼ່ງຂໍ້ມູນທີສອງ *n.* ການບັນທຶກ ເຫດການ (ທາງປະຫວັດສາດ) ທີ່ຂຽນ ໂດຍບຸກຄົນ ທີ່ບໍ່ໄດ້ ຕິດແທດໄພເຫດການຕໍ່ຈິງດ້ວຍຕົນເອງ.

Seljuk Turk / ເຊັນຈຸກ ເທີກ *n.* ຊາວຕໍອກກ໌ ຜູ້ທີ່ຄອບຄອງເອ ເຊຍ ກາງ ແລະ ຕາເວັນຕົກ ໃນລະຫວ່າງ ສັດຕະວັດທີ 11ແລະ 13.

serf / ຂ້າທາດ *n.* ຊາວນາທີ່ເປັນຂ້າທາດໃນສັງຄົມສັກດິນາ ຜູ້ທີ່ຮັບໃຊ້ ຂຸນນາງສັກດິນາ ເພື່ອໃຫ້ໄດ້ຮັບການປົກປ້ອງ.

Shakespeare, William / ວິນປະນັ້ນ ວິນລຽມ ເຊັກສະເປຍ *n.* ນັກຂຽນບົດລະຄອນອັງກິດ ທີ່ມີຊື່ສຽງທີ່ສຸດ ໃນຍຸກຟື້ນຟູສິນລະປະວິທະຍາການ ໂດຍມີລະຄອນທີ່ເປັນທີ່ຮູ້ຈັກຢ່າງໆ ກວ້າງຂວາງ ເຊັ່ນ: ໂຣມິໂອ ກັບ ຈຸລຽດ (Romeo and Juliet) ແລະ ແຮມເລັດ (Hamlet).

Shi'a / ເຊຍ *n.* ຊາວມຸດສະລິມກຸ່ມໜຶ່ງ ທີ່ຕົ້ງຕ້ານຄຳສັ່ງສອນຂອງ ຜະຍຸມາຍັດສ໌ (Umayyads) ໂດຍເຊື່ອວ່າ ຜູ້ສືບທອດຕຳ ແໜ່ງຂອງຜະມະຫະນັດ ຄວນແມ່ນເຊື້ອສາຍຂອງຜະມະຫະນັດເອງ.

Shinto / ລັດທິຊິນໂຕ *n.* ສາດສະໜາດັ້ງເດີມຂອງຍີ່ປຸ່ນ ທີ່ຊີ່ບໃຊ້ ການສັກການະບູຊາ ແລະ ພິທີ ທຳມະຊາດ ແລະ ບັນພະບູລຸດ.

shogun / ໂຊກຸນ *n.* ຜູ້ນຳທາງການທະຫານຂອງຍີ່ປຸ່ນ—ໜຶ່ງໃນ ບັນດາຜູ້ປົກຄອງ ທີ່ເຂົ້າກຳອຳນາດ ໃນປີ ຄ.ສ 1192 ແລະ ປົກຄອງ ໃນນາມຂອງຜະຈັກກະພັດ ແຕ່ຕາມປົກກະຕິແລ້ວ ຈະປົກຄອງເໜືອຜືນ ປະໂຫຍດ ຂອງຕົນເອງຫຼາຍກວ່າ.

Shona / ໂຊນາ *n.* ວັດທະນະທຳຂອງກຸ່ມຄົນ ທີ່ເວົ້າພາສາ ບັນທູ ກ່ອນປີ ຄ.ສ 1000 ຊຶ່ງໃນປະຈຸບັນ ແຍກອອກເປັນປະເທດ ບອດສະ ວານາ, ໂມຊຳບິກ ແລະ ຊິມບັບເວ.

Shotoku, Prince / ເຈົ້າຊາຍ ໂຊໂຕກຸ *n.* ຜູ້ສຳເລັດລາດຄະ ການ ທີ່ປົກຄອງຍີ່ປຸ່ນ ແຕ່ປີ ຄ.ສ 593 ຫາ 622 ແລະ ໄດ້ນຳເອົາ ວັດທະນະທຳຈີນເຂົ້າໄປເຜີຍແຜ່ໃນຍີ່ປຸ່ນ—ໂດຍສະເພາະແໜ່ນ ສາ ດສະໜາພຸດ.

Silk Roads / ຖະໜົນສາຍໄໝ *n.* ເສັ້ນທາງການຄ້າໃນສະ ໄໝບູຮານ ທີ່ເຊື່ອມຕໍ່ ຢູໂຣບ ແລະ ຈີນ.

slash-and-burn agriculture / ກະສິກຳແບບເຮັດໄຮ່ ເລື່ອນລອຍ *n.* ກະສິກຳປະເພດທີ່ມີການຖາງປ່າເຮັດໄຮ່.

Songhai / ຊົງໄຮ *n.* ຊາວອາຟຣິກາທາຕາເວັນຕົກ ທີ່ມີຜູ້ປົກຄອງເປັນຜູ້ສ້າງ ຈັກກະວັດອັນຍິ່ງໃຫຍ່ ໃນລະຫວ່າງ ສັດຕະວັດທີ 15 ແລະ 16.

sponsor / ຜູ້ສະໜັບສະໜູນ *n.* ຜູ້ທີ່ໄດ້ຈາກທຸ່ນສິນ ເງິນຄຳ ເພື່ອຊ່ວຍ ເຫຼືອ ບຸກຄົນ ຫຼື ໂຄງການໃດໜຶ່ງ.

standing army / ກອງປະຈຳການ *n.* ກອງທະຫານທີ່ປະຈຳການ ບໍ່ວ່າຈະເປັນຍາມສົ້ນຮົບ ຫຼື ສະຫງົບສຸກ.

stele / ອະນຸສາວະລີ *n.* ແທ່ນຫີນແກະສະຫຼັກ ທີ່ໃຊ້ເພື່ອສັນລະເສີນ ວັນ ຫຼື ເຫດການສຳຄັນ ໃດໜຶ່ງ.

Stoicism / ລັດທິ ສະໂຕອິຊິດຊຶ່ມ *n.* ປັດຊະຍາຂອງກຣີກ ທີ່ສັ່ງສອນກ່ຽວກັບ ຄຸນນະທຳ, ຄວາມຮັບຜິດຊອບ ແລະ ຄວາມອົດກົ້ນ ຊຶ່ງ ມີອິດທິພົນ ອ້ອມຂ້າງໆຫຼາຍ ຕໍ່ອານາຈັກ ໂຣມັນບູຮານ.

Suleyman I / ສຸລະຕ່ານ ສຸໄລມານ ທີ I *n.* ສຸລະຕ່ານ ແຫ່ງ ຈັກກະວັດອົດໂຕມັນ (ຄ.ສ. 1520 ຫາ 1566) ອົງທີ່ສົ່ງ ເສີມສິນລະປະ ວັດທະນະທຳ ແລະ ສ້າງຕັ້ງລະບົບກົດໝາຍ.

Sundiata / ຊຸນດ້ຽຕາ *n.* ຜູ້ປົກຄອງຊາວມາລີ ໃນສະໄໝບູຮານ ຊຶ່ງເປັນຜູ້ຍຶດຄອງການຄ້າທອງ ຂອງການຄ້າ ແລະ ແຜ່ອະຫຍາຍຈັກກະ ຫວັດ ອອກໄປຢ່າງກວ້າງໄກ.

Sunnah / ຄຳສອນຊຸນນາ *n.* ຄຳສອນ ແລະ ຫຼັກປະຕິບັດ ຂອງຜະມະຫະນັດ ເພື່ອສອນຊາວມຸດສະລິມ ດຳລົງຊີວິດ ໃຫ້ຖືກຕ້ອງຕາມຄອງທຳ.

Sunni / ຊຸນນິ *n.* ຊາວມຸດສະລິມ ກຸ່ມທີ່ຍອມຮັບການປົກຄອງຂອງ ຜູ້ສືບທອດຜະມະຫະນັດທີ່ໄດ້ຮັບລັດເລືອກ ແລະ ບໍ່ໄດ້ຕຳ່ນ ອຸມາຍັດສ໌ (Umayyads).

Swahili / ພາສາ ຊຸະວາຮີລີ *n.* ພາສາອາຟຣິກາພາສາໜຶ່ງ ທີ່ເກີດ ຈາກ ການປະສົມປະສານ ລະຫວ່າງ ພາສາບັນທູ ແລະ ພາສາອາຫຣັບ.

T

Tenochtitlán / ມະລອນ ເທນົດຕິດລັນ *n.* ນະລອນຂອງແອັດສະ ເຫັກບູຮານ ທີ່ໄດ້ຮັບການສ້າງຕັ້ງ ໃນປີ ຄ.ສ. 1325 ຢູ່ເກາະນ້ອຍໆ ກາງທະເລສາຍ ເທັກໂກໂກ (Texcoco).

Thomas Aquinas / ທ່ານ ໂທມັດສ໌ ອາທິມັດສ໌ *n.* ບັນດິດຊາວອິຕາລີ ຜູ້ທີ່ຮອບຮອມປັດຊຸຍາດັ່ງເດີມ ແລະ ວິຊາສາດສະໝາຂອງຊາວອຣິໂຕສ໌.

Timbuktu / ມະຄອນ ທິມບຸກຕຸ *n.* ນະຄອນຂອງມາລິກາງໆ ໃນອາຟຣິກາຕາເວັນຕົກ ຊຶ່ງໄດ້ຮັບການສ້າງຕັ້ງ ໃນສັດຕະວັດທີ 13 ແລະ ເປັນສູນກາງທາງການຄ້າ ແລະ ວັດທະນະທຳ.

Tokugawa Shogunate / ໂຕກູກາວາ ໂຊກຸນະເຕ *n.* ການປົກຄອງຍີ່ປຸ່ນ ຂອງ ໂຕກູກາວາ ແລະ ຜູ້ສືບທອດ ຊຶ່ງເລີ່ມຕົ້ນ ໃນປີ ຄ.ສ. 1603 ແລະ ເຮັດໃຫ້ປະເທດສະຫງົບສຸກ ເຖິງ 250 ປີ.

Treaty of Tordesillas / ສົນທິສັນຍາ ແຫ່ງ ທໍເດຊີບຍາ *n.* ຂໍ້ຕົກລົງ ລະຫວ່າງ ສະເປນ ແລະ ປໍຣຕຸຍການ ໃນປີ 1494 ເພື່ອ ແບ່ງອານາເຂດຂອງ ໂລກ ຕາມເສັ້ນແບ່ງຈາກເໜືອເຖິງໃຕ້ ເພື່ອໃຫ້ ຊາວສະເປນ ເຂົ້າຄອບຄອງທາງທິດຕາເວັນຕົກ ແລະ ປໍຣຕຸຍການ ແມ່ນທາງທິດຕາເວັນອອກ.

triangular trade / ສາມຫຼ່ຽມການຄ້າ *n.* ການແລກປ່ຽນສິນຄ້າ ແລະ ຂ້າທາດ ຂ້າມມະຫາສະໝຸດແອັດລັງຕິກ ລະຫວ່າງ ທະວີບອາເມລິກາ, ຍູໂຣບ ແລະ ອາຟຣິກາ.

tribute / ເຄື່ອງບັນນາການ *n.* ການເສຍສ່ວຍ ຈາກປະເທດໜຶ່ງ ແກ່ປະເທດອື່ນ ເພື່ອສະແດງຄວາມເຄົາລົບນັບຖື.

U, V, W, X, Y, Z

universal gravitation / ແຮງດຶງດູດແຫ່ງຈັກກະວານ *n.* ທິດສະດີຂອງ ໄອຊັກ ນິວຕັນ (Isaac Newton) ທີ່ວ່າ ແຮງດຶງ ດູດແມ່ນເກີດຂຶ້ນກັບ ວັດຖຸສິ່ງຂອງຕ່າງໆ ໃນຈັກກະວານ.

vassal / ຂ້າທາດ *n.* ຂ້າທາດ ໃນສັງຄົມສັກດິນາ ຜູ້ທີ່ສາມາດນຳ ໃຊ້ທີ່ດິນທຳກິນ ແລະ ໄດ້ຮັບການປົກປ້ອງ ຈາກເຈົ້າຂອງທີ່ດິນ ເພື່ອແລກ ປ່ຽນກັບຄວາມຈິງຮັກພັກດີ.

vegetation zone / ເຂດພືດສາສາດ *n.* ຊົງເຂດທີ່ມີພືດພັນ ບາງຊະນິດ ເນື່ອງຈາກມີ ດິນ ແລະ ພູມອາກາດ ສະເພາະ.

vernacular / ພາສາພື້ນເມືອງ *n.*

weather / ພູມອາກາດ *n.* ສະພາບຂອງບັນຍາກາດ ໃນສະຖານທີ່ ແລະ ເວລາໃດໜຶ່ງ.

wood-block printing / ອຸປະກອນພິມພັ້ງສີ *n.* ລະບົບການພິມທີ່ໄດ້ຮັບການພັດທະນາ ໂດຍຊາວຈີນບູຮານ ເພື່ອໃຊ້ກາບໄມ້ແກະສະຫຼັກ ພິມຕົວພັ້ງສີ ໃສ່ໝຶກ ທັງໝັ້ງໆຂອງເຈ້ຍ.

Yucatán Peninsula / ແຫຼມຍຸກາຕ່ານ *n.* ອານາເຂດຍຸກກາງຕາເວັນອອກສ່ຽງໃຕ້ຂອງແມັກຊິໂກ ທີ່ກວມເອົາອ່າວແມັກຊິໂກ ແລະ ທະເລແຄຣິບຽນ.

Zen / ສາດສະໝາພຸດ ນິກາຍມະຫາຍານ *n.* ສາດສະໝຸດ ນິກາຍມະຫາຍານໃນຍີ່ປຸ່ນ ທີ່ສັ່ງສອນກ່ຽວກັບ ການບັງຄັບຕົນເອງ, ດຳລົງຊີວິດແບບງ່າຍໆ ແລະ ການນັ່ງສະມາທິ.

Zheng He / ຜົນເຊກ ເຊັ້ງ ເຣ *n.* ນາຍຜົນເຊກທະຫານເຮືອຊາວຈີນ ຜູ້ທີ່ເດີນເຮືອ ໃນລະຫວ່າງໆປີ ຄ.ສ. 1405 ແລະ 1433 ແລະ ແຜ່ຂະ ຫຍາຍ ການຄ້າຕ່າງໆປະເທດ ແລະ ຊື່ສຽງຂອງຊາວຈີນ ອອກໄປຢ່າງກວ້າງໄກ.

فهرس بالعربية

هذا الفهرس هو قائمة أدرجت حسب الترتيب الأبجدي لكثير من الكلمات الرئيسية المذكورة في الفصول مع تفسير معانيها. الخلاصات المدرجة في هذا الفهرس وشرحها طبقت على الشكل الذي وردت فيه الكلمات في هذا الكتاب. يعطي الفهرس النوع الصرفي لكل من الكلمات. استخدمت الإختصارات التالية:

adj. = صفة   **n.** / = اسم   **v.** / = فعل

A

n. Abd al-Malik / عَبد المَلِك حَاكم مسلم أصبح خليفة في عام ٦٨٥ميلادية وجعل العَربية لغة الحكومية الرسمية في جميع بِلاد المسلمين.

n. Abd al-Rahman III / عبد الرَحمن الثالث أمير الأندَلس الثامن وصلت الأندلس في عَهده أوج عَظمتها.

n. Afonso I / أفونسو الأول مَلِك من ملوك الكونغو بدأ حكمه في ١٥٠٦ بعد الميلاد تأثر بالبرتغاليين واشترك في تجارة العبيد.

n. al-Andalus / الأندَلس منطقة في أسبانيا وقعت تحت حُكم المسلمين ما بين السبعمائيات إلى ١٤٩٢ بعد الميلاد.

n. Allah / الله الرَب في الديانة الإسلامية.

n. alluvial soil / التُربة الطَميه تُربة غَنية وخصبة جداً تترسب على جَانبي النَهر.

n. Almoravids / المرابطون سلالة إسلامية من شَمال إفريقيا حاولت أن ترغم الشعوب المجاورة بما في ذلك الغرب وإسبانيا وغَانا على تغيير دينها.

n. anatomy / علم التَشريح الدراسة العلمية لأشكال وتركيبة الإنسان والنبات والحيوان.

n. Angkor Wat / أنجكور واط مجمع من الهياكل في جَنوب شرق آسيا شيد في القرن الحادي عشر بعد الميلاد يغطي تقريباً مساحة ميل مربع وهو أيضاً أكبر الهياكل الدينية في العالم.

n. anthropology / الأنثروبولوجية علم الإنسان والثقافات الإنسانية.

n. aqueduct / قَناة مائية بناء يستخدم لِجلب المياه العذبة إلى المدينة أو البَلدة.

n. archaeology / علم الآثار استرداد ودراسة الأدلة المادية من الماضي.

n. artifact / نتاج صنعي شئ من صنع الإنسان.

---

n. Askia Muhammad / أسكيا مُحَمد حَاكم الإمبراطورية السونغية ما بين ١٤٩٣–١٥٢٨ بعد الميلاد قام بتوسيع الإمبراطورية وتنظيم حكومتها.

n. astrolabe / الأُسطرولاب آله فَلَكية استخدمت لقياس ارتفاع النجوم فوق الأفق لمساعدة الملاحين على قياس مداهم.

n. Augustus / أغسطس أول إمبراطور لروما حكم من ٢٧ قبل الميلاد إلى ١٤ ميلادية وقام بتوسيع حجم الإمبراطورية الرومانية ونفوذها بصورة كَبيرة.

B

n. Baghdad / بَغداد مدينة واقعة فيما هو معروف اليوم بالعِراق كانت عاصمة الخِلافة العَباسية.

n. Bantu migrations / هجرة البانتو حَركة للشعوب الناطقة بالبانتو بدأت نحو ألف قبل الميلاد من غَرب أفريقيا إلى الجنوب والشرق. أدت إلى انتشار لغاتهم وثقافاتهم.

n. bubonic plague / الطَاعون الدبلي مَرض أصاب أوراسيا الغَربية في منتصف القرن الثالث عشر وعرف تَفشيه بالموت الأسود.

n. Buddhism / البوذية نظام مُعتقدات مَبني على تَعاليم سيدارتا غواتاما المعروف شَهواتها في الدنيا. أيضاً ببوذا يركز على ضَرورة تَحرير النفس من شهواتها الدنيوية.

n. bureaucracy / البيروقراطية نظام حكومي منظم في دوائر ووكالات تقوم بأعمال الحكومة.

n. bushido / البوشيدو القانون الأخلاقي للمحاربين اليابانيين المعروفين بالساموراي يتطلب منهم الكرم والشَجاعة والإخلاص.

n. Byzantine Empire / الإمبراطورية البيزنطية الإمبراطورية الرومانية الشَرقية التي اتخذت من القسطنطينية مقراً لها وامتدت من القرن الرابع إلى القرن الخامس عشر.

n. cacao / **الكاكاو** شَجرة استوائية أمريكية تستخدم بذورها لِصنع الشوكولاتة.

n. caliph / **الخَليفة** حَاكم مجتمع المسلمين اعتبر خَليفة للنبي محمد.

n. calligraphy / **الخطاطة** فن الكتابة الحسنة باليد.

n. Calvin, John / **جون كالفن** زَعيم حَركة الإصلاح الديني البروتستانتي عاش ما بين ١٥٠٩ و ١٥٦٤ ميلادية وركز على مبدأ القَضاء والقَدر.

n. capitalism / **الرأسمَالية** نظام اقتصادي مبني على الملكية الخاصة للموارد الاقتصَادية واستخدام تلك الموارد لجني الرِبح.

n. caravel / **المركب الشراعي الصغير (الكرافيل)** نوع من السُفن الشراعية البرتغالية له أشرعة مربعة ومثلثة تم تطويرها للرحلَات البعيدة.

n. cartography / **الخَرائطية** المَهارات والطرق المستخدمة في صُنع الخَرائط.

n. celadon / **السيلادون** نَوع من الفُخار الكوري عادة مصنوع باستخدام اللون الأخضر المائل إلى الأزرق.

n. Charlemagne / **شَارلمان** مَلك الفرنجة (من ٧٦٨ ميلادية) غَزا معظم أوروبا ونَشر المَسيحية في المناطق المغزوة.

n. chasqui / **شاسكي** عدَّاء في زمن إمبراطوريةَ الانكا حمل الرسائل على امتداد الإمبراطورية.

n. chivalry / **الفروسية** نظام أخلاقي لفرسان أوروبا في القرون الوسطى ركز على الشَجاعة والشَهامة واحترام النِساء والمستضعفين.

n. Christianity / **المَسيحية** ديانة مبينة على حياة المَسيح وتَعاليمه.

v. circumnavigate / **الإبحار** حول العَالم الذهاب في رِحلة كاملة حول العَالم.

n. clan / **العشيرة** مجموعة من الناس تجمعها صِلات الدم أو النَسب.

n. clergy / **رجال الدين** الأشخاص الذين يَتمتعون بِصلاحيات دينية في أية ديانة.

n. climate / **المُناخ** نَمط معين من ظروف الطَقس في موقع مُعين على مدى فترة طويلة من الزَمن.

n. Clovis / **كلوفيس** زَعيم الفرنجة غَزا مقاطعة غول الرومانية في ٤٨٦ ميلادية وأسَس فيما بعد مملكة الفَرنجة المتسعة والقوية.

n. codex / **مخطوطة (كوديكس)** كتاب مثل النوع الذي استخدمته الحَضارات الميسو أمريكية لتسجيل الأحداث التاريخية الهامة.

n. Columbian Exchange / **التبادل الكولومبي** حَركة النبات والحيوان وغيرها من الكائنات الحية بين نصَف الكرة الأرضي الشرقي والغربي بعد رحلة كولومبوس إلى الأمريكيتين في ١٤٩٢ ميلادية.

n. Confucianism / **الكونفوشية** نظام معتقدات مَبني على تَعاليم كونفوشيوس وهو عَالم درَس القيم الأخلاقية.

n. Constantine / **قسطنطين** إمبراطور الرومان من ٣٠٦ إلى ٣٣٧ ميلادية أنهى اضطهاد المَسيحيين ونقل عاصمة الإمبراطورية إلى البيزنطية (التي عُرفت لاحقاً بالقسطنطينية).

n. continent / **القارة** واحدة من كُتل أرضية كبيرة من الكرة الأرضية – أمريكا الشمالية وأمريكا الجَنوبية وأوروبا وآسيا وأفريقيا وأستراليا والمتجمد الجنوبي.

v. convert / **تَغيير المذهب** إقناع شخص ما بتغيير دينه أو دينها أو معتقداته أو معتقداتها.

n. Córdoba / **قُرطبة** عَاصمة الأندلس.

n. Cortés, Hernán / **كورتيز هيرنان** المكتشف الأسباني الذي غَزا حَضارة الأزتيك في المكسيك في ١٥٢١ ميلادية.

n. covenant / **مُعاهدة** اتفاقية ملزمة.

n. Crusades / **الغَزوات الصليبية** مجموعة من الحَملات العَسكرية شَنها المَسيحيون في أوروبا على فَلسطين ما بين القرن الحادي عشر والثالث عشر بعد الميلاد.

n. culture / **الثَقافة** طريقة حياة تشترك فيها مجموعة من الناس.

D

n. daimyo / **ديميو** سيد ياباني يملك أراض شاسعة وجيش خاص من محاربي الساموراي لم يدفع الضَرائب إلى الحكومة.

Daoism .n / **الداوية** نَظام معتقدات بدأ في الصين نحو ٥٠٠ قبل الميلاد يؤكد على التآلف مع الطبيعة والشعور الداخلي.

Declaration of Independence .n / **إعلان الاستقلال** وثيقة أعلنت من خلالها المستعمرات الأمريكية استقلالها عن بريطانيا العظمى.

Declaration of the Rights of Man and of the Citizen .n / **إعلان الاستقلال** وثيقة أعلنت استقلال المُستعمرات الأمريكية عن بريطانيا العظمى.

dissection .n / **التشريح** فتح النباتات والحيوانات عن طريق القص لدراسة وتفحص أجزاءها.

divan .n / **الديوان** مَجلس عَالي قدم النُصح للسلطان خلال الإمبراطورية العُثمانية.

E

elevation .n / **الارتفاع** ارتفاع الأرض فوق مستوى الماء.

elite .n / **النُخبة** الأفراد الأعلى مكانه أو الأغنى في مجتمع أو جماعة ما.

Elizabethan Age .n / **العَصر الأيليزبيثي** فترة حُكم الملكة اليزابيث الأولى في إنكلترا من ١٥٥٨ إلى ١٦٠٣.

embassy .n / **سَفارة** مَكتب بلد ما أو حكومة ما في بلد آخر.

emperor .n / **إمبراطور** حَاكم الإمبراطورية.

empire .n / **إمبراطورية** مجموعة ثَقافات أو أراض مختلفة يقود حَاكم واحد يتمتع بكامل النفوذ.

enlightened despot .n / **الحَاكم المطلق المُستنير** حَاكم تمتع بكامل السُلطة لكنه راعى الأفكار السياسية التي جاءت بها حَركة التنوير الفلسفية وحاول الحكم بصورة عَادلة ومُثقفة.

Enlightenment .n / **حَركة التنوير** حَركة فلسفية ازدهرت في القرن الثامن عشر استخدم خلالها الفلاسفة العقل لفهم حقيقة الطبيعة الإنسانية.

epic poem .n / **الشِعر المَلحمي** شِعر طَويل يَروي قِصة مُغامرات بطولية.

excavation .n / **حَفريات** عَملية حَفر وإخراج أشياء ذات أهمية تاريخية من أجل دِراستها.

F

faction .n / **فئة** مَجموعة صغيرة من الناس تتضارب مَصالحها مع مَصالح المجموعة الأكبر التي هي جُزء منها.

federalism .n / **الفدرالية** تَقاسم السُلطة بين مؤسسة أو حكومة ما وأفرادها.

feudalism .n / **الإقطاعية** نظام سياسي واجتماعي سَاد أوروبا في العصور الوسطى أعطى خلَاله الأسياد الأراضي التوابع مقابل الخدمة والولاء.

Forbidden City .n / **المُحرمة المدينة** مجموعة من القصور مُحاطة بالأسوار شيدت لإمبراطور الصين في أوائل القرن الخامس عشر بعد الميلاد في العَاصمة بكين.

Francis of Assisi, Saint .n / **سَانت فرانسيس أسيسي** إيطالي أسس الأخوية الفرانسيسكانية الدينية في أوائل القرن الثاني عشر بعد الميلاد.

G

Genghis Khan .n / **جنكيس غان** زعيم مَغولي وحد القبائل المغولية نحو عام ١٢٠٦ ميلادية ثم بدأ حملة من الغزوات مكوناً إمبراطورية غَطت شمال الصين وآسيا الوسطى.

geocentric theory .n / **نَظرية مركزية الأرض** نظرية أن الأرض هي مَركز الكون.

geography .n / **الجغرافيا** دراسة المزايا الطبيعة للأرض.

Ghana .n / **غَانا** منطقة تقع بين الصحراء الكُبرى وغَابات جنوب أفريقيا الغربية ازدهرت فيها العديد من الثَقافات القَديمة.

glyph .n / **الصورة الرمزية المنقوشة** رمز عادة ما يكون منحوتا أو منقوشا يمثل مقطع أو كلمة كاملة.

golden age .n / **العَصر الذهبي** حقبة من الزمن يَصل فيها مجتمع أو حضارة ما إلى أوجه.

Great Enclosure .n / **التَسييج العظيم** أكبر قسم من أقسام مستوطنة شونا الثلاثة في زيمبابوي العَظيمة أغلب الظن قصر ملكي.

n. Great Schism / الانشقاق العظيم انقسام في الكنيسة الكاثوليكية الرومانية وقع ما بين ١٣٧٨ و ١٤١٧ ميلادية عندما انقسم قُطبي السلطة في الكنيسة أفينون وروما وانتخبا بابا مختلف لكل منهما.

n. Great Zimbabwe / زمبابوي العَظيمة مستعمرة مركزية لإمبراطورية الشونا في إفريقيا محاطة بأسوار حَجرية عالية تغطي نحو ١٠٠ آكراً بِتعداد سكاني يتراوح ما بين ١٠ إلى ٢٠ ألفاً.

n. Gregory VII, Pope / بابَا غريغوري السابع رئيس الكنيسة الكاثوليكية الرومانية ما بين ١٠٧٣ و ١٠٨٥ تنازع مع الإمبراطور هنري الرابع على السُلطة.

n. griot / الجريوت راوي قصص رسمي في الثقافة الإفريقية.

n. guild / نقابة الحرفيين مؤسسة تتألف من أشخاص لهم تجارة أو حرفة مشتركة تهدف إلى السيطرة على نوعية وكمية الإنتاج وحِماية مصالحهم.

n. Gutenberg, Johann / غوتنبرغ يوهان ألماني اخترع آلة طابعة لها حروف متحركة في منتصف القرن الرابع عشر.

H

n. habeas corpus / حق المثول أمام المَحكمة حق الناس في ألا يسجنوا بصورة غير قانونية.

n. haiku / هايكو نوع من الأشعار اليابانية يتضمن ١٧ مقطعاً مرتب في ثلاثة أسطر الأول منها يتألف من ٥ مقاطع والثاني ٧ من مقاطع والثالث من ٥ مقاطع.

n. harmony / التآلف التقاء العناصر مع بعضها البعض لتكون وحدة كاملة مُرضية.

adj. heliocentric / شمسي المركز اعتبار الشمس مركزا.

n. hemisphere / نصف الكرة الأرضية أحد نصفي الأرض المتساويين مقسم وفق خط الطول أو الخط الاستوائي.

n. Henry IV, Emperor / الإمبراطور هنري الرابع حاكم من حُكام الإمبراطورية الرومانية المقدسة في القرن الحادي عشر تنازع على السلطة مع البابا غريغوري السابع.

n. Hijrah / الهجرة انتقال مُحمد وأتباعه من مكة إلى مَدينة يَثرب في سنة ٦٢٢ ميلادية.

n. historian / مُؤرخ شَخص يَدرس ويُفسر الماضي.

n. history / التاريخ دراسة الأحداث الماضية.

n. humanism / الحَركة الإنسانية حَركة في النهضة الأوروبية احتفلت بإمكانيات الإنسان وإنجازاته وأكدت على دراسة مواضيع مثل التاريخ والقواعد والأدب والفلسفة.

n. Hundred Years' War / حرب المائة سنة مجموعة من الحروب بين إنجلترا وفرنسا استمرت من ١٣٣٧ إلى ١٤٥٣ ميلادية.

I

n. Iberian Peninsula / شبة جَزيرة أيبريا أقصى نقطة في جنوب غرب أوروبا حيث تقع اليوم أسبانيا والبرتغال.

n. Ignatius of Loyola, Saint / سانت أغناطيوس ليولا إسباني أسس حركة اليسوعيين الدينية في أوائل الثلاثينيات من القرن الخامس عشر ميلادي.

adj. imperial / إمبراطوري مرتبط بإمبراطورية أو إمبراطور.

n. indulgence / الغُفران غفران على المعاصي تمنحه الكنيسة الكاثوليكية الرومانية يسمح للشخص تفادي عقاب الله في الحياة والآخرة.

n. Inquisition / محاكم التفتيش محكمة أسستها الكنيسة الكاثوليكية الرومانية في عام ١٥٤٢ ميلادية للتحقيق مع الأشخاص الذين قد يكونوا قد حادوا عن الديانة الكاثوليكية الرومانية ولتعزيز سلطة الكنيسة.

n. Islam / الإسلام ديانة توحيدية مبنية على تعاليم محمد.

J

n. janissary / الإنكشاري عضو في قوة مقاتلة من النخبة في الإمبراطورية العثمانية مؤلفة بشكل رئيسي من العبيد.

n. Jesuit / اليسوعي عضو في جمعية المسيح وهو تنظيم أخوي ديني أسسه القديس أغناطيوس ليولا في الثلاثينيات من القرن الخامس عشر.

n. Joan of Arc / جان دارك بنت من الفلاحين الفرنسيين قادت الفرنسيين إلى النصر على الإنكليز في أورلينز في عام ١٤٢٩ ميلادية.

ARABIC

n. landform / تشكيلة أرضية ميزة فوق سطح الأرض مكونة بصورة طبيعية مثل الجُزر والجبال أو الهِضاب.

n. latitude / خط العرض قياس المسافة إلى شمال أو جنوب خط الاستواء.

n. Leonardo da Vinci / ليوناردو دي فينشي رسام إيطالي عاش في عصر النهضة ولد في عام ١٤٥٢ميلادية ورسم العديد من الروائع مثل الموناليزا والعشاء الأخير وأبدع كذلك في البحث العلمي.

n. longbow / القوس الطويل سلاح تنطلق منه سِهام تستطيع أن تخترق درع الفارس.

n. longitude / خط الطول قياس المسافة إلى شرق أو غرب خط الطول الرئيسي.

n. lord / اللورد نبيل قوي يملك أراض.

n. Luther, Martin / مارتن لوثر عالم ديني ألماني ولد في عام ١٤٨٣ ميلادية قاد حركة الإصلاح ونادى بالخلاص عن طريق الإيمان بالله عوضا عن القيام بالأعمال الحسنة.

M

n. Magna Carta / الماغنا كارتا قائمة حقوق كتبها النبلاء في إنكلترا وقام الملك جون بتوقيعها في ١٢١٥ ميلادية.

n. maize / ذرة الميز نوع من الذرة تزرعها الحضارات الأمريكية الأصلية.

n. Mali / مالي إمبراطورية في غرب أفريقيا أسسها شعب المالينكة.

n. Manchu / المانشو عضو في شعب صيني عاش في شمال الشرق قام بغزو الصين في ١٦٤٤ ميلادية وبدأ السلالة الأخيرة في التاريخ الصيني عرفت بسلالة التشينغ.

n. manor / العزية منزل نبيل إقطاعي عادة ما يشتمل على بناية محصنة أو قصر.

n. Mansa Musa / مانسا موسى إمبراطور مالي قام بحج مشهور إلى مكة في عام ١٣٢٤ ميلادية.

adj. maritime / ملاحي له علاقة بالبحر.

n. Maya / مايا حضارة جنوب المكسيك وشمال أمريكا الوسطى وصلت أوجها ما بين ٢٥٠ و ٩٠٠ ميلادية.

n. Mbanza / إمبانزا المدينة العاصمة لمملكة الكونغو الإفريقية القديمة.

n. John, King / الملك جون ملك إنكلترا قام بتوقيع الماغنا كارتا في ١٢١٥ ميلادية.

n. Justinian / جستنيان حاكم الإمبراطورية الرومانية الشرقية من ٥٢٧ إلى ٥٦٥ ميلادية حكم مع زوجته ثيودورا واستعاد أراض كانت الإمبراطورية قد خسرتها.

n. Justinian Code / قانون جستيان قانون وضع بناءً على أوامر إمبراطور البيزنطيين جستيان ونظم معظم نواحي الحياة في البيزنطية.

K

n. Kabuki / كابوكي نوع من الدراما اليابانية تم تطويرها في القرن السادس عشر ميلادية تحتوي على غناء ورقص ميلودرامي ويتميز بالمكياج الكثيف ولبس أزياء مزخرفة.

n. Khmer Empire / إمبراطورية الخمير أقوى وأطول مملكة في جنوب شرقي آسيا تركزت فيما هو معروف اليوم بكمبوديا.

n. Kilwa / كلوة دولة مدينية قديمة في الساحل الشرقي لإفريقيا استوطن فيها أناس من إيران وشبه الجزيرة العربية وصلت أوجها في أواخر القرن الثاني عشر ميلادية.

n. kinship / القَرابة رابطة دم أو نَسب أو تَبني تجمع أناس معينون.

n. knight / فارس مُحارب متمرس يركب فرسا عمل في خدمة نبيل من نبلاء القصور الوسطى في أوروبا.

n. Kongo / الكونغو مملكة قديمة على الساحل الغربي لإفريقيا استوطنها شعوب الكونغو الناطقة بالبانتو قبل القرن الرابع عشر ميلادية.

n. Koryo / كوريو مملكة قامت في شبه جزيرة الكونغو في ٩٣٥ ميلادي بعد انهيار مملكة السيلا.

n. Kublai Khan / كبلاخان حفيد جنكيس خان تولى الحكم في جنوب الصين في ١٢٦٠ ميلادية وهزم جيش السونغ في ١٢٧٩ مانحاً المغول السيطرة على جميع أراضي الصين.

L

n. labor specialization / التخصص الوظيفي قيام عمال متدربين أو أولئك الذين يتمتعون بمعرفة معينة بنوع معين من العمل.

n. mercantilism / الروح التجارية (المركنتلية)
سياسة اقتصادية مبنية على فكرة أن قوه دولة ما تعتمد على ثروتها.

n. mercenary / المرتزقة جندي يتلقى المال كي يُحارب.

n. Meso-America / ميسو أمريكا منطقة تشمل الجزء الجنوبي من المكسيك ومعظم أمريكا الوسطى.

n. Michelangelo / مايكل أنجيلو فنان عاش في عصر النهضة الإيطالية ولد في ١٤٧٥ ميلادية عمل بشكل رئيسي كنحات لكنه رسم أعمال مشهورة مثل سقف كنيسة سيستين في روما.

n. Middle Ages / العصور الوسطى حقبه من التاريخ الأوروبي استمرت ما بين انهيار روما والنهضة من عام ٥٠٠ إلى ١٤٥٠ ميلادية.

n. missionary / المُبشر شخص يسافر إلى بلد أجنبي للقيام بعمل ديني.

n. monastery / الدير مكان يمارس فيه أعضاء تنظيم ديني حياة الصلاة والعبادة.

n. Mongol Ascendancy / صعود المغول حقبة قام فيها المغول بالسيطرة على جميع آسيا الوسطى وأمنوا طرق التجارية البرية والسفر.

n. monotheism / التوحيد الإيمان بإله واحد.

n. Montezuma II / مونيتزوما الثاني آخر إمبراطور الأزتيك حكم من ١٥٠٢ إلى ١٥٢٠ قام الأسبان بقلب حكمة.

n. mosaic / الموزايك صورة مصنوعة من خزف أو قطع من الزجاج الملون.

n. mosque / المَسجد بناء لعبادة المسلمين مصمم بحيث يقابل مدينة مكة.

n. mother culture / الثقافة الأم ثقافة تشكل وتؤثر في عادات وأفكار ثقافات لاحقة.

n. movable type / الحرف المتحرك قطعة صغيرة من المعدن أم الخشب لها حرف واحد بارز يستخدم في طباعة النصوص.

n. Murasaki Shikibu, Lady / ليدي موراساكي شيكيبو كاتبة يابانية عاشت في أوائل الألفية الميلادية الأولى ألفت «قصة جينجي» التي تعتبر أول رواية في العالم.

n. Muslim / مُسلم شخص يتبع الديانة الإسلامية يؤمن بالله كإله واحد.

---

n. Mutapa / موتابا مملكة قديمة قامت فيما هو اليوم زيمبابوي أسسها أول ملك من ملوك الشونا نحو ١٤٤٠ ميلادية الذي حكم مملكة الموتابا.

N

n. Nam Viet / نات فيت مملكة فيتنامية غزتها الصين في ١١١ قبل الميلاد.

n. natural rights / الحقوق الطبيعية الحقوق التي يتمتع الناس بها عند الولادة مثل الحق في الحياة والحرية والملكية وفق أفكار الفيلسوف جون لوك الذي عاش في القرن الثامن عشر.

n. Noh / نو نوع من الدراما اليابانية ظهرت في القرن الثالث عشر الميلادي عادة ما تشتمل على إعادة رواية أساطير وخرافات شعبية على لسان ممثلين يلبسون أقنعة خشبية ملونة.

n. nomad / البدوي الشخص الذي ينتقل من مكان لآخر بدلاً من التوطن بصورة دائمة.

O

n. oasis / الواحة منطقة خصبة في وسط الصحراء.

n. Olmec / أولميك أولى الثقافات الميسو أمريكية المعروفة ازدهرت ما بين ١٢٠٠ و ٤٠٠ قبل الميلاد وتمركزت في جنوب شرق المَكسيك.

n. Omar Khayyám / عُمر الخيام شاعر مسلم ولد في إيران كتب أشعار تتألف من مقطوعات رباعية الأبيات وتفوق في الرياضيات كذلك.

n. oral history / التاريخ الشفهي رواية غير مكتوبة للأحداث متناقلة شفوياً مثل حكاية تنتقل من جيل لآخر.

adj. Orthodox / أرثوذ وكسي مرتبط بالكنيسة المسيحية التي ظهرت في زمن الإمبراطورية البيزنطية ولم تخضع لسلطة البابا.

n. Osman / عثمان زعيم تركي أسس الإمبراطورية العُثمانية في أوائل القرن الثالث عشر الميلادي.

P

n. Pacal II / باكال الثاني ملك حكم مدينة البالينك في حضارة المايا لمدة بلغت تقريباً ٧٠ سنة (من ٦١٥ ميلادية) وواحد من أعظم ملوك المايا.

n. Pachacuti / باشاكوتي حاكم الأنكا التاسع اعتلى الحكم في ١٤٣٨ ميلادية وقام بتوسيع إمبراطورية الأنكا.

n. parliament / البرلمان مجموعة من الممثلين يتمتعون ببعض صلاحيات الحكومة.

n. patron / الراعي شخص يرعى نشاطا أو مؤسسة ما عن طريق تقديم التمويل المالي.

n. Peace of Westphalia / اتفاقية سلام ويستفاليا اتفاقية عقدت في ١٦٤٨ ميلادية اعترفت بالتقسيم الدائم لأوروبا الغربية إلى شعوب كاثوليكية وبروتستانتية وأنهت عدة حروب دينية كانت قائمة حينذاك.

n. perspective / الرسم المنظوري أسلوب في التلوين تم تطويره خلال حقبه النهضة يمثل الأشياء في فراغ من ثلاثة أبعاد.

n. philosophe / فيلسوف مفكر عاش في القرن الثامن عشر حاول تطبيق الطرق العلمية على المشاكل الاجتماعية.

n. pilgrimage / الحج رحلة إلى مكان مقدس أو معبد.

n. Pizarro, Francisco / بيزارو، فرانسيسكو مكتشف إسباني وصل إلى البيرو في ١٥٣٢ ميلادية وغزا إمبراطورية الأنكا مع حلول عام ١٥٣٥.

n. Polo, Marco / ماركو بولو تاجر من البندقية سافر عبر طرق الحرير ووصل إلى الصين نحو ١٢٧٥ ميلادية وأصبح مساعداً لكبلاخان وقام لاحقاً بنشر كتاب مشهور حول مغامراته.

n. porcelain / البورسيلان مادة مصنوعة من السيراميك الأبيض تسمى عادة بالخزف.

n. predestination / القبول بالقضاء والقدر مبدأ أن الله يختار أشخاصا معينين للخلاص والعقاب قبل أن يولدوا وأن الأفراد لا يملكون القدرة على تغيير حكم الله.

n. primary source / المصدر الأساس وثيقة أو شئ من صنع الإنسان مصنوع في فترة تاريخية معينة.

n. printing press / الطابعة آله لضغط الورق على طابعة متحركة تحتوي على حبر.

n. projection / الاختطاط أسلوب لتصوير سطح الأرض المنحني على خارطة منبسطة مع تقليل إمكانية التشويه.

n. Protestant / بروتستانتي عضو في جماعة مسيحية خرجت على الكنيسة الكاثوليكية خلال أو بعد القرن السادس عشر.

Q

n. quipu / ذات العقد (الكيبو) أداة مؤلفة من حبل وعقد صغيرة استخدمها الانكا القدماء للحساب.

n. Qur'an / القرآن كتاب المسلمين المقدس يتألف من سور أوحاها الله إلى محمد وقام أتباعه بتسجيلها بعد مماته.

R

n. rationalism / المذهب العقلي الفكرة القائلة أن على الناس أن يستخدموا العقل أو التفكير المنطقي لفهم العالم.

n. Reconquista / إعادة الغزو مجموعة من الحملات انتهت في عام ١٤٩٢ ميلادية قامت خلالها الجيوش المسيحية بإخراج حكام المسلمين من إسبانيا.

n. Reformation / حركة الإصلاح الديني حركة معارض للكنيسة الكاثوليكية الرومانية ابتداء من القرن السادس عشر.

n. regent / العاهل شخص يحكم مكان ما في غياب الملك أو في حال كونه دون السن القانوني.

n. religious order / الأخوية الدينية مجموعة من الناس تعيش وفق قانون ديني معين.

n. Renaissance / النهضة فترة من الإحياء والإبداع في الفنون والكتابة والفكر استمرت من ١٣٠٠ إلى ١٦٠٠ بدأت في إيطاليا واستمرت في جميع أنحاء أوروبا.

n. republic / الجمهورية نوع من الحكومة تكون السلطة فيه للشعب الذي ينتخب ممثليه.

v. reunify / إعادة توحيد إعادة تجميع شئ ما إلى وضعه الأول.

adj. Roman Catholic / كاثوليكي روماني مرتبط بالكنيسة المسيحية في القرن التي تخضع لسلطة البابا.

S

n. Sahara / الصحراء صحراء كبيرة في شمال أفريقيا تمتد من الساحل الأطلسي إلى وادي النيل.

n. Saladin / صلاح الدين قائد عسكري وحد المسلمين لقتال المسيحيين في فلسطين في القرن الثاني عشر الميلادي.

salon / n. صالون التقاء المفكرين والفنانين لمناقشة قضايا وتبادل الأفكار خلال فترة التنوير.

samurai / n. ساموراي محارب متمرس عمل لحساب الأرستقراطية اليابانية.

savanna / n. السفانا أرض عشبية منبسطة ينمو فيها قليل من الأشجار تقع في منطقة استوائية.

schism / n. انشقاق انقسام رسمي بين مجموعتين.

scholar-official / n. عالم - موظف إنسان مثقف يحتل مركزاً حكومياً.

scientific method / n. المنهج العلمي منهج في البحث العلمي تدخل فيه المراقبة عن قرب وعمل وامتحان الفرضيات والتوصل إلى نتيجة تؤكد أو تعدل هذه الفرضية.

Scientific Revolution / n. الثورة العلمية حقبة من الزمن بدأت في أوائل القرن الخامس عشر قام خلالها العلماء الأوروبيين بإثارة أسئلة حول الأفكار الكلاسيكية و المعتقدات المسيحية.

secondary source / n. المصدر الثانوي عمل حول حدث تاريخي كتبه شخص لم يشهد الواقعة بأم عينيه.

Seljuk Turk / n. تركي سلجوقي عضو في شعب تركي سيطر على وسط غرب آسيا من القرن الحادي عشر إلى الثالث عشر.

serf / n. القن مزارع فلاح في المجتمع الإقطاعي عمل لنبيل من النبلاء مقابل الحماية وحقوق أخرى معينة.

Shakespeare, William / n. شكسبير، وليام أشهر كاتب إنكليزي في عهد النهضة اشتهر بمسرحياته روميو وجوليت وهامليت.

Shi'a / n. الشيعية مجموعة مسلمة قاومت حكم الأمويين وآمنت بأن الخليفة يجب أن يكون من أقرباء النبي محمد.

Shinto / n. شينتو الديانة التقليدية في اليابان قائمة على عبادة واحترام الطبيعة والأجداد.

shogun / n. شوغان زعيم عسكري ياباني وعضو في جماعة جاءت إلى الحكم في ١١٩٢ ميلادية وحكمت بالنيابة عن الإمبراطور ولكنها راعت مصالحها الخاصة في الأساس.

Shona / n. الشونا ثقافة ناطقة بالبانتو ازدهرت في المناطق التي تحتلها اليوم بوستوانا موزمبيق وزمبابوي نحو عام ألف ميلادية.

Shotoku, Prince / n. الأمير شوتوكو عاهل حكم اليابان من ٥٩٣ إلى ٦٢٢ ميلادية وأدخل عناصر من الثقافة الصينية ولا سيما الديانة البوذية إلى البلاد.

Silk Roads / n. طرق الحرير الطرق التجارية القديمة التي وصلت أوروبا بالصين.

slash-and-burn agriculture / n. الشرط بالسكين والحرق نوع من الزراعة يَتم فيه إعداد قطع من الأراضي للزراعة عن طريق قطع وحرق النباتات الطبيعية.

Songhai / n. سونغاى شعب في غرب إفريقيا قام زعماؤه ببناء إمبراطورية في القرن الخامس عشر والسادس عشر ميلادية.

sponsor / n. الراعي شخص يقدم الأموال لدعم شخص أو مشروع ما.

standing army / n. الجيش القائم قوة محاربة قائمة في زمن الحرب والسلم.

stele / n. عمود حجري عمود منحوت منتصب على الأرض عادة كنصب تذكاري لشخص أو واقعة معينة.

Stoicism / n. الرواقية فلسفة يونانية أكدت على أهمية الفضيلة والواجبات والتحمل كان لها نفوذ كبير في روما القديمة.

Suleyman I / n. سليمان الأول سلطان الإمبراطورية العثمانية من ١٥٢٠ إلى ١٥٦٦ ميلادية شجع الفنون ووضع نظاماً قانونياً.

Sundiata / n. سوندياتا حاكم شعب المالينكة القديم استولى على عاصمة غانا وقام بتوسيع الإمبراطورية بشكل كبير.

Sunnah / n. السنة أقوال النبي محمد وأفعاله التي تعمل كمرشد للمسلمين على العيش الصحيح.

Sunni / n. سني عضو في جماعة مسلمة تقبلت حكم الخلفاء المنتخبين ولم تقاوم الأمويين.

Swahili / n. سواحيلي لغة إفريقية تجمع ما بين البانتو والعربية.

T

Tenochtitlán / n. تنوكتيتلان مدينة ازتكية قديمة أسست في ١٣٢٥ ميلادية على جزيرة صغيرة في بحيرة تكسكوكو.

n. Thomas Aquinas / توماس أقوانياس عالم إيطالي جمع ما بين الفلسفة الكلاسيكية والديانة المسيحية.

n. Timbuktu / تمباكتو مدينة في أواسط مالي في شرق إفريقيا أسست في القرن الثالث عشر وعملت كمركزاً للتجارة والثقافة.

n. Tokugawa Shogunate / توكوغاوا شوغونيت حكم توكوغاوا إساسو وخلفائه في اليابان الذي بدأ في ١٦٠٣ ميلادية وأدخل فترو ٢٥٠ عاماً من الاستقرار إلى البلاد.

n. Treaty of Tordesillas / معاهدة تورديسالاس اتفاقية بين إسبانيا والبرتغال وقعت في ١٤٩٤ أسست خطاً وهمياً من الجنوب إلى الشمال حول العالم وسمحت لإسبانيا بالمطالبة بأراضي غرب الخط وللبرتغال بمطالبة بأراضي إلى الشرق من الخط.

n. triangular trade / التجارة الثلاثية تبادل البضائع والعبيد عبر المحيط الأطلسي بين الأمريكيتين وأوروبا وأفريقيا.

n. tribute / الجزية مبلغ تدفعه بلد ما إلى أخرى كمؤشر على الاحترام.

U, V, W, X, Y, Z

n. universal gravitation / الجاذبية الكونية نظرية اسحق نيوتن القائلة بأن الجاذبية تؤثر على جميع الأشياء في الكون.

n. vassal / المقطع في المجتمع الإقطاعي هو شخص تتلقى الأراضي والحماية من الإقطاعي مقابل الولاء.

n. vegetation zone / منطقة النباتات الطبيعية منطقة تنمو فيها أنواع متميزة من النباتات بسبب تربتها ومناخها.

n. vernacular / اللغة العامية لغة الشخص الأصلية.

n. weather / الطقس حالة الجو في مكان وزمان معين.

n. wood-block printing / الطباعة عن طريق استخدام القوالب الخشبية نظام طباعة طوره الصينيون القدامى بحيث حفرت حروف خشبية على قوالب خشبية بحيث طبعت صفحات كاملة.

n. Yucatán Peninsula / شبة جزيرة اليوكاتان منطقة في جنوب شرق المكسيك تمتد إلى البحر الكاريبي وخليج المكسيك.

n. Zen / زين نوع ياباني من البوذية يركز على الانضباط الذاتي والبساطة والتأمل.

n. Zheng He / تشينغ هي أدميرال صيني عملت رحلاته الواسعة ما بين ١٤٠٥ و ١٤٣٣ ميلادية بتوسيع تجارة وسمعة الصين الخارجية.

GLOSÈ KREYÒL AYISYEN

Glosè a se yon lis ki nan lòd alfabetik ki genyen anpil nan tèm enpòtan ki nan chapit yo, ak tout definisyon yo. Definisyon ki liste nan Glosè a se yo ki aplike pou jan mo yo sèvi nan liv sa a. Glosè a bay klasifikasyon chak mo. Abrevyasyon sila yo itilize:

adj. = adjektif   **n.** = non   **v.** = vèb

A

Abd al-Malik n. yon chèf mizilman ki te tounen kalif nan ane 685 avan Jezikri epi ki te fè lang arab la tounen lang ofisyèl gouvènman nan tout tè mizilman.

Abd al-Rahman III / Abd al-Ramann III n. wityèm emi nan peyi al-Andalis; pandan peryòd sa a al-Andalis rive atenn pi wo pouvwa li te janm genyen.

Afonso I n. yon wa nan peyi Kongo ki te sou pouvwa depi ane 1506 apre Jezikri. Li te enfliyanse pa ras pòtigè epi te patisipe nan kòmès esklavaj.

al-Andalus / al-Andalis. n. zòn nan peyi Lespay ki te anba kontwòl mizilman depi ane 700 jouk ane 1492 avan Jezikri yo.

Allah / Ala. n. Bondye nan relijyon izlam.

alluvial soil / tè alivyal n. yon tè rich epi fètil ki depoze lè dlo fin desann.

Almoravids / Almoravid n. yon dinasti islamik nan lamerik dinò ki te eseye konvèti pèp vwazen ni yo, ak tout moun Mawòk, Lespay, ak Gana.

anatomy / anatomi n. Etid syantifik sou fòm ak estrikti imen, plant, ak zannimo.

Angkor Wat / Angkò Wat n. yon seri tanp nan sidès Lazi, yo te konstwi nan ane 1100 apre Jezikri yo, ki kouvri prèske yon mil kare epi ki se pi gwo estrikti relijye nan lemonn.

Anthropology / antwopoloji n. etid imen ak kilti imen.

aqueduct / akedik n. yon estrikti ki deziyen pou pote dlo fre nan yon vil oubyen vilaj.

archaeology / akeyoloji n. dekouvèt ak etid objè ki te egziste nan tan lontan.

artifact / objè da n. yon objè ke yon imen fabrike.

Askia Muhammad / Askya Mowamèd n. chèf anpi Songay depi ane 1493 rive jouk ane 1528 apre Jezikri, ki te agrandi anpi a epi ki te òganize gouvènman an.

astrolabe / astwolab n. yon enstriman ki itilize pou mezire ang etwal yo anlè lorizon an, pou ede maren kalkile latitid yo.

Augustus / Ogistis n. premye anprè nan peyi Wòm, ki te dirije depi 27 avan Jezikri jouk 14 apre Jezikri; li te vreman agrandi epi enfliyanse anpi women an.

B

Baghdad / Bagdad n. yon vil, sitiye kote ki rele Irak kounyela, ki te kapital anpi abasi.

Bantu migrations / migrasyon bantu n. deplasman pèp ki te pale bantu depi Lafrik delwès jouk nan sid ak nan lès epi te pwolonje lang yo ak kilti yo; mouvman sa a te kòmanse nan peryòd ane 1000 avan Jezikri.

bubonic plague / pès bibonik n. yon maladi ki te afekte lwès peyi Erazi nan mitan ane 1300 yo, ki te koze yon epidemi yo te rele Lanmò Nwa.

Buddhism / Boudis n. sistèm kwayans ki te baze sou sa Bouda ki te rele Sidata Gwatama te ansey ; li konsantre sou libere tèt ou de dezi sou latè.

bureaucracy / biwokrasi n. yon sistèm depatman ak ajans ki fè travay yon gouvènman.

bushido / bouchido n. kòd kondwit gerye samourè yo, ki te mande pou yo jenere, brav, epi fidèl.

Byzantine Empire / Anpi bizanten n. Anpi women delès, peyi Kostantinòp te kontwole de 4yèm syèk jouk 15yèm syèk.

C

cacao / kakawo n. yon pyebwa twopikal ameriken ki gen grenn ki sèvi pou pwodwi chokola.

Caliph / kalif n. yon chèf kominote mizilman an, ke yo te konsidere kòm siksesè Mowamèd.

calligraphy / kaligrafi n. la bèl ekriti.

Calvin, John / Kalven, Jan *n.* yon chèf refòmasyon pwotestan, ki te viv de 1509 jouk 1564 apre Jezikri epi ki te souliye doktrin predestinasyon an.

capitalism / kapitalis *n.* yon sistèm ekonomik ki baze sou posesyon prive resous ekonomik ak itilizasyon resous sa yo pou fè yon pwofi.

caravel / karavèl *n.* yon kalite bato avwal pòtigè ak de vwal kare epi fòm triyang, ki te devlope pou vwayaj ki long.

cartography / katografi *n.* abilite ak metòd ki itilize pou fè kat.

celadon / seladon *n.* yon kalite potri koreyen, ki trè souvan gen yon koulè ble vèt.

Charlemagne / Chalmay *n.* yon wa pèp frank yo (de 768 apre Jezikri) ki te konkeri anpil nan Lewòp epi ki te simaye krisyanis nan rejyon li te konkeri yo.

chasqui / Chaskwi *n.* yon mesaje nan anpi Enka a ki te pote mesaj alevini pandan dire anpi a.

chivalry / galantri *n.* kòd kondwit chevalye epòk medyeval ewopeyen, ki santre sou kouraj, onè, ak respè anvè lafam ak lòt moun ki fèb.

Christianity / Krisyanis *n.* yon relijyon ki baze sou lavi ak sa Jezikri anseye.

circumnavigate / navige toutotou *v.* fè yon vwayaj konpètman otou dimonn.

clan / klan *n.* yon gwoup moun ki alye nan san oswa nan maryaj.

clergy / klèje *n.* moun ki genyen otorite tankou prèt nan yon relijyon.

climate / klima *n.* kondisyon tanperati nan yon kote presi pandan anpil tan.

Clovis / Klovis *n.* yon chèf pèp frank yo, ki te konkeri pwovens women nan peyi Gòl nan ane 486 apre Jezikri, epi apresa te etabli yon wayòm frank ki te gran e pwisan.

codex / kodèks *n.* yon kalite liv premye sivilizasyon mezo-ameriken yo te itilize pou anrejistre evènman istorik enpòtan yo.

Columbian Exchange / Echanj kolonbyen *n.* mouvman plant, bèt, ak lòt èt vivan ant emisfè lès ak lwès apre vwayaj Kolon pou Lamerik yo nan ane 1492 apre Jezikri.

Confucianism / Konfisyanis *n.* yon sistèm kwayans baze sou sa Konfisiyis anseye ; li te yon filozòf chinwa ki te anseye lavèti ak etik moral.

Constantine / Konstanten *n.* anprè women de 306 jouk 337 apre Jezikri, ki te sispann pèsekisyon kretyen yo epi ki te deplase kapital anpi a jouk peyi Bizantentium (ki vin rele Konstantinòp apresa).

continent / kontinan *n.* youn nan sèt gwo moso tè sou latè—Lamerik dinò, Lamerik disid, Lewòp, Lazi, Lafrik, Lostrali, ak Lantatik.

convert / konvèti *v.* konvenk yon moun pou li adopte yon nouvo relijyon oswa kwayans.

Córdoba / Kòdoba *n.* kapital peyi al-Andalis.

Cortés, Hernán / Kòtèz, Èrnann *n.* eksploratè espayòl ki te konkeri sivilizasyon aztèk Meksik la nan ane 1521.

covenant / angajman *n.* yon akò obligatwa.

Crusades / Kwazad yo *n.* yon seri ekspedisyon militè depi peyi Lewòp kretyen jouk Palestin ant 11yèm ak 13yèm syèk apre Jezikri.

culture / kilti *n.* yon estil devi yon gwoup moun pataje.

D

daimyo / dayimyo *n.* yon mèt japonè ak anpil tè epi yon lame samurè prive, ki pat peye okenn enpo bay gouvènman an.

Daoism / Dawoyis *n.* yon sistèm kwayans ki te kòmanse nan peyi Lachin ozanviwon ane 500 avan Jezikri, ki te souliye lamoni ak lanati epi emosyon entèn.

Declaration of Independence / Deklarasyon Endepandans *n.* yon dokiman ki te deklare endepandans koloni ameriken yo de Grann Bretay.

Declaration of the Rights of Man and of the Citizen / Deklarasyon dwa delòm ak dwa sitwayen *n.* yon dokiman gouvènman revolisyonè fransè te adopte nan ane 1789, ki te souliye dwa pèp la.

dissection / diseksyon *n.* koupe plant ak bèt pou etidye epi envestige pati nan kò yo.

divan *n.* yon konsèy enperyal ki te bay siltan anpi otomann nan konsèy.

E

elevation / elevasyon *n.* wotè ki anlè nivo lanmè.

elite / elit *n.* manm ki pi siperyè oswa ki pi rich nan yon sosyete oswa nan yon gwoup.

Elizabethan Age / Epòk Elizabeten *n.* peryòd rèy rèn Elizabèt I nan peyi Langletè, depi 1558 jouk 1603.

embassy / anbasad *n.* yon biwo pou gouvènman yon peyi ki sitiye nan yon lòt peyi.

emperor / anprè *n.* chèf ki dirije yon peyi.

empire / anpi *n.* yon gwoup kilti oswa teritwa diferan yon sèl chèf ki gen tout pouvwa dirije.

enlightened despot / diktatè eklere *n.* yon chèf ki te gen pouvwa absoli men ki te prete atansyon sou ide politik epòk eklèsisman an epi ki te eseye dirije yon jan ki onèt epi enstwi.

Enlightenment / Eklèsisman *n.* yon mouvman filozofi nan 18yèm syèk lè filozòf yo te itilize larezon pou konprann verite sou lanati imen.

epic poem / powèm epik *n.* yon powèm ki long epi ki bay yon istwa avanti ewoyik.

excavation / ekskavasyon *n.* pwosesis detere objè ki gen valè istorik pou pèmèt etid yo.

F

faction / faksyon *n.* yon ti gwoup piti ki fè pati de yon pi gwo gwoup, men ki opoze a enterè gwoup sa a.

federalism / federalis *n.* pataj pouvwa ant yon òganizasyon oswa yon gouvènman ak manm ni yo.

feudalism / fewodalis *n.* sistèm politik ak sosyal nan epòk mwayen nan Lewòp, lè mèt yo te bay vasal yo tè annechanj pou sèvis ak fidelite.

Forbidden City / Vil entèdi *n.* yon gwoup palè klotire yo te bati pou anprè chinwa yon ti tan apre 1400 apre Jezikri nan vil kapital Bejing.

Francis of Assisi, Saint / Franswa Dasiz, Sen *n.* yon italyen ki te fonde lòd relijye fransisken yo nan kòmansman ane 1200 apre Jezikri yo.

G

Genghis Khan / Gengis Kann *n.* yon chèf mongòl ki te inifye tribi mongolè yo ozanviwon 1206 apre Jezikri, e ki te kòmanse yon kanpay konkèt ki te fòme yon anpi ki te kouvri nò Lachin ak Lazi santral.

geocentric theory / teyori jewosantrik *n.* teyori ki konsidere latè tankou sant inivè a.

geography / jewografi *n.* etid karakteristik natirèl Latè yo.

Ghana / Gana *n.* yon rejyon ant Saara ak forè nan sid Lafrik delwès, anpil ansyen kilti te konsidere tankou teritwa yo.

glyph / glif *n.* yon imaj ki reprezante yon mo, silab, oswa yon son.

golden age / epòk dore *n.* yon peryòd lè yon sosyete oswa yon kilti nan nivo pi elve ni.

Great Enclosure / Gran Kloti *n.* pi gwo nan twa zòn prensipal etablisman Chona nan Gran Zimbabwe —pwobableman yon rezidans wayal.

Great Schism / Gran Chis *n.* yon divizyon nan legliz katolik de 1378 jouk 1417, ki te fòme lè toulède sant pouvwa legliz yo, Avinyon ak Wòm, te separe epi te eli pap diferan.

Great Zimbabwe / Gran Zimbabwe *n.* etablisman santral nan anpi Chona nan Lafrik, ki antoure pa yon gran kloti siman, ki te kouvri plis pase 100 ekta, epi ki te genyen yon popilasyon ant 10.000 ak 20.000.

Gregory VII, Pope / Gregori VII, Pap *n.* chèf legliz katolik depi 1073 jouk 1085, ki te goumen ak anprè Anri IV pou pouvwa a.

griot / griyo *n.* yon moun ki rakonte istwa ofisyèlman nan yon sivilizasyon afriken

guild / gild *n.* yon asosyasyon moun ki pataje yon komès oswa yon metye, ki devlope pou kontwole kalite ak kantite pwodiksyon yo epi tou pou pwoteje enterè yo.

Gutenberg, Johann / Gutenbèg, Jowann *n.* yon alman ki, nan mitan ane 1400 yo, te envante yon aparèy pou enprime ak senbòl mobil.

H

habeas corpus / habeas corpus *n.* dwa moun genyen pou yo pa pran prizon ilegalman.

haiku / haykou *n.* yon kalite powèm japonè, ki gen 17 silab epi ki ranje nan twa liy 5, 7, epi 5 silab.

harmony / amoni *n.* konbinezon eleman pou fòme yon rezilta antye ki agreyab.

heliocentric / elyosantrik *adj.* ki gen solèy la tankou sant li.

hemisphere / emisfè *n.* youn nan de mwatye egal latè a, ki trase selon ekwatè a oswa meridyen prensipal la.

Henry IV, Emperor / Anri IV, Anprè *n.* yon chèf 11yèm syèk nan Anpi Women Sakre, ki te toujou nan goumen ak Pap Gregori VII pou pran pouvwa a.

Hijrah / Ijra *n.* deplasman Mowamèd ak disip li yo soti Meka rive jouk vil Yatrib la nan ane 622 apre Jezikri.

historian / istoryen *n.* yon moun ki etidye epi ki entèprete tan pase.

history / istwa *n.* etid evènman ki fin pase.

humanism / imanis *n.* yon mouvman nan renesans Lewòp, ki selebre potansyèl ak akonplisman imen, epi ki souliye etid sijè tankou istwa, gramè, literati, ak filozofi.

Hundred Years' War / Gè Santan *n.* yon seri gè ant Langletè ak Lafrans, pandan ane 1337 jouk 1453.

I

Iberian Peninsula / Penensil Iberyen *n.* pwent nan sidwès Lewòp, kote nasyon modèn Lespay ak Pòtigal sitiye.

Ignatius of Loyola, Saint / Ignasiyis de Loyola, Sen *n.* yon Panyòl ki te fonde òd relijye jezwit yo nan kòmansman ane 1530 apre Jezikri yo.

imperial / enperyal *adj.* ki gen rapò ak yon anpi oswa yon anprè.

indulgence / endiljans *n.* yon padon legliz katolik bay pou peche ki pèmèt yon moun evite pinisyon nan men Bondye apre lanmò.

Inquisition / Enkizisyon *n.* yon tribinal legliz katolik te etabli nan ane 1542 apre Jezikri pou envestige moun ki te gen dwa fè move chimen selon relijyon katolik la epi pou ranfòse pouvwa legliz.

Islam *n.* yon relijyon monoteyis [yon sèl Bondye] ki baze sou sa Mowamèd anseye.

J

janissary / janisari *n.* yon manm nan yon fòs batay nan anpi otomann nan, ki te pi plis genyen esklav ladan ni.

Jesuit / Jezwit *n.* yon manm nan sosyete Jezikri, yon òd relijye Sen Ignasiyis de Loyola te fonde nan kòmansman ane 1530 apre Jezikri yo.

Joan of Arc / Jan Dak *n.* yon peyizàn fransèz ki te dirije fransè yo a viktwa sou angle yo nan Òleyan nan ane 1429.

John, King / Jan, Wa *n.* wa peyi Langletè ki te siyen Grann Chat la [Magna Carta] nan ane 1215.

Justinian / Jistinyen *n.* Chèf anpi women delès la nan ane 527 jouk 565 apre Jezikri, ki te dirije ak madanm ni, Teyodora, epi te repran teritwa ki te pèdi yo pou anpi a.

Justinian Code / Kòd jistinyen *n.* yon kòd legal, prepare anba dirijans anprè bizanten Jistinyen, ki te regle anpil nan lavi bizanten.

K

Kabuki / Kabouki *n.* yon kalite dram japonè ki te devlope nan ane 1600 apre Jezikri yo, ki te monte chan ak dans melodramatik, anpil makiyaj ak degizman byen fen.

Khmer Empire / Anpi Kmè *n.* anpi ki te pi pwisan epi ki te dire pi lontan sou tè prensipal nan sidès Lazi, ki sitiye kote Kanbòj ye jodiya.

Kilwa *n.* yon ansyen vil-eta sou kòt lès Lafrik, kote moun ki soti Iran ak Arabi te etabli, epi ki te rive nan somè li nan fen ane 1200 yo.

kinship / parante *n.* yon koneksyon ant moun pa san, maryaj, oswa pa adopsyon.

knight / chevalye *n.* yon gèrye ki sou cheval epi ki byen antrene e ki sèvi yon nòb pandan mwayennaj nan peyi Lewòp.

Kongo *n.* yon ansyen wayòm sou kòt lwès Lafrik, kote pèp Kongo ki te pale bantou te etabli, yon ti tan anvan 14yèm syèk apre Jezikri.

Koryo *n.* yon wayòm sou penensil koreyen, ki te etabli nan ane 935 apre Jezikri apre wayòm Sila te fin tonbe.

Kublai Khan / Koublay Kann *n.* pitit pitit Gengis Kann ki te pran pouvwa nan sid Lachin nan ane 1260 apre Jezikri epi te gen viktwa sou lame Song nan ane 1279; sa te bay Mongòl yo kontwòl sou tout Lachin.

L

labor specialization / espesyalizasyon travay *n.* travayè kalifye oswa ak konesans ki ap fè yon kalite travay presi.

landform / fòm tè *n.* yon karakteristik natirèl ki fòme sou sifas latè, tankou yon il, yon mòn, oswa yon plato.

latitude / latitid *n.* yon mezi distans onò oswa osid ekwatè a.

Leonardo da Vinci / Lewona da Vinchi *n.* yon pent epòk renesans, ki te fèt nan ane 1452 apre Jezikri, ki te pentire plizyè chedèv, tankou Mona Lisa ak Dènye Soupe a, epitou ki te avanse nan rechèch syantifik.

longbow / ak long *n.* yon zam ki kapab tire epe epi ki kapab penetre zam yon chevalye.

longitude / lonjitid *n.* yon mezi distans alès oswa alwès meridyen prensipal la.

lord / seyè *n.* yon pwopriyetè nòb ak anpil pouvwa.

Luther, Martin / Loutè, Maten *n.* yon teyologis alman, ki te fèt nan ane 1483 apre Jezikri, ki te yon chèf Refòmasyon epi ki te anseye delivrans ak lafwa nan Bondye atravè bon bagay.

M

Magna Carta / Grann Chat *n.* yon lis dwa noblès Langletè te ekri epi wa Jan te siyen nan ane 1215 apre Jezikri.

maize / mayi *n.* yon kalite mayi yo kiltive nan sivilizasyon ameriken natif yo.

Mali *n.* yon anpi Lafrik delwès pèp Malinke te etabli.

Manchu / Manchou *n.* yon manm nan yon pèp nòdès chinwa, ki te konkeri Lachin nan ane 1644 apre Jezikri epi ki te kòmanse dènye dinasti chinwa nan listwa, ki te rele Dinasti King.

manor / manwa *n.* domèn yon nòb fewodal, ki pi souvan enkli yon batiman oswa yon chato fòtifye.

Mansa Musa / Mannsa Mousa *n.* yon anprè nan peyi Mali ki te fè yon pelerinaj fame rive jouk Meka nan ane 1324 apre Jezikri.

maritime / maritim *adj.* ki gen rapò ak lanmè.

Maya *n.* yon sivilizayon sidès Meksik ak nò Lamerik santral, ki te atenn pi wo moman li ant ane 250 ak 900 apre Jezikri yo.

Mbanza *n.* vil kapital ansyen wayòm Afriken peyi Kongo.

mercantilism / mèkantilis *n.* yon règleman ekonomik ki baze sou ide ke pouvwa yon nasyon depann sou richès li.

mercenary / mèsenè *n.* yon solda ki resevwa lajan pou goumen.

Meso-America / Mezo-Amerik *n.* yon rejyon ki enkli pati sid nan peyi Meksik epi anpil nan Amerik Santral.

Michelangelo / Mikèlanj *n.* yon atis epòk Renesans, ki te fèt nan ane 1475 apre Jezikri, ki te travay pi plis tankou yon eskiltè men ki te pentire plizyè chedèv tankou plafon Chapèl Sistin nan peyi Wòm tou.

Middle Ages / Mwayennaj *n.* peryòd nan listwa ewopeyen ant fayit Wòm ak Renesans lan, ki te dire apeprè de 500 jouk 1450 apre Jezikri.

missionary / misyonè *n.* yon moun ki vwayaje pou ale nan yon peyi etranje pou fè travay relijye.

monastery / monastè *n.* yon kote kote manm yon òd relijye pratike yon vi priyè ak adorasyon.

Mongol Ascendancy / Asandans mongòl *n.* peryòd lè Mongòl yo te kontwole tout Lazi santral, ki te fè kòmès sou tè ak vwayaj pi an sekirite.

monotheism / monoteyis *n.* kwayans nan yon sèl Bondye.

Montezuma II / Montezima II *n.* dènye anprè aztèk, ki te dirije depi ane 1502 rive jouk ane 1520 epi ki te tonbe apre koudeta Espayòl yo.

mosaic / mozayik *n.* yon imaj ki fèt ak plizyè ti moso kawo oswa moso vè kolore.

mosque / mòsk *n.* yon batiman pou adorasyon mizilman, yo te bati pou l fasafas ak vil Meka.

mother culture / kilti mè *n.* yon kilti ki estriktire epi ki enfliyanse koutim ak ide lòt kilti ki vin apre yo.

movable type / tip mobil *n.* yon ti blòk an metal oswa an bwa ak yon sèl senbòl ki soulve pou enprime tèks.

Murasaki Shikibu, Lady / Mourasaki Chikibou, Dam *n.* yon ekriven japonè nan kòmansman ane 1000 yo ki te ekri Istwa Gennji, ke yo konsidere tankou youn nan premye woman.

Muslim / Mizilman *n.* yon moun ki swiv relijyon islam, epi ki aksepte Ala tankou Bondye inik.

Mutapa / Moutapa *n.* yon ansyen wayòm ki sitiye kote peyi Zimbabwe ye kounyela, yon wa Chona te etabli ozanviwon 1440 apre Jezikri; li se yon chèf wayòm sila a tou.

N

Nam Viet / Nam Vyèt *n.* yon wayòm vyetnamyen chinwa te konkeri nan 111 avan Jezikri.

natural rights / dwa natirèl *n.* dwa tout moun genyen lè nesans yo—tankou dwa a lavi, libète, ak pwopriyete selon filozòf 18yèm syèk la ki te rele Jan Lòk.

Noh / No *n.* yon kalite dram japonè ki te devlope nan ane 1300 apre Jezikri yo, ki te trè souvan rakonte ankò lejann ak istwa tradisyonèl aktè, ki te mete mask an bwa kolore, te prezante.

nomad *n.* yon moun ki te deplase soti yon kote al nan yon lòt olye li rete yon kote an pèmanans.

O

oasis / owasis *n.* yon zòn fètil nan mitan yon dezè.

Olmec / Olmèk *n.* premye kilti mezo-ameriken ki koni, ki te devlope ant ane 1200 jouk 400 avan Jezikri, epi ki te sitiye nan sidès Meksik.

Omar Khayyám / Oma Kayam *n.* yon powèt mizilman ki ne pèsan, ki dabitid te ekri an fòm kwatren epi ki te yon gran matematisyen tou.

oral history / istwa oral *n.* yon kont vèbal sou evènman, tankou yon istwa ki pase de jenerasyon an jenerasyon.

Orthodox / Òtodòks *adj.* ki gen rapò ak legliz kretyen ki te devlope nan anpi Bizanten epi ki pa anba otorite pap la.

Osman / Osmann *n.* chèf tik ki te fonde anpi otomann nan nan kòmansman ane 1300 apre Jezikri yo.

P

Pacal II / Paka II *n.* yon wa ki te dirije vil maya nan Palenk pandan prèske 70 ane (depi 615 avan Jezikri)—youn nan pi gran wa Maya yo.

Pachacuti / Pachakiti *n.* nevyèm chèf enka, ki te pran pouvwa an 1438 apre Jezikri epi ki te agrandi anpi a.

parliament / paleman *n.* yon gwoup reprezantan ki genyen sèten pouvwa nan gouvènman an.

patron / patwon *n.* yon moun ki bay sipò finansyè pou ankouraje yon aktivite oswa yon enstitisyon.

Peace of Westphalia / Lapè Wèstfali *n.* yon akò yo te fè an 1648 apre Jezikri, ki te rekonèt divizyon pèmanan Lewòp delwès antanke nasyon katolik ak pwotestan epi ki te sispann plizyè gè relijye.

perspective / pèspektiv *n.* yon teknik nan penti, ki te devlope pandan epòk Renesans, ki te reprezante aspè objè an twa dimansyon.

philosophe / filozòf *n.* youn nan pansè 18yèm syèk yo ki te eseye aplike metòd syantifik la a plizyè pwoblèm sosyal.

pilgrimage / pelerinaj *n.* yon vwayaj pou ale yon kote sakre oswa pou ale nan yon tonbo.

Pizarro, Francisco / Pizawo, Fransis *n.* yon eksploratè panyòl ki te rive nan Pewou an 1532 apre Jezikri epi ki te konkeri anpi enka avan 1535.

Polo, Marco / Polo, Mako *n.* yon komèsan venisyen ki te vwayaje Wout Swa yo epi te rive nan Lachin ozanviwon 1275 apre Jezikri. Li te tounen yon èd pou Koublay Kann epi apresa te pibliye yon liv popilè sou avanti li yo.

porcelain / pòslèn *n.* yon materyèl seramik blan ki di, ke yo trè souvan rele tchayna.

predestination / predestinasyon *n.* dokrin ki di Bondye chwazi moun pou delivrans ak malediksyon anvan yo fèt epi moun sa a pa genyen okenn pouvwa pou chanje sa Bondye vle.

primary source / sous prensipal *n.* yon dokiman oswa yon objè fabrike, ki kreye pandan yon peryòd istorik presi.

printing press / enprimant *n.* yon aparèy pou prese papye kont yon senbòl mobil ak lank.

projection / pwojeksyon *n.* yon jan pou respekte sifas koube sou latè sou yon kat ki plat e ki kenbe defòmasyon ki konsistan epi ke yo kapab manye.

Protestant / Pwotestan *n.* yon manm nan yon gwoup kretyen ki te kite legliz katolik pandan oswa apre 16yèm syèk la.

Q

quipu / kwipou *n.* yon zouti ansyen sivilizasyon enka ki te sèvi pou konte, epi ki te genyen ne nan plizyè kote.

Qur'an / Kouran *n.* bib mizilman yo, ki konpoze de revelasyon Ala te bay e disip Mowamèd yo te kolekte apre lanmò li.

R

rationalism / rasyonalis *n.* ide ki di moun dwe rezone, oswa itilize panse lojik, pou konprann lemonn.

Reconquista / Rekonkista *n.* seri kanpay, ki te fini an 1492 apre Jezikri, ki te pèmèt lame kretyen yo mete chèf mizilman yo deyò Lespay.

Reformation / Refòmasyon *n.* yon mouvman ki te opoze legliz katolik, ki te kòmanse nan 16yèm syèk.

regent / rejan *n.* yon moun ki dirije nan plas yon monak ki absan oswa ki anbazaj.

religious order / òd relijye *n.* yon gwoup moun ki viv selon yon règ relijye.

Renaissance / Renesans *n.* yon peryòd renesans ak kreyativite nan la, ekriti, ak panse depi apeprè 1300 apre Jezikri jouk 1600, ki te kòmanse nan Itali epi ki te evantyèlman pwolonje atravè Lewòp.

republic / repiblik *n.* yon kalite gouvènman kote pouvwa a nan men sitwayen yo, epi yo vote pou eli chèf yo.

reunify / reyinifye *v.* mete ansanm ankò.

Roman Catholic / Katolik Women *adj.* ki gen rapò ak legliz kretyen nan lwès ki anba otorite pap la.

S

Sahara / Saara *n.* yon gwo dezè nan Lafrik dinò, ki etann depi kòt atlantik la jouk vale nil la.

Saladin / Saladen *n.* yon chèf militè ki te ini mizilman yo pou goumen ak kretyen yo nan Palestin pandan 12yèm syèk apre Jezikri.

salon *n.* yon rankont ak pansè epi atis pou diskite pwoblèm epi pou pataje ide pandan peryòd Eklèsisman.

samurai / samourè *n.* yon gerye kalifye nan aristokrasi japonè.

savanna / savann *n.* yon preri plat nan yon rejyon twopikal, ki pa genyen anpil pyebwa.

schism / chis *n.* yon separasyon ofisyèl ant de gwoup.

scholar-official / entelektyèl-ofisyèl *n.* yon moun edike ki genyen yon pozisyon nan gouvènman.

scientific method / metòd syantifik *n.* yon apwòch a envestigasyon syantifik ki enkli fè obsèvasyon atantif, fè epi teste yon ipotèz, epi tire yon konklizyon ki konfime oswa modifye ipotèz la.

Scientific Revolution / Revolisyon syantifik *n.* yon peryòd ki te kòmanse nan ane 1500 apre Jezikri yo, lè entelektyèl ewopeyen yo te kòmanse kesyone ide syantifik klasik yo ak kwayans kretyen yo.

secondary source / sous segondè *n.* yon zèv yon moun pwodwi sou yon evènman istorik ke li pat viv.

Seljuk Turk / Seljik Tik *n.* manm yon pèp tik ki te kontwole Lazi santral ak lwès depi 11yèm jouk 13yèm syèk.

serf / sèf *n.* yon peyizan fèmye nan yon sosyete fewodal, ki te travay pou yon nòb annechanj pou pwoteksyon ak sèten dwa.

Shakespeare, William / Chekspè, Wilyam *n.* ekriven anglè pi fame nan epòk Renesans ki pi koni pou pyès teyat Womeyo e Jilyèt epi Amlèt.

Shi'a / Chiya *n.* gwoup mizilman ki te reziste rèy imayad yo, epi ki te kwè kalif la sipoze yon pwofèt ki fanmi ak Mowamèd.

Shinto / Chinto *n.* relijyon tradisyonèl nan peyi Japon, ki baze sou adorasyon ak respè pou lanati ak zansèt yo.

shogun / chogonn *n.* yon chèf militè japonè— youn nan premye gwoup ki te pran pouvwa an 1192 apre Jezikri ki te dirije pou anprè a men pi souvan pou pwòp enterè yo.

Shona / Chona *n.* yon kilti ki te pale bantou ki tap pwospere avan ane 1000 apre Jezikri, kote peyi Bostwana, Mozanbik, ak Zimbabwe ye kounyela.

Shotoku, Prince / Chotoki, Prens *n.* yon rejan ki te dirije peyi Japon de 593 jouk 622 apre Jezikri epi te pote eleman kilti chinwa yo—sitou relijyon boudis la—nan peyi a.

Silk Roads / Wout Swa yo *n.* ansyen wout komès ki te konekte Lewòp ak Lachin.

slash-and-burn agriculture / agrikilti koupe epi boule *n.* yon kalite agrikilti kote moso tè prepare pou plante lè yo fin koupe epi boule vejetasyon natirèl la.

Songhai / Songay *n.* pèp Afrik delwès ak chèf ki te kreye yon gran anpi nan 15yèm ak 16yèm syèk apre Jezikri yo.

sponsor / parenn *n.* yon moun ki bay lajan pou bay yon moun oswa yon pwojè sipò li.

standing army / lame kanpe *n.* yon fòs pou batay ki toujou la nan peryòd lapè tankou tou nan tan lagè.

stele / estèl *n.* yon wòch dekoupe ki sèvi tankou mak pou komemore dat oswa gan evènman enpòtan.

Stoicism / Estoyisis *n.* yon filozofi grèk ki te souliye enpòtans vèti, devwa, ak andirans epi ki te sitou enfliyanse ansyen Wòm.

Suleyman I / Souleymann I *n.* siltan anpi otomann nan ant ane 1520 ak 1566 apre Jezikri ki te ankouraje la epi ki te devlope yon kòd legal.

Sundiata / Soundiyata *n.* yon ansyen chèf pèp malenk, ki te kapital Sana epi ki te pwolonje anpi a anpil.

Sunnah / Souna *n.* pawòl epi aksyon Mowamèd, ki sèvi tankou gid pou mizilman kapab viv byen.

Sunni / Souni *n.* manm nan yon gwoup mizilman ki te aksepte règ kalif ki eli yo epi ki pat reziste imayad yo.

Swahili / Swayili *n.* yon lang afriken ki melanje eleman bantou ak eleman arab yo.

T

Tenochtitlán / Tenoktitlàn *n.* yon ansyen vil aztèk ki sitiye sou yon ti il nan lak tekskoko, ki te fonde an 1325 apre Jezikri.

Thomas Aquinas / Toma Akinas *n.* yon entelektyèl italyen ki te fè yon melanj ant filozofi klasik ak teyoloji kretyen.

Timbuktu / Timbòktou *n.* yon vil nan Mali santral nan Lafrik delwès, ki te fonde nan 13yèm syèk epi ki te sant komès ak kilti.

Tokugawa Shogunate / Tokougawa Chogounat *n.* rèy Tokougawa Iyeyasou ak siksesè li yo nan peyi Japon, ki te kòmanse nan ane 1603 apre Jezikri epi ki te mennen yon peryòd establilite nan peyi a pandan 250 ane.

Treaty of Tordesillas / Akò Tòdesiyas *n.* yon akò ant Lespay ak Pòtigal an 1494, ki trase yon liy imajinè toutotou lemonn ki soti nan nò rive jouk nan sid, epi ki te bay Lespay tè ki alwès liy nan epi tè alès yo bay Pòtigal.

triangular trade / komès triyangilè *n.* echanj machandiz epi esklav atravè Oseyan Atlantik la ant peyi Lamerik yo, Lewòp, ak Lafrik.

tribute / omaj *n.* yon peman yon peyi bay yon lòt kòm siy respè.

U, V, W, X, Y, Z

universal gravitation / gravitasyon inivèsèl *n.* Teyori Isaac Newton ki deklare ke gravite aji nan tout objè ki nan inivè a.

vassal / vasal *n.* nan sosyete fewodal, yon moun ki resevwa tè ak pwoteksyon yon seyè annechanj pou fidelite.

vegetation zone / zòn vejetasyon *n.* yon rejyon ki genyen de plant espesyal akòz tè ak klima li.

vernacular / vènakilè *n.* lang natal yon moun.

weather / tanperati *n.* kondisyon nan atmosfè a nan yon kote pandan yon lè byen presi.

wood-block printing / enpresyon ak blòk -bwa *n.* yon sistèm enprimant ansyen chinwa yo te devlope, kote blòk an bwa te grave ak ase karaktè pou enprime tout yon paj.

Yucatán Peninsula / Penensil Youkatan *n.* yon zòn nan sidès Meksik ki pwolonje jouk Lanmè Karayib la ak Gòlf Meksik.

Zen / Zenn *n.* fòm boudis japonè ki baze sou disiplin pèsonèl, senplisite, ak meditasyon.

Zheng He / Zeng E *n.* yon amiral chinwa ki te fè yon pakèt vwayaj ant ane 1405 ak 1433 apre Jezikri yo; vwayaj sa yo te agrandi komès ak repitasyon etranjè Lachin.

РУССКИЙ ГЛОССАРИЙ

Глоссарий — это алфавитный указатель ключевых терминов разделов, вместе с описанием их значения. Определения, указанные в глоссарии, пояснх том понятии, в котором он использовался в данной книге. В глоссарии указывается часть речи каждого термина. В глоссарии используются следующие сокращения:

глаг. = глагол   **прилаг.** = прилагательное   **сущ.** = существительное

A

Abd al-Malik / Абд аль-Малик, *сущ.*, мусульманский правитель, ставший халифом в 685 г. н. э. и провозгласивший арабский язык официальным языком правительств всех мусульманских территорий.

Abd al-Rahman III / Абд Аль-Рахман III, *сущ.*, восьмой эмир аль-Андалуса, во время правления которого аль-Андалус достиг наибольшего могущества.

Afonso I / Афонсо I, *сущ.*, король Конго, взошедший на престол в 1506 г. н. э. Находился под большим влиянием португальцев, участвовал в торговле рабами.

Andalus / Андалусия, *сущ.*, территория Испании, находившаяся под контролем мусульман с 700-х годов по 1492 г. н. э.

Allah / Аллах, *сущ.*, Бог в исламской религии.

alluvial soil / аллювиальная почва, *сущ.*, очень плодородная, богатая микроэлементами почва, образованная речными отложениями.

Almoravids / Альморавиды, *сущ.*, северо-африканская исламская династия, пытавшаяся насильственно обратить в мусульманскую веру население соседствующих стран, в том числе Марокко, Испании и Ганы.

anatomy / анатомия, *сущ.*, наука о формах и строении человека, растений и животных.

Angkor Wat / Ангкор-Ват, *сущ.*, комплекс храмов в Юго-восточной Азии, построенный в 1100-ых гг. н. э., занимающий площадь почти в 1 квадратную милю. Самое грандиозное по размеру религиозное строение в мире.

anthropology / антропология, *сущ.*, наука о людях и их культуре.

aqueduct / акведук, *сущ.*, сооружение, по которому чистая вода поступает в город.

archaeology / археология, *сущ.*, восстановление и изучение материальных остатков прошлой жизни.

artifact / артефакт, *сущ.*, объект созданный человеком.

Askia Muhammad / Аския Мухаммед, *сущ.*, правитель империи Сонгай с 1493 г. по 1528 г. н. э., расширивший территорию империи и создавший ее правительство.

astrolabe / астролябия, *сущ.*, инструмент для измерения углов расположения звезд над горизонтом, что позволяет морякам определять их местонахождение.

Augustus / Август, *сущ.*, первый император Рима, правивший с 27 г. до н. э. до 14 г. н. э., значительно расширивший территорию и влияние Римской империи.

B

Baghdad / Багдад, *сущ.*, город в нынешнем Ираке, ранее столица Аббасидской империи.

Bantu migrations / переселения Банту, *сущ.*, миграция банту-говорящих народностей из Западной Африки на юг и восток. Началась примерно в 1000 г. до н. э. и способствовала распространению языка и культуры этих народов.

bubonic plague / бубонная чума, *сущ.*, болезнь, поразившая западную часть Евразии в середине 1300-х гг., вспышка этой болезни известна как "черная смерть".

Buddhism / Буддизм, *сущ.*, система верований, основанная на учениях Сиддхартхи Гаутамы, иначе Будды, особое значение в которой придается освобождению личности от мирских желаний.

bureaucracy / бюрократия, *сущ.*, система департаментов и агентств, исполняющих функции правительства.

bushido / бусидо, *сущ.* моральный кодекс самураев, требовавший от них быть щедрыми, храбрыми и преданными.

Byzantine Empire / Византийская империя, *сущ.*, Восточная Римская империя со столицей Константинополь, существовавшая в период с IV по XV века.

C

cacao / какао, *сущ.*, дерево тропических лесов Америки, семена которого используются в производстве шоколада.

caliph / халиф, *сущ.*, правитель мусульманского государства, считающийся потомком Мухаммеда.

calligraphy / каллиграфия, *сущ.*, искусство красивого письма.

Calvin, John / Жан Кальвин, *сущ.*, (1509-1564 гг. н. э.) лидер протестантской реформации, развивший учение о предопределении.

capitalism / капитализм, *сущ.*, экономическая система, основанная на частной собственности экономических ресурсов и их использовании для извлечения прибыли.

caravel / каравелла, *сущ.*, разновидность португальского морского судна для длительных плаваний, имеет квадратные и треугольные паруса.

cartography / картография, *сущ.*, навыки и методы, применяемые в составлении карт.

celadon / селадон, *сущ.*, вид корейского фарфора, часто голубовато-зеленоватого цвета.

Charlemagne / Карл Великий, *сущ.*, король франков (с 768 г.), захвативший большую часть территории Европы и распространивший христианство на завоеванных территориях.

chasqui / часки, *сущ.*, гонец в империи Инка, переносивший послания по всей территории империи.

chivalry / галантность, *сущ.*, нормы поведения рыцарей в Европе в Средние века, основными из которых были мужество, честь, уважение к женщинам и слабым.

Christianity / Христианство, *сущ.*, религия, основанная на жизнеописании и учении Иисуса.

circumnavigate / совершать кругосветное путешествие, *глаг.*, совершить путешествие вокруг всего земного шара.

clan / клан, *сущ.*, группа людей, связанных кровным родством или браком.

clergy / духовенство, *сущ.*, в религии люди с приличествующими духовному лицу обязанностями.

climate / климат, *сущ.*, многолетний характер погодных условий в определенной местности.

Clovis / Хлодвиг, *сущ.*, правитель франков, одержавший победу над Римской империей в сражении за контроль над Галлией в 486 г. н. э., а позже основавший могущественное и влиятельное Франкское королевство.

codex / рукопись, *сущ.*, вид книги, использовавшийся первыми мезо-американскими народами для записи важных исторических событий.

Columbian Exchange / Колумбийский обмен, *сущ.*, обмен растениями, животными или другими биологическими формами между восточным и западным полушариями, произошедший после открытия Америки Колумбом в 1492 г. н. э.

Confucianism / конфуцианство, *сущ.*, вера, основанная на учениях Конфуция, философа, распространявшего идеи благодетели и моральной этики.

Constantine / Константин, *сущ.*, римский император (306-337 гг. н. э.), прекративший гонения на христиан и перенесший столицу империи в Византию (позже стала именоваться Константинополем).

continent / континент, *сущ.*, один из семи материков Земли: Северная Америка, Южная Америка, Европа, Азия, Африка, Австралия и Антарктида.

convert / обращать в веру, *глаг.*, убеждать кого-либо принять новую религию или убеждения.

Córdoba / Кордоба, *сущ.*, столица государства Аль-Андалус.

Cortés, Hernán / Эрнандо Кортес, *сущ.*, испанский конкистадор, одержавший победу над ацтеками в Мексике в 1521 г. н. э.

covenant / договор, *сущ.*, обязывающее соглашение.

Crusades / крестовые походы, *сущ.*, серия военных походов христиан из Европы в Палестину в период между XI и XIII веками.

culture / культура, *сущ.*, стиль жизни, разделяемый группой людей.

D

daimyo / даймио, *сущ.*, японский феодал, владеющий большими участками земли, имеющий личную армию самураев и не плативший налоги правительству.

Daoism / Даосизм, *сущ.*, вера, зародившаяся в Китае примерно в 500 г. до н. э., придающая особое значение жизни в гармонии с природой и внутренним миром.

Declaration of Independence / Декларация независимости, *сущ.*, документ провозгласивший независимость американских колоний от Великобритании.

Declaration of the Rights of Man and of the Citizen / Декларация прав человека и гражданина, *сущ.*, документ, принятый французским революционным правительством в 1789 году, декларировавший права людей.

dissection / вскрытие, *сущ.*, препарирование животного или растения для диагностики и изучения его органов или частей.

divan / диван, *сущ.*, имперский совет при султане в Османском государстве.

E

elevation / высота над уровнем моря, *сущ.*, высота расположения суши над уровнем моря.

elite / элита, *сущ.*, расположенные выше других по социальному статусу или самые богатые представители или группы общества.

Elizabethan Age / Елизаветинский век, *сущ.*, период правления королевы Елизаветы I с 1558 г. по 1603 г. в Англии.

embassy / посольство, *сущ.*, представительство правительства какой-либо страны в другом государстве.

emperor / император, *сущ.*, человек, правящий империей.

empire / империя, *сущ.*, группа различных территорий или культур под контролем одного верховного правителя.

enlightened despot / просвещенный деспот, *сущ.*, правитель обладающий абсолютной властью, но воодушевленный политический идеями Просвещения и потому старающийся править справедливо и основывать решения на знаниях.

Enlightenment / Просвещение, *сущ.*, философское движение XVIII века, когда философы искали причинно-следственные связи для понимания истин человеческой природы.

epic poem / эпическая поэма, *сущ.*, длинная поэма, рассказывающая о подвигах героев.

excavation / раскопки, *сущ.*, процесс выемки грунта с целью нахождения ценных материальных остатков прошлой жизни для их изучения.

F

faction / фракция, *сущ.*, небольшая группа, чьи интересы противоречат интересам большей по размерам группы, частью которой она является.

federalism / федерализм, *сущ.*, разделение власти между организацией или правительством и его членами.

feudalism / феодализм, *сущ.*, политическая и социальная система в средневековой Европе, при которой лендлорд наделял вассалов землей в обмен на их службу и преданность.

Forbidden City / Запретный город, *сущ.*, группа обнесенных стеной дворцов, построенных для китайского императора в начале 1400-х годов н. э. в столице Китая Пекине.

Francis of Assisi, Saint / святой Франциск Ассизский, *сущ.*, итальянец, основатель ордена францисканцев в начале 1200-ых годов н. э.

G

Genghis Khan / Чингисхан, *сущ.*, татаро-монгольский правитель, примерно в 1206 г. н. э. объединивший татаро-монгольские племена, начавший завоевательную кампанию и создавший империю, простиравшуюся с севера Китая в Центральную Азию.

geocentric theory / теория геоцентризма, *сущ.*, теория, утверждающая, что Земля – центр вселенной.

geography / география, *сущ.*, наука о природных характеристиках Земли.

Ghana / Гана, *сущ.*, регион, расположенный между Сахарой и южными лесами Западной Африки, родина многих древних культур.

glyph / глиф, *сущ.*, изображение, представляющее собой слово, слог или звук.

golden age / золотой век, *сущ.*, период, во время которого общество или культура достигают наибольшего расцвета.

Great Enclosure / Великое ограждение, *сущ.*, самое большое из трех главных частей поселения народа Шона в Великом Зимбабве, возможно, резиденция короля.

Great Schism / Великий раскол, *сущ.*, разделение в Римской католической церкви в 1378-1417 гг., произошедшее когда два центра церковной власти - Авиньон и Рим разделились и избрали разных пап.

Great Zimbabwe / Великое Зимбабве, *сущ.*, центральное поселение народов Шона за высокой каменной стеной, на территории более 100 акров. Его население составляло от 10000 до 20000 человек.

Gregory VII, Pope / Григорий VII, папа римский, *сущ.*, глава Римской католической церкви с 1073 г. по 1085 г., боровшийся за власть с императором Генрихом IV.

griot / гриот, *сущ.*, профессиональный сказитель в африканской культуре.

guild / гильдия, *сущ.*, союз людей, занимающихся торговлей или ремеслом, основной целью которого являлось поддержание качества и количества поставляемой ими продукции, а также защита интересов членов союза.

Gutenberg, Johann / Гуттенберг Иоганн, *сущ.*, немец, в середине 1400-ых годов изобретший пресс для печатания с наборными литерами.

H

habeas corpus / хабеас корпус, *сущ.*, право людей не быть незаконно заключенными в тюрьму.

haiku / хокку, *сущ.*, японская поэтическая форма, состоящая из 17 слогов, расположенных в три строки из 5, 7 и 5 слогов.

harmony / гармония, *сущ.*, сочетание элементов, образующих приятное целое.

heliocentric / гелиоцентрический, *прилаг.*, имеющий солнце в качестве центра.

hemisphere / полушарие, *сущ.*, одна из двух половин Земли, отделенных друг от друга экватором или нулевым меридианом.

Henry IV, Emperor / император Генрих IV, *сущ.*, правитель Священной Римской империи в XI в., постоянно боровшийся за власть с папой римским Григорием VII.

Hijrah / Хиджра, *сущ.*, переселение Мухаммеда и его последователей из Мекки в Медину в 622 г. н. э.

historian / историк, *сущ.*, человек, изучающий и истолковывающий прошлое.

history / история, *сущ.*, изучения событий, произошедших в прошлом.

humanism / гуманизм, *сущ.*, течение в эпоху Ренессанса в Европе, прославлявшее возможности и достижения человека и уделявшее особое внимание таким наукам, как история, литература, грамматика и философия.

Hundred Years' War / Столетняя война, *сущ.*, череда войн между Англией и Францией в 1337-1453 гг. н. э.

I

Iberian Peninsula / Пиренейский полуостров, *сущ.*, юго-западная оконечность Европы, где сегодня располагаются Испания и Португалия.

Ignatius of Loyola, Saint / святой Игнатий Лойола, *сущ.*, испанец, основавший религиозный орден иезуитов в начале 1530-х годов.

imperial / имперский, *прилаг.*, имеющий отношение к империи или императору.

indulgence / индульгенция, *сущ.*, прощение грехов Римской католической церковью, позволяющее человеку избежать Божьего наказания в загробном мире.

Inquisition / Инквизиция, *сущ.*, суд, учрежденный Римской католической церковью в 1542 г. н. э., чтобы преследовать людей, отошедших от римской католической веры и усилить влияние Церкви.

Islam / Ислам, *сущ.*, монотеистическая религия, основанная на учениях Мухаммеда.

J

janissary / янычар, *сущ.*, член элитной военной единицы в Османской империи, состоящей в основном из рабов.

Jesuit / иезуит, *сущ.*, член "Общества Иисуса", религиозного ордена, основанного в начале 1530-х годов святым Игнатием Лойолой.

Joan of Arc / Жанна д'Арк, *сущ.*, французская крестьянская девушка, возглавившая армию и приведшая Францию к победе над Англией в Орлеане в 1429 г. н. э.

John, King / король Иоанн, *сущ.*, король Англии, подписавший Великую Хартию Вольностей в 1215 г. н. э.

Justinian / Юстиниан, *сущ.*, император Восточной Римской империи, правивший с 527 г. по 565 г. до н. э. вместе со своей женой Теодорой и отвоевавший ранее утраченные территории империи.

Justinian Code / Кодекс Юстиниана, *сущ.*, кодекс римского права, пересмотренный по приказу византийского императора Юстиниана, и охватывающий большинство вопросов, касающихся жизни в Византии.

K

Kabuki / кабуки, *сущ.*, японский вид драмы, основанный в 1600-ых годах н. э., в котором сюжет раскрывается с помощью эмоциональных песен и танцев, большого количества макияжа и замысловатых костюмов.

Khmer Empire / Империя кхмеров, *сущ.*, самое могущественное и просуществовавшее дольше других на своем материке царство, располагавшееся в Юго-восточной Азии на территории, где сейчас находится Камбоджа.

Kilwa / Килва, *сущ.*, древний город-государство на восточном побережье Африки, основанный людьми из Ирана и Аравии, достигший расцвета в конце 1200-х годов.

kinship / родство, *сущ.*, связь между людьми, кровная или созданная в результате брака или усыновления.

knight / рыцарь, *сущ.*, в средневековой Европе хорошо обученный конный воин, находящийся на службе у дворянина.

Kongo / Конго, *сущ.*, древнее королевство на западном побережье Африки, основанное банту-говорящими народами незадолго до начала XIV века.

Koryo / Корё, *сущ.*, королевство на Корейском полуострове, образованное в 935 г. н. э. после краха королевства Силла.

Kublai Khan / Кублайхан, *сущ.*, внук Чингисхана, пришедший к власти в южном Китае в 1260 г. и разгромивший армию Сонг в 1279 г., в результате чего монголо-татары получили контроль над всем Китаем.

L

labor specialization / разделение труда, *сущ.*, распределение различных видов трудовой деятельности между специально обученными работниками.

landform / суша, *сущ.*, естественно сформированная разновидность земной поверхности, например остров, гора или плато.

latitude / широта, *сущ.*, единица измерения расстояния от экватора до какой-либо точки на севере или юге от него.

Leonardo da Vinci / Леонардо да Винчи, *сущ.*, итальянский художник эпохи Возрождения, родившийся в 1452 г. н. э. Создал многие шедевры, в том числе картины "Мона Лиза" и "Тайная вечеря", а также написал блестящие научные работы.

longbow / лук, *сущ.*, оружие, пускающее стрелы, способные пробить ,броню рыцаря.

longitude / долгота, *сущ.*, единица измерения расстояния от нулевого меридиана до какой-либо точки на востоке или западе от него.

lord / лорд, *сущ.*, влиятельный дворянин, обладающий большими земельными владениями.

Luther, Martin / Лютер, Мартин, *сущ.*, немецкий теолог, родившийся в 1483 г. Лидер Реформации, распространявший идеи спасения через веру в Бога, а не через совершение хороших поступков.

M

Magna Carta / Великая Хартия Вольностей, *сущ.*, перечень прав, созданный английскими дворянами и утвержденный королем Иоанном в 1215 г.

maize / маис, *сущ.*, сорт кукурузы, который выращивали цивилизации коренных американцев.

Mali / Мали, *сущ.*, Западно-африканская империя, основанная народом Малинке.

Manchu / Маньчжур, *сущ.*, представитель группы северо-восточных китайцев, покорившей Китай в 1644 г. и давшей начало последней династии в истории Китая – династии Цин.

manor / поместье, *сущ.*, владение феодала, обычно с укрепленным строением или замком.

Mansa Musa / Манса Муса, *сущ.*, император Мали, совершивший известное паломничество в Мекку в 1324 г. н. э.

maritime / морской, *прилаг.*, имеющий отношение к морю.

Maya / Майя, *сущ.*, цивилизация на юге Мексики и севере Центральной Америки, достигшая расцвета в 250-900 гг. н. э.

Mbanza / Мбанза, *сущ.*, столица древне-африканского королевства Конго.

mercantilism / меркантилизм, *сущ.*, экономическая политика, основанная на идее, что мощь нации зависит от ее богатства.

mercenary / наемник, *сущ.*, солдат, нанимаемый для участия в боевых действиях.

Meso-America / Мезо-Америка, *сущ.*, регион, в который входит южная часть Мексики и большая часть Центральной Америки.

Michelangelo / Микеланджело, *сущ.*, итальянский художник эпохи Возрождения, родившийся в 1475 г. н. э. В основном был скульптором, но также известен как художник своей росписью свода Сикстинской Капеллы в Риме.

Middle Ages / Средневековье, *сущ.*, период в истории Европы между падением Рима и началом эпохи Возрождения, длившийся примерно с 500 г. по 1450 г. н. э.

missionary / миссионер, *сущ.*, человек, путешествующий в другие страны для распространения своих религиозных убеждений.

monastery / монастырь, *сущ.*, место, где члены религиозного ордена проводят жизнь в молении и поклонении.

Mongol Ascendancy / Монголо-Татарское господство, *сущ.*, период, во время которого монголо-татары контролировали всю территорию Средней Азии, сделав ее безопасной для торговли и перемещений.

monotheism / монотеизм, *сущ.*, вера в одного Бога.

Montezuma II / Монтесума II, *сущ.*, последний император ацтеков, чье правление длилось с 1502 г. по 1520 г. н. э., был свергнут испанцами.

mosaic / мозаика, *сущ.*, картина, созданная из мелких кусочков цветного стекла или плиток.

mosque / мечеть, *сущ.*, здание, в котором молятся мусульмане. Строят таким образом, чтобы оно было обращено лицом к Мекке.

mother culture / материнская культура, *сущ.*, культура, предопределяющая обычаи и представления последующих культур.

movable type / наборные литеры, *сущ.*, небольшая металлическая или деревянная пластина лишь с одним выступающим символом, использовавшаяся в книгопечатании.

Murasaki Shikibu, Lady / леди Мурасаки Сикибу, *сущ.*, японская писательница начала 1000-х годов н. э., написавшая "Гендзи-моногатари", один из первых романов в истории человечества.

Muslim / Мусульманин, *сущ.*, человек, чьей религией является ислам, а единственным Богом - Аллах.

Mutapa / Мутапа, *сущ.*, древнее королевство на территории нынешнего государства Зимбабве, основанное королем народа Шона примерно в 1440 г. н. э. Также имя правителя королевства.

N

Nam Viet / Нам Виет, *сущ.*, вьетнамское королевство, завоеванное китайцами в 111 г. до н. э.

natural rights / естественные права, *сущ.*, в соответствии с философом XVIII в. Джоном Локком, это права, которыми наделены все люди с рождения. Например, право на жизнь, свободу и собственность.

Noh / Ноо, *сущ.*, японский драматический жанр, появившийся в 1300-х годах н. э., в котором часто актеры в разрисованных деревянных масках пересказывают легенды и сказки.

nomad / кочевник, *сущ.*, человек, не имеющий постоянного места жительства и перемещающийся из одного места в другое.

O

oasis / оазис, *сущ.*, район с плодородной почвой посреди пустыни.

Olmec / Ольмеки, *сущ.*, самая ранняя из известных мезо-американских цивилизаций, сконцентрированная на юго-востоке Мексики и процветавшая в 1200-400 гг. до н. э.

Omar Khayyám / Омар Хайям, *сущ.*, мусульманин, уроженец Персии, писавший четверостишия. Также талантливый математик.

oral history / неписанная история, *сущ.*, незафиксированное на бумаге описание события, например история переходящая из уст в уста от поколения к поколению.

Orthodox / Православный, *прилаг.*, имеющий отношение к христианской церкви, получившей развитие в Византийской империи и не находящейся под контролем папы римского.

Osman / Осман, *сущ.*, турецкий правитель, основавший Османскую империю в начале 1300-х годов.

P

Pacal II / Пакал II, *сущ.*, король, правивший в Паленке, городе народов майя, в течение почти 70 лет (с 615 г. н. э.)—один из величайших королей цивилизации майя.

Pachacuti / Пачакути, *сущ.*, девятый правитель инков, пришедший к власти в 1438 г. н. э. и увеличивший территорию империи инков.

parliament / парламент, *сущ.*, группа представителей народа, наделенных некоторой правительственной властью.

patron / покровитель, *сущ.*, человек, поддерживающий какую-либо деятельность или организацию посредством предоставления финансовой поддержки.

Peace of Westphalia / Вестфальский мир, *сущ.*, соглашение, достигнутое в 1648 г. н. э., о признании постоянного деления западной Европы на католиков и протестантов. Способствовало завершению многих религиозных войн.

perspective / перспектива, *сущ.*, техника в живописи, появившаяся в эпоху Возрождения, с помощью которой объекты изображаются в трехмерном измерении.

philosophe / философ, *сущ.*, представитель группы мыслителей 18-го века, пытавшихся применить научный подход к вопросам общественной жизни.

pilgrimage / паломничество, *сущ.*, путешествие в священное место или место поклонения.

Pizarro, Francisco / Писарро, Франсиско, *сущ.*, испанский конкистадор, в 1532 году высадившийся на землю Перу и к 1535 году покоривший империю инков.

Polo, Marco / Поло, Марко, *сущ.*, венецианский купец, прибывший по Шелковому пути в Китай в 1275 г. н. э. Стал помощником Кублайхана и позже издал известную книгу о своих приключениях.

porcelain / фарфор, *сущ.*, прочный белый керамический материал.

predestination / предназначение, *сущ.*, теория о том, что Бог дарует избранным людям спасение, а другим проклятие еще до их рождения и о том, что люди не в силах изменить волю Божью.

primary source / первоисточник, *сущ.,* документ или артефакт, созданный во время определенного исторического периода.

printing press / печатный пресс, *сущ.,* машина для прижима бумаги к покрытым чернилами наборным литерам.

projection / проекция, *сущ.,* способ представления изогнутой поверхности Земли на плоскости карты, чтобы искажение не противоречило реальности.

Protestant / Протестант, *сущ.,* представитель группы христиан, отделившихся от Римской католической церкви в XVI в. или позже.

Q

quipu / кипу, *сущ.,* инструмент для счета у древних инков, состоящий из веревок с узелками, расположенными на различном расстоянии.

Qur'an / Коран, *сущ.,* священная книга мусульман, состоящая из откровений Аллаха, собранных последователями Мухаммеда после его смерти.

R

rationalism / рационализм, *сущ.,* убеждение, что люди должны использовать разум или логическое мышление для понимания мира.

Reconquista / Реконкиста, *сущ.,* ряд военных кампаний христианских армий, завершившихся в 1492 г вытеснением мусульманских правителей из Испании.

Reformation / Реформация, *сущ.,* движение против Римской Католической церкви, начавшееся в XVI веке.

regent / регент, *сущ.,* человек, правящий вместо отсутствующего или слишком юного монарха.

religious order / религиозный орден, *сущ.,* группа людей, живущих по какому-либо религиозному принципу.

Renaissance / Возрождение, *сущ.,* период возрождения и развития искусства, литературы и мышления в XIV-XVII вв., начавшийся в Италии и в последствии распространившийся на всю Европу.

republic / республика, *сущ.,* форма правления, в которой власть остается у граждан, избирающих своих руководителей путем голосования.

reunify / воссоединить, *глаг.,* вновь соединить воедино.

Roman Catholic / Римский Католический, *прилаг.,* имеющий отношение к христианской церкви на Западе, находящейся под властью папы римского.

S

Sahara / Сахара, *сущ.,* большая пустыня на севере Африки, простирающаяся от Атлантического побережья до долины Нила.

Saladin / Саладин, *сущ.,* военный лидер, объединивший мусульман для борьбы с христианами в Палестине в XII в. н. э.

salon / салон, *сущ.,* в эпоху Просвещения собрание мыслителей и людей искусства для обсуждения вопросов и обмена идеями.

samurai / самурай, *сущ.,* воин, обученный для службы японским феодалам.

savanna / саванна, *сущ.,* ровная травянистая равнина в тропических районах с небольшим количеством деревьев.

schism / раскол, *сущ.,* официальное разделение на две группы.

scholar-official / ученый-чиновник, *сущ.,* высокообразованный человек на правительственном посту.

scientific method / научный подход, *сущ.,* подход к научному исследованию, включающий точные наблюдения, обоснование и проверку гипотезы и формирование заключения, которое подтверждает гипотезу или вносит поправки в нее.

Scientific Revolution / Научная революция, *сущ.,* период, начавшийся в 1500-х годах н. э., когда европейские мыслители начали подвергать сомнению классические научные идеи и христианские верования.

secondary source / вторичный источник, *сущ.,* описание исторического события, созданное не очевидцем.

Seljuk Turk / Сельджук, Турк, *сущ.*, представитель династии турков, под контролем которых находилась центральная и западная Азия с XI по XIII вв.

serf / крепостной, *сущ.*, в феодальном обществе крестьянин, занимающийся сельским хозяйством для дворянина в обмен на его защиту и определенные права.

Shakespeare, William / Уильям Шекспир, *сущ.*, самый известный английский писатель эпохи Возрождения. Особо известен своими пьесами "Ромео и Джульетта" и "Гамлет".

Shi'a / Шиизм, *сущ.*, группа мусульман, оказывавшая сопротивление правящим Умайядам, утверждая, что халифом должен быть родственник пророка Мухаммеда.

Shinto / Синтоизм, *сущ.*, традиционная религия Японии, основанная на поклонении природе и предкам.

shogun / сёгун, *сущ.*, японский военный предводитель, член группы, впервые пришедшей к власти в 1192 г. н. э. и правившей от имени императора, но обычно в своих личных интересах.

Shona / Шона, *сущ.*, народность, говорящая на языке банту, процветавшая примерно в 1000-х годах н. э. на территории современных Ботсваны, Мозамбика и Зимбабве.

Shotoku, Prince / принц Шотоку, *сущ.*, регент, правивший Японией в 593-622 гг. н. э. и внесший в культуру Японии элементы культуры Китая, в частности, Буддизм.

Silk Roads / Шелковый путь, *сущ.*, древние сухопутные торговые пути, соединявшие Европу и Китай.

slash-and-burn agriculture / подсечно-огневое земледелие, *сущ.*, тип сельскохозяйственных работ, когда участок земли подготавливается к посеву путем срезания и выжигания естественной растительности.

Songhai / Сонгаи, *сущ.*, западноафриканская империя, благодаря своим правителям достигшая своего расцвета в XV и XVI вв. н. э.

sponsor / спонсор, *сущ.*, человек, дающий деньги в поддержку другого человека или проекта.

standing army / регулярная армия, *сущ.*, вооруженные силы, сохраняемые и поддерживаемые как в мирное время, так и во время военных действий.

stele / стела, *сущ.*, древняя высеченная из камня мемориальная доска, устанавливаемая в память о важной дате или великом событии.

Stoicism / Стоицизм, *сущ.*, греческая философия, придающая особое значение важности добродетели, долга и терпения. Была особенно влиятельной в Древнем Риме.

Suleyman I / Сулейман I, *сущ.*, султан Османской империи в 1520-1566 гг., способствовал развитию искусства и создал кодекс законов.

Sundiata / Сундиата, *сущ.*, древний правитель народа Малинке, захвативший столицу Ганы и значительно расширивший территорию империи.

Sunnah / Сунна, *сущ.*, слова и поступки Мухаммеда, служащие мусульманам руководством к праведной жизни.

Sunni / Суннит, *сущ.*, представитель группы мусульман, одобрявших избрание халифов и противостоящих Умайядам.

Swahili / Суахили, *сущ.*, африканский язык, содержащий в себе элементы языка банту и арабского языка.

T

Tenochtitlán / Теночтитлан, *сущ.*, древний город ацтеков, основанный в 1325 г. н. э. на небольшом острове на озере Тескоко.

Thomas Aquinas / Фома Аквинский, *сущ.*, итальянский мыслитель, соединивший классическую философию и христианскую теологию.

Timbuktu / Тимбукту, *сущ.*, город в центральной части Мали в Западной Африке, основанный в XIII в., торговый и культурный центр.

Tokugawa Shogunate / Сёгунат Токугава, *сущ.*, правление Токугава Иэясу и его потомков в Японии, начавшееся в 1603 г. и ознаменовавшее 250-летний период стабильности в стране.

Treaty of Tordesillas / Договор Тордесиллас, *сущ.*, соглашение между Испанией и Португалией в 1494 году о том, что все новые территории, которые будут открыты к западу от воображаемой линии в Атлантическом океане, будут принадлежать Испании, а все земли, которые будут открыты к востоку от этой линии, будут принадлежать Португалии.

triangular trade / треугольная торговля, *сущ.*, трансатлантический обмен товарами и рабами между двумя Америками, Европой и Африкой.

tribute / подношение, *сущ.*, платеж одной страны другой в знак уважения.

U, V, W, X, Y, Z

universal gravitation / всемирное тяготение, *сущ.*, теория Исаака Ньютона о действии гравитации на все предметы вселенной.

vassal / вассал, *сущ.*, в феодальном обществе, человек, получавший надел земли и защиту от лендлорда в обмен на свою преданность.

vegetation zone / зона растительности, *сущ.*, регион, имеющий отличительные типы растений из-за своей почвы и климата.

vernacular / родной язык, *сущ.*, язык, на котором человек говорил с рождения.

weather / погода, *сущ.*, состояние атмосферы в определенном месте в определенное время.

wood-block printing / печатание с деревянного клише, *сущ.*, разработанная в древнем Китае система печатания, в которой на деревянных клише вырезались все буквы, содержащиеся на одной странице.

Yucatán Peninsula / полуостров Юкатан, *сущ.*, территория юго-восточной Мексики, выступающая в Карибское море и Мексиканский залив.

Zen / Дзен, *сущ.*, японское ответвление буддизма, основной акцент в котором делается на самодисциплину, скромность и медитацию.

Zheng He / Чжен Хе, *сущ.*, китайский адмирал, чьи продолжительные плавания в 1405-1433 годах н. э. способствовали значительному увеличению оборота китайской внешней торговли и повышению репутации страны.

GLOSSÁRIO PORTUGUÊS

O Glossário é uma lista alfabética de muitos dos termos chaves dos capítulos, junto com seus significados. As definições listadas no Glossário são as que se adequam à maneira como as palavras são usadas neste livro. O Glossário indica a classe gramatical da palavra. As seguintes abreviações são usadas:

adj. = adjetivo **s.** = substantivo **v.** = verbo

A

Abd al-Malik / Abd Al-Malik s. governante muçulmano que tornou-se califa no ano de 685 e fez do árabe a língua oficial do governo em todas as terras muçulmanas.

Abd al-Rahman III / Abd Al-Ramán III s. oitavo emir de al-Andalus, durante cujo reinado al-Andalus alcançou o apogeu de seu poder.

Afonso I s. rei do Congo cujo governo inicia-se no ano de 1506. Foi influenciado pelos portugueses e participou do tráfico de escravos.

al-Andalus s. área da Espanha sob controle muçulmano entre os 700s e 1492.

Allah / Alá s. Deus na religião islâmica.

alluvial soil / solo de aluvião s. solo muito rico e fértil depositado por fluxos d'água.

Almoravids / Almorávidas s. dinastia islâmica do norte da África que tentou converter à força os povos vizinhos, incluindo o Marrocos, a Espanha e Gana.

anatomy / anatomia s. estudo científico das formas e estruturas dos humanos, plantas e animais.

Angkor Wat / Angkor Vat s. conjunto de templos no sudeste da Ásia, construído nos anos 1100, com quase 1 milha quadrada e que é a maior estrutura religiosa do mundo.

anthropology / antropologia s. o estudo dos humanos e das culturas humanas.

aqueduct / aqueduto s. estrutura desenhada para transportar água fresca para cidades ou vilas.

archaeology / arqueologia s. a recuperação e o estudo de evidência física do passado.

artifact / artefato s. objeto feito pelo homem.

Askia Muhammad s. governante do império Songai do ano 1493 ao 1528, que expandiu o império e organizou seu governo.

astrolabe / astrolábio s. instrumento usado para medir os ângulos das estrelas acima do horizonte, ajudando, desta forma, os marinheiros a determinar sua latitude.

Augustus / Augusto s. o primeiro imperador de Roma, que governou de 27 A.C. ao ano 14, e expandiu grandemente o tamanho e a influência do Império Romano.

B

Baghdad / Bagdá s. cidade localizada no que é hoje o Iraque, que foi a capital do império Abássida.

Bantu migrations / migrações banto s. movimento, que se iniciou cerca de 1000 A.C., dos povos bantos da África Ocidental para o sul e para o leste, difundindo suas línguas e culturas.

bubonic plague / peste bubônica s. doença que atingiu a Eurásia ocidental em meados dos anos 1300, em surto conhecido como a Peste Negra.

Buddhism / budismo s. sistema de crenças baseado nos ensinamentos de Sidarta Gautama, o Buda, cuja ênfase é a liberação individual dos desejos mundanos.

bureaucracy / burocracia s. sistema de departamentos e agências que executam as tarefas de um governo.

bushido s. código de conduta dos guerreiros samurai, que requeria que fossem generosos, bravos, e leais.

Byzantine Empire / Império Bizantino s. O Império Romano do Oriente, que foi governado a partir de Constantinopla, do 4° século ao 15° século.

C

cacao / cacau s. árvore americana cujas sementes são usadas para produzir chocolate.

caliph / califa s. governante de comunidade muçulmana, visto como sucessor de Maomé.

calligraphy / caligrafia *s.* a arte da escrita humana com elegância.

Calvin, John / João Calvino *s.* um dos líderes da Reforma Protestante, que viveu do ano 1509 ao 1564, e enfatizou a doutrina da predestinação.

capitalism / capitalismo *s.* sistema econômico baseado na propriedade privada dos recursos econômicos e seu uso para gerar lucros.

caravel / caravela *s.* tipo de embarcação à vela portuguesa, com velas tanto quadradas quanto triangulares, projetada para grandes viagens.

cartography / cartografia *s.* técnicas e métodos usados na confecção de mapas.

celadon / céladon *s.* tipo de porcelana coreana, freqüentemente de cor verde-azulada.

Charlemagne / Carlos Magno *s.* rei dos francos (a partir de 768) que conquistou grande parte da Europa e divulgou o cristianismo nas regiões conquistadas.

chasqui / chasque *s.* mensageiro no império Inca que portava mensagens, correndo, por toda a extensão do território do império.

chivalry / fidalguia *s.* código de conduta dos cavaleiros medievais europeus, que enfocava bravura, honra e respeito pelas mulheres e pelos mais fracos.

Christianity / Cristianismo *s.* religião baseada na vida e ensinamentos de Jesus.

circumnavigate / circunavegar *v.* fazer uma viagem ao redor do globo terrestre inteiro.

clan / clã *s.* grupo de pessoas relacionadas por sangue ou casamento.

clergy / clérigo *s.* pessoas com autoridade sacerdotal numa religião.

climate / clima *s.* o padrão das condições de tempo numa certa localidade por um longo período de tempo.

Clovis / Clóvis *s.* líder dos Francos, que conquistou a província romana da Gália no ano 486 e mais tarde estabeleceu um grande e poderoso império franco.

codex / códice *s.* livro do tipo usado pelas civilizações mesoamericanas primitivas para registrar importantes eventos históricos.

Columbian Exchange / Intercâmbio Colombino *s.* o movimento de plantas, animais e outras coisas vivas entre os hemisférios oriental e ocidental depois da viagem de Colombo às Américas no ano de 1492.

Confucianism / Confucionismo *s.* sistema de crenças baseado nos ensinamentos de Confúcio, escolarca que ensinou virtudes morais e éticas.

Constantine / Constantino *s.* imperador romano do ano 306 ao 337, que terminou com a perseguição aos cristãos e mudou a capital do império para Bizâncio (mais tarde conhecida como Constantinopla).

continent / continente *s.* uma das sete grandes massas de terra da Terra—América do Norte, América do Sul, Europa, Ásia, África, Austrália e Antártica.

convert / converter *v.* persuadir alguém a adotar uma nova religião ou crença.

Córdoba / Córdova *s.* a capital de al-Andalus.

Cortés, Hernán / Hernán Cortés *s.* explorador espanhol que conquistou a civilização Asteca do México no ano de 1521.

covenant / convenção *s.* um acordo vinculatório.

Crusades / Cruzadas *s.* série de expedições militares da Europa Cristã à Palestina entre os séculos 11 e 13.

culture / cultura *s.* modo de vida compartilhado por um grupo de pessoas.

D

daimyo / daimiô *s.* nobre japonês grande proprietário de terras com grande exército particular de samurais, que não pagava impostos ao governo.

Daoism / Taoísmo *s.* sistema de crenças originário da China em 500 A.C., que enfatiza a harmonia com a a natureza e os sentimentos interiores.

Declaration of Independence / Declaração de Independência *s.* documento que declarou a independência das colônias americanas da Grã Bretanha.

Declaration of the Rights of Man and of the Citizen / Declaração dos Direitos do Homem e do Cidadão *s.* documento adotado pelo governo revolucionário francês em 1789, delineando os direitos das pessoas.

dissection / dissecação *s.* secção de plantas e animais para estudar e investigar suas partes internas.

divan / divã *s.* conselho imperial que aconselhava o sultão, no império Otomano.

E

elevation / elevação *s.* a altura da terra acima do nível do mar.

elite *s.* membros superiores ou mais ricos de uma sociedade ou grupo.

Elizabethan Age / Era Elisabetana *s.* período de governo da Rainha Elisabete I na Inglaterra, de 1558 a 1603.

embassy / embaixada *s.* escritório do governo de um país em outro país.

emperor / imperador *s.* o governante de um império.

empire / império *s.* grupos de culturas ou territórios diferentes liderados por um governante todo-poderoso.

enlightened despot / déspota esclarecido *s.* governante que tinha poder absoluto, mas também prestava atenção à idéias políticas do Iluminismo e tentava governar de modo justo e educado.

Enlightenment / Iluminismo *s.* movimento filosófico do século 18 em que filósofos usavam a razão para entender as verdades sobre a natureza humana.

epic poem / poema épico *s.* longo poema que conta uma história de aventuras heróicas.

excavation / escavação *s.* processo de cavar-se a terra à cata de objetos significativamente históricos com o propósito de estudá-los.

F

faction / facção *s.* pequeno grupo cujos interesses vão de encontro àqueles de um grupo maior do qual fazem parte.

federalism / federalismo *s.* divisão de poder entre uma organização ou governo e seus membros.

feudalism / feudalismo *s.* sistema sócio-político da Idade Média na Europa, em que os nobres davam terra aos vassalos em troca de serviços e lealdade.

Forbidden City / Cidade Proibida *s.* grupo de palácios fortificados construído para o imperador da China logo depois do ano 1400, na capital Pequim.

Francis of Assisi, Saint / São Francisco de Assis *s.* italiano que fundou a ordem religiosa dos Franciscanos no início dos anos 1200.

G

Genghis Khan / Gengis Khan *s.* líder mongol que uniu a Mongólia e suas tribos em cerca de 1206 e iniciou uma campanha de conquistas, fundando um império que cobria o norte da China e da Ásia Central.

geocentric theory / teoria geocênctrica *s.* a teoria de que a Terra está no centro do Universo.

geography / geografia *s.* o estudo das características naturais da Terra.

Ghana / Gana *s.* região entre o Saara e as florestas do sul da África Ocidental, berço de muitas culturas antigas.

glyph / glifo *s.* figura que representa uma palavra, sílaba ou som.

golden age / era dourada *s.* período em que uma sociedade ou cultura está em seu apogeu.

Great Enclosure / Grande Cercado *s.* a maior das três grandes seções do povoamento shona do Grande Zimbábue—provavelmente uma residência real.

Great Schism / Grande Cisma *s.* uma divisão na Igreja Católica Apostólica Romana do ano 1378 até 1417, ocorrida quando os dois centros de poder da Igreja, Avignon e Roma, separaram-se e elegeram dois papas diferentes.

Great Zimbabwe / Grande Zimbábue *s.* estabelecimento central do império shona na África, cercado por grande muro de pedra, cobrindo mais de 100 acres, com população entre 10,000 a 20,000.

Gregory VII, Pope / Papa Gregório VII *s.* chefe da Igreja Católica Apostólica Romana de 1073 a 1085, que lutou com o imperador Henrique IV pelo poder.

griot / griô *s.* contador de estórias oficial em civilizações africanas.

guild / associação *s.* grupo de pessoas que compartilham um negócio ou ofício, e que pretende controlar a quantidade e a qualidade de sua produção e proteger seus interesses.

Gutenberg, Johann / Johanes Gutenberg *s.* alemão que inventou a prensa para impressão com tipos móveis em meados dos anos 1400.

H

habeas corpus *s.* o direito das pessoas de não serem presas indevidamente.

haiku / haikai *s.* forma de poema japonês, contendo 17 sílabas arrumadas em três linhas, com 5, 7 e 5 sílabas.

harmony / harmonia *s.* combinação de elementos para formar um todo agradável.

heliocentric / heliocêntrico *adj.* tendo o sol como centro.

hemisphere / hemisfério *s.* qualquer das duas metades iguais da Terra, divididas pelo equador ou pelo meridiano-origem.

Henry IV, Emperor / Imperador Henrique IV *s.* governante do Santo Imperio Romano no século XI, que lutou contínuamente com o Papa Gregório VII pelo poder.

Hijrah / Hégira *s.* a fuga de Maomé e seus seguidores, de Meca para Medina no ano 622.

historian / historiador *s.* pessoa que estuda e interpreta o passado.

history / História *s.* o estudo de eventos passados.

humanism / humanismo *s.* movimento na Europa renascentista, que celebrava as conquistas e o potencial humano, enfatizando o estudo de matérias como a História, a Gramática, Literatura e Filosofia.

Hundred Years' War / Guerra dos Cem Anos *s.* série de guerras entre a Inglaterra e a França, de 1337 a 1453.

I

Iberian Peninsula / Península Ibérica *s.* ponta sudoeste da Europa, onde as modernas nações de Espanha e Portugal estão localizadas.

Ignatius of Loyola, Saint / Santo Inácio de Loyola *s.* espanhol que fundou a ordem religiosa dos Jesuítas no início dos anos 1530.

imperial *adj.* relativo a um império ou imperador.

indulgence / indulgência *s.* perdão por pecado, concedido pela Igreja Católica Apostólica Romana, permitindo que uma pessoa evite ser punido por Deus no pós-morte.

Inquisition / inquisição *s.* tribunal estabelecido pela Igreja Católica Apostólica Romana no ano de 1542 para investigar pessoas que pudessem ter desgarrado da fé Católica Romana e para fortalecer o poder da Igreja.

Islam / Islã *s.* religião monoteísta baseada nos ensinamentos de Maomé

J

janissary / janízaro *s.* membro de uma força guerreira de elite do império Otomano, composta principalmente de escravos.

Jesuit / Jesuíta *s.* membro da Sociedade de Jesus, ordem religiosa fundada no início dos anos 1530 por Santo Inácio de Loyola.

Joan of Arc / Joana D'Arc *s.* camponesa francesa que liderou os franceses à vitória sobre a Inglaterra em Orleans no ano DE 1429.

John, King / Rei João *s.* rei da Inglaterra que assinou a Magna Carta no ano de 1215.

Justinian / Justiniano *s.* governante do Império Romano do Oriente de 527 a 565, governando com sua mulher, Teodora, reconquistando territórios perdidos para o império.

Justinian Code / Código de Justiniano *s.* código legal, preparado sob a direção do imperador Justiniano, de Bizâncio, que regulava muito da vida bizantina.

K

Kabuki *s.* forma japonesa de drama desenvolvida nos anos 1600, caracterizada por canto e dança melodramáticos, pesada maquiagem e trajes elaboradas.

Khmer Empire / império Khmer *s.* o mais poderoso e duradouro reino da parte continental do sudeste da Ásia, centrado no que é hoje o Camboja.

Kilwa *s.* antiga cidade-estado da costa oriental da África, estabelecida por povos do Irã e da Arábia, que alcançou seu apogeu no fim dos anos 1200.

kinship / parentesco *s.* uma conexão entre pessoas seja pelo sangue, casamento, ou adoção.

knight / cavaleiro *s.* altamente treinado guerreiro eqüestre, a serviço de um nobre durante a Idade Média européia.

Kongo / Congo *s.* antigo reino ao longo da costa ocidental da África, estabelecido pelo povo Congo de língua banto algum tempo antes do século 14 da era cristã.

Koryo *s.* reino da península Coreana, estabelecido no ano de 935 depois do colapso do reino Silla.

Kublai Khan *s.* neto de Gengis Khan, que tomou o poder no sul da China no ano 1260 e derrotou o exército Song em 1279, dando aos mongóis o controle sobre toda a China.

L

labor specialization / trabalho especializado *s.* execução de categorias específicas de trabalhos por trabalhadores treinados ou instruídos.

landform / acidente geográfico *s.* característica naturalmente formada da superfície da Terra, como uma ilha, montanha ou um planalto.

latitude *s.* medida de distância ao norte ou ao sul do equador.

Leonardo da Vinci *s.* pintor Renascentista italiano, nascido em 1452, que pintou muitas obras-primas, como a Mona Lisa ou a Última Ceia, e também brilhou na pesquisa científica.

longbow / arco *s.* arma que atirava flechas capazes de perfurar a armadura de um cavaleiro.

longitude *s.* medida de distância a leste ou oeste do meridiano-origem.

lord / senhor feudal *s.* poderoso nobre dono de terras.

Luther, Martin / Martinho Lutero *s.* teólogo alemão, nascido em 1483, que foi o líder da Reforma e ensinou a salvação mais pela fé em Deus do que por fazer o bem.

M

Magna Carta *s.* lista de direitos escrita pela nobreza da Inglaterra e assinada pelo rei João no ano de 1215.

maize / milho amarelo *s.* tipo de milho cultivado pelas civilizações dos Índios americanos.

Mali *s.* império africano ocidental estabelecido pelo povo malinqué.

Manchu *s.* membro de um povo do nordeste da China que conquistou o país em 1644 e iniciou a última dinastia da história chinesa, chamada a Dinastia Qing.

manor / herdade *s.* terras de um nobre feudal, incluindo usualmente uma construção fortificada ou um castelo.

Mansa Musa *s.* imperador de Mali que fez uma famosa peregrinação a Meca em 1324.

maritime / marítimo *adj.* relativo ao mar.

Maya / Maia *s.* civilização do sul do México e norte da América Central, que alcançou seu apogeu entre os anos 250 e 900.

Mbanza / Mbanza Congo *s.* capital do antigo reino africano do Congo.

mercantilism / mercantilismo *s.* política econômica baseada na idéia de que o poder de uma nação depende de sua riqueza.

mercenary / mercenário *s.* soldado que é pago para lutar.

Meso-America / Mesoamérica *s.* região que inclui a parte sul do México e muito da América Central.

Michelangelo *s.* artista renascentista italiano, nascido em 1475, que trabalhou principalmente como escultor mas também pintou obras famosas como o teto da Capela Sistina em Roma.

Middle Ages / Idade Média *s.* período da história européia entre o colapso de Roma e a Renascença, que durou de 500 a 1450, grosso modo.

missionary / missionário *s.* pessoa que viaja a outro país para fazer trabalho religioso.

monastery / monastério *s.* lugar onde os membros de uma ordem religiosa mantêm vida de preces e adoração.

Mongol Ascendancy / Ascendência Mongol *s.* período em que os mongóis controlaram toda a Ásia central, tornando seguros o comércio e as travessias continentais.

monotheism / monoteísmo *s.* crença em um Deus.

Montezuma II *s.* o último imperador Asteca, que governou de 1502 a 1520 e foi derrubado pelos espanhóis.

mosaic / mosaico *s.* a figura feita de muitos pequenos azulejos ou peças de vidro coloridos.

mosque / mesquita *s.* construção para adoração islâmica, projetada para ficar de frente para Meca.

mother culture / cultura matriz *s.* cultura que forma e influencia os costumers e idéias de culturas posteriores.

movable type / tipo móvel *s.* pequeno bloco de metal ou madeira, com um único caractere em relevo, usado para impressão de textos.

Murasaki Shikibu, Lady / Lady Murasaki Shikibu *s.* escritora japonesa do início dos anos 1000, que escreveu A História de Genji, considerado um dos primeiros romances do mundo.

Muslim / muçulmano *s.* pessoa que segue a religião do Islã, aceitando Alá como o deus único.

Mutapa / mutapa *s.* antigo reino no terrítório do atual Zimbábue, estabelecido por um rei shona em cerca de 1440; também, o governante deste reino.

N

Nam Viet *s.* reino vietnamita conquistado pela China em 111 A.C.

natural rights / direitos naturais *s.* direitos com que todas as pessoas nascem—como o direito à vida, à liberdade e à propriedade, de acordo com John Locke, filósofo do século 18.

Noh / Nô *s.* forma de drama japonês desenvolvido no ano 1300s, caracterizado freqüentemente pela recontagem de lendas e estórias populares apresentadas por atores com máscaras de madeira pintada.

nomad / nômade *s.* pessoa que se movimenta de lugar para lugar ao invés de manter estabelecimento permanente.

O

oasis / oásis *s.* área fértil no meio de um deserto.

Olmec *s.* a mais primitiva cultura mesoamericana conhecida, que floresceu de 1200 a 400 A.C. centrada no sudeste do México.

Omar Khayyám / Omar Kayyam *s.* poeta persa muçulmano, que usualmente escrevia em forma de quartetos, e foi também grande matemático.

oral history / história oral *s.* relato verbal não-escrito de eventos, como uma estória que é passada de geração em geração.

Orthodox / Ortodoxo *adj.* relacionado à igreja cristã que se desenvolveu no Império Bizantino e não está sob a autoridade do Papa.

Osman *s.* líder turco que fundou o império Otomano no início dos anos 1300.

P

Pacal II *s.* rei que governou a cidade maia de Palenque por quase 70 anos (desde 615)—um dos grandes reis maias.

Pachacuti *s.* o nono governante inca, entronizado em 1438, que expandiu o Império Inca.

parliament / parlamento *s.* grupo de representantes com alguns dos poderes do governo.

patron / patrono *s.* pessoa que suporta uma atividade ou instituição, através do fornecimento de ajuda financeira.

Peace of Westphalia / Paz de Westphalia *s.* acordo feito em 1648, que reconheceu como permanentre a divisão da Europa ocidental em nações Protestantes e Católicas e terminou com muitas guerras em andamento à época.

perspective / perspectiva *s.* técnica de pintura, desenvolvida durante a Renascença, que representa a aparência dos objetos num espaço tridimensional.

philosophe / filósofo *s.* um dos pensadores do século 18 que tentaram aplicar métodos científicos aos problemas sociais.

pilgrimage / peregrinação *s.* jornada a um lugar ou santuário sagrado.

Pizarro, Francisco / Francisco Pizarro *s.* explorador espanhol que chegou no Peru em 1532, e que em 1535 já havia conquistado o Império Inca.

Polo, Marco / Marco Pólo *s.* comerciante veneziano que viajou através das Rotas da Seda e chegou na Cuina em cerca de 1275. Tornou-se um ordenança de Kublai Khan e mais tarde publicou um popular livro sobre suas aventuras.

porcelain / porcelana *s.* material cerâmico branco e duro, freqüentemente chamado de louça.

predestination / predestinação *s.* doutrina que diz que Deus escolhe pessoas para a salvação ou danação antes de que nasçam, e de que os indivíduos não tem poder para mudar a vontade de Deus.

primary source / recurso primário *s.* documento ou artefato criado durante um período histórico em particular.

printing press / prensa de impressão *s.* máquina para imprimir papel contra tipos móveis entintados.

projection / mapa-múndi *s.* modo de representar a superfície curva da Terra em mapa plano, mantendo ao mesmo tempo distorção consistente e controlável.

Protestant / Protestante *s.* membro de grupo cristão the rompeu com a Igreja Católica Apostólica Romana durante ou depois do século 16.

Q

quipu / quipo *s.* ferramentas para fazer contas do antigo império Inca, feita de cordões com nós em vários pontos.

Qur'an / Alcorão *s.* o livro santo muçulmano, consistindo das revelações de Alá colecionadas pelos adeptos de Maomé depois de sua morte.

R

rationalism / racionalismo *s.* a idéia de que as pessoas deveriam usar a razão, ou o pensamento lógico, para entender o mundo.

Reconquista / reconquista *s.* série de campanhas, que terminou em 1492, em que os exércitos cristãos expulsaram os governantes muçulmanos da Espanha.

Reformation / Reforma *s.* movimento de oposição à Igreja Católica Apostólica Romana, que começou no século 16.

regent / regente *s.* pessoa que governa por um monarca ausente ou de menor idade.

religious order / ordem religiosa *s.* grupo de pessoas que vive segundo uma regra religiosa.

Renaissance / Renascença *s.* período de renascimento e criatividade na arte, na escrita e no pensamento , de 1300 a 1600, que começou na Europa e eventualmente espalhou-se através da Europa.

republic / república *s.* forma de governo em que o poder fica com os cidadãos, que votam para eleger seus líderes.

reunify / reunificar *v.* juntar novamente.

Roman Catholic / Católica Romana *adj.* relativo à igreja cristã do ocidente que está sob autoridade do Papa.

S

Sahara / Saara *s.* grande deserto do norte da África, estendendo-se desde a costa Atlântica ao Vale do Nilo.

Saladin / Saladino *s.* líder militar que uniu os muçulmanos para lutar contra os cristãos na Palestina durante o século 12.

salon / salão *s.* reunião de pensadores e artistas para discutir questões e trocar idéias durante o Iluminismo.

samurai *s.* guerreiro treinado da aristocracia japonesa.

savanna / savana *s.* campina plana, com poucas árvores, numa região tropical.

schism / cisma *s.* cisão oficial entre dois grupos.

scholar-official / oficial-escolástico *s.* pessoa educada, com cargo no governo.

scientific method / método científico *s.* uma abordagem à investigação científica que envolve fazer cuidadosas observações, formulando e testando uma hipótese, e chegando a uma conclusão que confirma ou modifica a hipótese.

Scientific Revolution / Revolução Científica *s.* período, iniciado nos anos 1500, durante o qual os eruditos europeus começaram a questionar idéias científicas clássicas e as crenças cristãs.

secondary source / fonte secundária *s.* atrabalho sobre evento histórico, produzido por alguém que não estava presente ao evento.

Seljuk Turk / Turco Seljuk *s.* membro de povo turco que controlava a Ásia ocidental do século 11 ao 13.

serf / servo *s.* fazendeiro camponês numa sociedade feudal, que trabalhava para um nobre em troca de proteção e alguns direitos.

Shakespeare, William / William Shakespeare *s.* o mais famoso escritor inglês da Renascença, mais conhecido por suas peças Romeu e Julieta e Hamlet.

Shi'a / shia *s.* grupo muçulmano que resistiu ao governo dos Omayadas, acreditando que o califa devesse ser parente do profeta Maomé.

Shinto / xintoísmo *s.* tradicional religião do Japão, baseadda na adoração e respeito pela natureza e pelos ancestrais.

shogun *s.* líder militar japonês—um de um grupo que primeiro chegou ao poder em 1192 e governou em nome do imperador, mas normalmente em seu próprio interesse.

Shona *s.* cultura de língua banto que floresceu no ano 1000, no que é hoje o território de países como Botswana, Moçambique e Zimbábue.

Shotoku, Prince / Príncipe Shotoku *s.* regente que governou o Japão de 593 a 622 e trouxe elementos da cultura chinesa—em particular, a religião budista—para o país.

Silk Roads / Rota da Seda *s.* as antigas rotas de comércio que conectavam a Europa e a China.

slash-and-burn agriculture / agricultura de desmatamento e queima *s.* tipo de cultivo em que lotes de terra são preparados para o plantio através do desmatamento e queima da vegetação natural.

Songhai / songai *s.* povo da África Ocidental cujos líderes criaram um grande império nos séculos 15 e 16.

sponsor / patrocinador *s.* pessoa que dá dinheiro em apoio a uma pessoa ou projeto.

standing army / exército permanente *s.* força guerreira que é manutenida em tempos de paz e em tempos de guerra.

stele / estela *s.* antigo marco monolítico entalhado para comemorar data importante ou grande evento.

Stoicism / estoicismo *s.* filosofia grega que enfatizava a importância da virtude, do dever e da resignação, e que foi especialmente influente na antiga Roma.

Suleyman I / Suleiman I *s.* sultão do Império Otomano de 1520 a 1566, que fomentou as artes e organizou um código legal.

Sundiata *s.* antigo governante do povo malinqué, que capturou a capital de Gana e expandiu enormemente o império.

Sunnah / suna *s.* palavras e feitos de Maomé, que servem como guia dos muçulmanos para uma vida apropriada.

Sunni / Suni *s.* membro do grupo muçulmano que aceitou ser governado pelos califas eleitos e não resisitiu aos Omayadas.

Swahili / suaíli *s.* língua africana que mistura elementos Banto e Árabes.

T

Tenochtitlán *s.* antiga cidade asteca, fundada em 1325 numa pequena ilha do Lago Texcoco.

Thomas Aquinas / Tomás de Aquino *s.* escolarca italiano que fez uma síntese de filosofia clássiva e teologia cristã.

Timbuktu *s.* cidade do Mali central na África ocidental, que foi fundada no século 13 e era centro de comércio e cultura.

Tokugawa Shogunate / Shogunato Tokugawa *s.* governo de Tokugawa Ieyasu e seus sucessores no Japão, que iniciou em 1603 e trouxe um príodo de 250 anos de estabilidade ao país.

Treaty of Tordesillas / Tratado de Tordesilhas *s.* acordo entre Espanha e Portugal em 1494, eatabelecendo uma linha imaginária de norte a sul em torno do mundo, que permitia à Espanha reclamar as terras a oeste da linha e Portugal as terras a leste da linha.

triangular trade / comércio triangular *s.* troca de mercadorias e escravos através do oceano Atlântico, entre as Américas, Europa e África.

tribute / tributo *s.* pagamento feito por um país a outro como sinal de respeito.

U, V, W, X, Y, Z

universal gravitation / gravitação universal *s.* teoria de Sir Isaac Newton de que a gravidade age em todos os objetos através do universo.

vassal / vassalo *s.* na sociedade feudal, uma pessoa que recebia terra e proteção de um senhor feudal em troca de lealdade.

vegetation zone / zona de vegetação *s.* uma região que, devido ao seu solo e ao seu clima, tem tipos diferentes de plantas.

vernacular / vernáculo *s.* língua nativa de uma pessoa.

weather / tempo *s.* condições atmosféricas num lugar e hora em particular.

wood-block printing / impressão por bloco de madeira *s.* sistema de impressão desenvolvido pelos antigos chineses, em que entalhavam-se blocos de madeira com caracteres suficientes para serem impressas páginas inteiras.

Yucatán Peninsula / Península de lucatán *s.* área do sudeste do México que se estende para o Mar do Caribe e o Golfo do México.

Zen *s.* forma japonesa de budismo, que é focada na autodisciplina, na simplicidade e na meditação.

Zheng He *s.* almirante chinês cujas extensas viagens entre 1405 e 1433 expandiram enormemente o comércio externo e a reputação chineses.

DAIM NTAWV TEEV COV NTSIAB LUS MIS KAS

Daim Ntawv Teev Cov Ntsiab Lus yog ib daim ntawv uas sau raws zus cov ntsiab lus los ntawm cov sob (chapters), nrog rau lawv lub ntsiab txhais. Cov ntsiab lus nyob hauv Daim Ntawv Teev Cov Ntsiab Lus yog cov uas siv raws li cov lus siv hauv phau ntawv kawm. Daim Ntawv Teev Cov Ntsiab Lus muaj ib feem ntawm cov lus hais rau txhua lo lus. Siv cov cim nram qab:

adj. = ib los lus piav txog tej yam dab tsi
n. = hais txog ib tug neeg, ib qho chaw, ib qho khoom
v. = lo lus hais txog kev ua tej yam dab tsi

A

Abd al-Malik *n.* Muslim ib tug neeg kav uas los ua ib tug kav txuas ntxiv thaum A.D. 685 thiab muab Arabic los ua hom lus siv ntawm cov tsoom fwv hauv tag nrho Muslim cov av.

Abd al-Rahman III *n.* tus neeg kav zus yim ntawm al-Andalus, uas nws zim txwv al-Andalus tau lub zog kav loj tshaj.

Afonso I *n.* tus huab tais ntawm Kongo uas pib tswj thaum A.D. 1506. Nws yaum tau los ntawm cov Portuguese thiab koom hauv kev ua lag luam qhev.

al-Andalus *n.* cheeb tsam ntawm Spain uas nyob qab tswj hwm ntawm Muslim thaum A.D. 700s thiab 1492.

Allah *n.* Tswv ntuj hauv Islamic qhov kev ntseeg.

alluvial soil / cov av uas zoo *n.* cov av uas zoo heev uas tso los ntawm tus dej uas ntws.

Almoravids *n.* ib lub kee tiam hauv North African Islamic uas yuam sim hloov cov neeg nyob ib ncig, nrog rau cov nyob hauv Morocco, Spain, thiab Ghana.

anatomy / tej yam ntawm cev *n.* ib qho kev kawm txog cov duab thiab kev ua ntawm tib neeg, xyoob ntoo, thiab cov tsiaj.

Angkor Wat *n.* ib cov tsev teev ntuj uas nyuab heev hauv Sab Qab Teb Sab Hnub Tuaj Hauv Asia, ua thaum A.D. 1100s, uas puv kwv yees li ib square mais thiab yog ib lub rau kev teev hawm uas loj tshaj plaws hauv lub ntiaj teb.

anthropology / kev kawm txog neeg *n.* kev kawm txog tib neeg thiab neeg cov kev coj noj coj ua.

aqueduct *n.* ib qho dab tsi los nqa cov dej tshiab rau hauv ib lub nroog los sis zos.

archaeology / kev kawm txog khoom qub *n.* kev nrhiav tau thiab kawm txog tej yam pov thawj los yav puag thaum ub los.

artifact / khoom *n.* ib qho khoom uas neeg txua.

Askia Muhammad *n.* tus tswv ntawm Songhai thaj av uas muaj ntau lub teb chaws thaum A.D. 1493 txog 1528, uas nthuav thaj av uas muaj ntau lub teb chaws thiab pab muab nws cov tsoom fwv los ua ib pawg.

astrolabe *n.* ib qho twj siv los ntsuas cov ces kaum ntawm cov hnub qub uas nyob saum toj ntawm ntim npoo ntuj, uas pab cov neeg caij nkoj kom lawv paub txog lawv txoj kab uas khiav ntsug.

Augustus *n.* thawj tus nom hauv Rome, uas kav thaum 27 B.C. txog A.D. 14 thiab nthuav qhov ntau thiab yaum tau hauv Roman Thaj Av Uas Muaj Ntau Lub Teb Chaws.

B

Baghdad *n.* ib lub nroog, uas nyob rau qhov tam sim uas yog Iraq, uas yog lub hauv paus loj ntawm Abbasid thaj av uas muaj ntau lub teb chaws.

Bantu migrations *n.* ib qho kev khiav, pib li thaum 1000 B.C., ntawm cov neeg hais lus Bantu-ntawm Sab Hnub Poob Africa mus rau sab qab teb thiab sab hnub tuaj, uas tshaj tawm lawv hom lus thiab cov kev coj noj coj ua.

bubonic plague / kis kab mob bubonic *n.* ib tug kab mos uas tshwm sim rau sab hnub poob Eurasia thaum nruab nrab ntawm 1300s, ib qho tshwm sim uas ua ua Tuag Dub.

Buddhism / hauj sam *n.* ib qho kev ntseeg raws li cov kev qhia ntawm Siddhartha Gautama, tus Buddha, uas hais txog qhov tso tus kheej tawm ntawm cov kev ntshaw hauv ntiaj teb.

bureaucracy / kev tuav laj kam teb chaws
n. ib qho kev siv ntawm cov caj meem fai thiab cov laj fai uas ua tsoom fwv cov hauj lwm.

bushido *n.* tus cwj pwm coj ntawm samurai cov tub rog, uas lawv yuav tsum siab zoo, siab tawv, thiab ncaj ncees.

Byzantine Empire / Byzantine Thaj Av Uas Muaj Ntau Lub Teb Chaws *n.* Romam Thaj Av Uas Muaj Ntau Lub Teb Chaws Nyob Sab Hnub Tuaj, uas kav thaum Constantinople thiab pib thiab tiam (century) 4 mus rau tiam (century) 15.

C

cacao *n.* ib tsob ntoo Mis Kas uas nws cov noob yog siv los ua chocolate.

caliph / tus kav txuas ntxiv *n.* tus kav hauv Muslim lub zej zos, uas pom tias yog tus los hloov Muhammad.

calligraphy / kev sau ntawv zoo nkauj *n.* txoj kev sau ntawv zoo nkauj.

Calvin, John *n.* ib tug thawj coj ntawm Protestant Reformation, uas nyob thaum A.D. 1509 txog 1564 thiab hais txog kev paub seb yuav zoo li cas ua ntej.

capitalism / fab nyiaj txiag *n.* ib qho kev ceev nyiaj txiag raws li kev ua tswv ntawm cov kev pab nyiaj txiag thiab kev siv cov kev pab ntawv los ua kom tau peev.

caravel *n.* Portuguese ib hom nkoj uas yog xwm fab xwm meem thiab caij yam zoo, tsim los kom caij tau ntev.

cartography / ua kab lig teb *n.* cov txuj ci thiab cov kev ua cov kab lig teb.

celadon *n.* ib hom huv Kaus lim, feem ntau yog yeej yuj xiav ntsuab tsawv.

Charlemagne *n.* tus huab tais ntawm Franks (thaum A.D. 768) uas tau feem ntau Europe thiab nthuav Christianity hauv cov cheeb tsam uas lawv txeeb tau.

chasqui *n.* tus neeg khiav hauv Inca thaj av uas muaj ntau lub teb chaws uas cev lus mus mus los los hauv thaj av uas muaj ntau lub teb chaws.

chivalry / cwj pwm tub rog *n.* tus cwj pwm coj ntawm European cov tub rog, hais txog kev muaj siab tawv, kev hwm, thiab kev hwm poj niam thiab cov uas tsis muaj zog.

Christianity *n.* ib qho kev ntseeg raws lub neej thiaab cov kev qhia los ntawm Yesxus.

circumnavigate / mus ncig teb chaws *v.* mus ncig ib lwm thoob plaws lub ntiaj teb.

clan / xeem *n.* ib pawg neeg uas sib txheeb raws roj ntsha los sis raws kev sib yuav.

clergy / xib fwb *n.* cov neeg uas muaj kev cai uas xib fwv hauv ib pawg ntseeg twg.

climate / huab cua *n.* tus qauv ntawm cov huab cua hauv ib cheeb tsam twg tau ntev heev.

Clovis *n.* ib tug thawj coj ntawm Franks, uas txeeb tau Roman lub xeev Gaul thaum A.D. 486 thiab tom qab tsim ib lub Frankish lub teb chaws uas loj thiab muaj zog.

codex *n.* ib phau ntawv uas siv los ntawm Meso-American kev ua kom vam meej thaum ub los sau tej yam uas tseem ceeb hauv keeb kwm.

Columbian Exchange *n.* qhov kev txav ntawm cov nroj tsuag, cov tsiaj, thiab lwm yam uas muaj sia ntawm ob sab hnub tuaj thiab sab hnub poob tom qab Columbus ncig hauv Teb Chaws Mis Kas hauv A.D. 1492.

Confucianism *n.* ib qho kev ntseeg raws qhov lus qhia ntawm Confucius, ib tug neeg txawj ntse uas tau qhia txog cov kev qhuab ntuas ua ncaj ncees thiab cov kev coj zoo.

Constantine *n.* Roman tus nom thaum A.D. 306 txog 337, uas tau xaus kev rau txim rau neeg ntawm cov Christians thiab txav lus hauv paus loj ntawm thaj av uas muaj ntau lub teb chaws mus rau Byzantium (tom qab hu ua Constantinople).

continent / thooj av *n.* ib thooj ntawm xya thooj av loj hauv ntiaj teb—North America, South America, Europe, Asia, Africa, Australia, thiab Antarctica.

convert / hloov *v.* haub yam ib tug neeg kom coj ib qhov kev ntseeg ntuj los sis kev ntseg tshiab.

Córdoba *n.* lub hauv paus loj hauv al-Andalus.

Cortés, Hernán *n.* cov neeg tshawb nrhiav uas yog Mev uas tau txeeb Aztec cov kev coj noj coj ua hauv Mev Teb thaum A.D. 1521.

covenant / kev cog lus *n.* ib qho kev cog lus.

Crusades *n.* ib co kev sib ntaus sib tua los ntawm Christian Europe mus rau Palestine thaum tiam (century) 11 thiab tiam (century) 13 A.D.

culture / kev coj noj coj ua *n.* ib txoj kev ua neej uas koom los ntawm ib pawg neeg.

D

daimyo *n.* ib tug tub rog Japanese uas muaj av ntau thiab ib pawg tub rog samurai, uas tsis them se rau tsoom fwv.

Daoism *n.* ib qho kev ntseeg uas tsim los hauv Suav Teb li thaj tsam ntawm 500 B.C., uas hais txog kev sib raug zoo nrog qhov uas ib txwm xeeb txawm los thiab cov kev xav sab hauv qab.

Declaration of Independence / Daim Ntawv Hais Txog Kev Ywj Pheej *n.* ib daim ntawv uas qhia tias Mis Kas cov zos tau kev ywj pheej ntawm Great Britain lawm.

Declaration of the Rights of Man and of the Citizen *n.* ib daim ntawv uas tsim los ntawm tsoom fwv Fab Kis thaum 1789, uas hais txog neeg cov cai.

dissection / kev phais *n.* qhov uas phais cov nroj tshuag thiab tsiaj es kawm txog lawv.

divan *n.* ib lub koom haum uas loj uas tawm tswv yim rau tus kav hauv Ottoman Thaj Av Uas Muaj Ntau Lub Teb Chaws.

E

elevation / qhov siab *n.* qhov siab ntawm ib daim av uas nyob siab tshaj dej.

elite / meej mom siab *n.* tus loj los sis muaj nyiaj tshaj ntawm cov neeg hauv zej zos los sis ib pawg neeg.

Elizabethan Age *n.* lub sij hawm ntawm cov cai ntawm Queen Elizabeth I hauv England, thaum 1558 txog 1603.

embassy / chav fai *n.* ib lub chav fai hauv ib lub teb chaws li tsoom fwv hauv lwm lub teb chaws.

emperor / tus nom *n.* tus neeg kav ntawm ib thaj av uas muaj ntau lub teb chaws.

empire / thaj av uas muaj ntau lub teb chaws *n.* ib pawg neeg uas muaj cov haiv neeg sib txawv los sis cov teb chaws uas coj los ntawm ib tus neeg kav uas muaj zog tshaj plaws.

enlightened despot *n.* ib tug neeg kav uas tau cov zog uas tag nrho tiam sis tseem mloog txog cov tswv yim kam teb kam chaw ntawm cov Enlightenment thiab sim tus cai yam ncaj ncees thiab muaj kev kawm.

Enlightenment *n.* ib qho kev sim tswv yim thaum tiam (century) 18 uas cov neeg kawm txhua yam siv cov kev paub los nkag siab txog qhov tseeb ntawm tib neeg.

epic poem / dab neeg *n.* ib zaj dab neeg ntev ntev uas qhia txog cov neeg muaj peev xwm.

excavation / kev tshawb *n.* txoj kev uas tshawb tej yam qub qub txheej thaum ub uas yog los kawm txog lawv.

F

faction / ib feem *n.* ib pab pawg me me uas lawv qhov kev nyiam yog los txiav cov pab pawg loj uas lawv yog ib feem.

federalism / kev sib koom *n.* kev sib koom zog kav ntawm ib lub koom haum los sis tsoom fwv thiab nws cov neeg koom.

feudalism / kev sib txeeb *n.* kev siv kam teb chaws thiab neeg ntawm Middle Ages hauv Europe, uas cov tub rog tau muab av rau cov nkoj los pauv lawv cov kev pab thiab kev ntseeg siab.

Forbidden City *n.* ib pawg tsev uas ua rau tus nom Suav tsis ntev tom qab A.D. 1400 hauv lub nroog Beijing uas yog lub hauv paus loj.

Francis of Assisi, Saint *n.* ib tug Italian uas nrhiav tau qhov kev ntseeg ntuj Franciscan thaum ntxov hauv A.D. 1200s.

G

Genghis Khan *n.* ib tug Mongol thawj coj uas ntsib Mongol cov pab pawg li ntawm A.D. 1206 thiab pib ib qho kev tawm tsawm sib txeeb, dag ib thaj av uas muaj ntau lub teb chaws uas npog sab qaum teb Suav Teb thiab Central Asia.

geocentric theory / kev xav txog lub ntiaj teb *n.* ib qho kev xav tias lub ntiaj teb yog nyob nruab nrab ntawm lub ntiaj teb no.

geography / qhov uas muaj nyob hauv lub ntiaj teb *n.* qhov kev kawm txog Lub Ntiaj Teb cov uas ib txwm xeeb txwm muaj.

Ghana *n.* ib cheeb tsam ntawm Sahara thiab cov hav zoov uas nyob sab qab teb ntawm West Africa, uas yog tsev rau ntau haiv neeg thaum ub.

glyph *n.* ib daim duab uas sawv cev ib lo lus, ib tug ntawv, los sis ib lub suab.

golden age *n.* ib lub sij hawm uas zej zos los sis haiv neeg nyob yam ntau tshaj.

Great Enclosure *n.* qhov loj tshaj ntawm peb seem hauv Shona settlement ntawm Great Zimbabwe—feem ntau yog ib tug neeg muaj koob nto npe.

Great Schism *n.* ib feem ntawm Roman Catholic Church thaum A.D. 1378 txog rau 1417, uas tshwm sim thaum lub Tsev Teev Ntuj ob qho zog nruab nrab, Avignon thiab Rome, sib caib thiab xaiv cov thawj coj hauv lub tsev teev ntuj txawv.

Great Zimbabwe *n.* qhov tuaj nyob yam nruab nrab ntawm Shona thaj av uas muaj ntau lub teb chaws hauv Africa, uas thaiv los ntawm sab phab ntsa uas ua pob zeb loj tshaj plaws, thaiv ntau tshaj 100 ev kawm, thiab muaj neeg coob li ntawm 10,000 txog 20,000.

Gregory VII, Pope *n.* tus thawj ntawm Roman Catholic Church thaum 1073 txog 1085, uas sib tw nrog Tus Nom Henry IV los txheeb lub zog kav.

griot / kws piav dab neeg *n.* ib tug neeg qhia dab neeg hauv African kev coj noj coj ua.

guild / lub koom haum *n.* ib lub koom haum uas cov neeg sib pauv lag luam los sis khoom, ua kom tswj qhov zoo thiab qhov ntau ntawm lawv cov khoom thiab los tiv qhov uas lawv nyiam.

Gutenberg, Johann *n.* ib tug German uas, thaum nruab nrab ntawm 1400s, tsim lub tshuab luam ntawv uas txav tau.

H

habeas corpus *n.* txoj cai ntawm neeg uas tsis pub coj mus kaw yam uas tsis raug cai.

haiku *n.* ib zaj dab neeg uas sau li Japanese, uas muaj 17 lo lus uas sau ua peb kab uas muaj 5, 7, thiab 5 lo lus.

harmony / kev sib haum *n.* qhov uas muab cov kev siv los sib tso ua ke kom ua ib qho uas txaus siab rau.

heliocentric / hnub nyob nruab nrab *adj.* muaj lub hnub uas qhov nruab nrab.

hemisphere / ib sab ntawm lub ntiaj teb *n.* ob sab ntawm lub ntiaj teb uas zoo ib yam, uas muaj txoj kab txiav lub ntiaj teb ua ob sab hnub tuaj thiab hnub poob koom sib npaug los sis txoj kab txiav kom sab qab teb thiab qaum teb sib npaug.

Henry IV, Emperor *n.* ib tug neeg kav thaum tiam (century) 11 tus neeg kav ntawm Roman Thaj Av Uas Muaj Ntau Lub Teb Chaws Uas Muaj Kev Dawb Huv, uas sib tw txuas mus rau lub zog kav nrog Pope Gregory VII.

Hijrah *n.* qhov txav ntawm Muhammad thiab nws cov neeg caum Mecca txog rau lub nroog Yathrib hauv A.D. 622.

historian / tus neeg kawm txog keeb kwm *n.* ib tug neeg uas kawm txog thiab txhais yav dhau los.

history / keeb kwm *n.* kev kawm txg tej yam uas tshwm sim yav dhau los.

humanism / tib neeg *n.* qhov kev txav hauv Renaissance Europe, muab kev pab zoo siab txog neeg lub peev xwm thiab kev ua tau thiab hais txog txoj kev kawm xws li keeb kwm, lus, dab neeg, thiab txhua yam hauv lub ntiaj teb.

Hundred Years' War / Tsov Rog Ib Puas Xyoo *n.* ib cov tsov rog ntawm England thiab Fab Kis, thaum A.D. 1337 txog 1453.

I

Iberian Peninsula *n.* qhov nte hauv uas nyob sab hnub poob sab qab teb ntawm Europe, uas tam sim no yog lub teb chaws Spain thiab Portugal nyob.

Ignatius of Loyola, Saint *n.* ib tug Mev uas tsim qhov kev ntseeg ntuj ntawm Jesuits thaum yav ntxov thaum A.D. 1530s.

imperial / ib qho uas loj *adj.* hais txog ib thaj av uas muaj ntau lub teb chaws los sis ib tug nom.

indulgence / kev zam *n.* ib qho kev zam rau qhov uas ua tsis yog los ntawm Roman Catholic Church, uas cia ib tug neeg nyob qhov kev raug txim los ntawm Tswv Ntuj tom qab tag sim neej.

Inquisition *n.* ib lub tsev hais plaub uas tsim los ntawm Roman Catholic Church thaum A.D. 1542 los soj ntsuam cov neeg uas tej zaum tau ncaim ntawm Roman Catholic txoj kev ntseg thiab mus ua kom lub zog kav ntawm lub Tsev Teev Ntuj kom muaj zog.

Islam *n.* ib qho kev ntseeg ntuj tias muaj ib tug tim tswv li qhov kev qhia los ntawm Muhammad.

J

janissary *n.* ib tug neeg koom ntawm ib pawg neeg sib ntaus uas muaj meej mom siab ntawm Ottoman Thaj Av Uas Muaj Ntau Lub Teb Chaws, uas feem ntau yog cov qhev.

Jesuit *n.* ib tug neeg koom hauv Society of Jesus, ib qho kev ntseeg ntuj uas nrhiav tau thaum yav ntxov ntawm A.D. 1530s los ntawm Saint Ignatius of Loyola.

Joan of Arc *n.* ib tug menyuam ntxhais Fab Kis uas coj cov Neeg Fab Kis mus yeej cov English tom Orléans thaum A.D. 1429.

John, King *n.* tus huab tais hauv England uas kos npe rau daim Magna Carta thaum A.D. 1215.

Justinian *n.* tus neeg kav hauv Roman Thaj Av Uas Muaj Ntau Lub Teb Chaws Nyob Sab Hnub Tuaj thaum A.D. 527 txog 565, uas ruled nrog nws tus poj niam, Theordora, thiab rov qab txeeb tau cov teb chaws uas poob rau thaj av uas muaj ntau lub teb chaws.

Justinian Code *n.* ib txoj cai, npaj los ntawm Byzantine tus nom Justinian, uas tswj feem ntau Byzantine lub neej.

K

Kabuki *n.* ib hom yeeb yam Japanese uas tsim thaum A.D. 1600s, uas muaj kev nqua yas suab thiab seev cev, pleev plhu ntau, thiab hnav cov tsoos tsho uas zoo nkauj heev.

Khmer Empire / Khmer Thaj Av Uas Muaj Ntau Lub Teb Chaws *n.* lub teb chaws uas muaj zog tshaj plaws thiab nyob ntev tshaj plaws hauv thaj av loj hauv Southeast Asia, nyob kiag qhov nruab nrab ntawm qhov uas hnub no Cambodia nyob.

Kilwa *n.* ib lub nroog hauv xeev txheej thaum ub uas nyob rau sab ntug dej sab hnub tuaj hauv Africa, uas cov neeg tuaj Iran thiab Arabia tuaj nyob, uas siab kawg nkaus thaum yav lig thaum A.D. 1200s.

kinship / sib txheeb *n.* ib qho kev sib txheeb los ntawm cov neeg raws roj ntsha, kev sib yuav, los sis kev coj mus tu.

knight / tub tus rog *n.* ib tug tub rog uas muaj peev xwm uas tau kev xyaum siab ntawm ib tug thawj coj loj, thaum lub sij hawm hauv European Middle Ages.

Kongo *n.* ib lub teb chaws txheej thaum ub raws sab ntug dej sab hnub poob hauv Africa, uas cov neeg uas hais lus Bantu los ntawm cov neeg Kongo tuaj nyob tej zuam tom qab tiam (century) 14 A.D.

Koryo *n.* ib lub teb chaws ntawm Korean thooj av, tsim thaum A.D. 935 tom qab Silla lub teb chaws poob.

Kublai Khan *n.* tus tub xeeb ntxwv ntawm Genghis Khan uas muaj zog kav hauv sab qab teb Suav Teb thaum A.D. 1260 thiab yeej cov tub rog Song thaum 1279, uas cia cov Mongols tswj thoob plaws Suav Teb.

L

labor specialization / kev ua ib hom hauj lwm *n.* ib qho kev ua tshwj xeeb los ntawm cov neeg ua hauj lwm uas tau kev xyaum los sis paub txog cov hauj lwm ntawv.

landform / ua av *n.* ib thaj av uas yeej ib txwm xeeb txawm hauv Lub Ntiaj Teb cov av, xws li lub pov txwv, ib lub roob, los sis ib thaj av.

latitude / txoj kab sawv ntsug *n.* ib qho kev ntsuas sab qaum teb los sis qab teb ntawm txog kab uas faib lub ntiaj teb kom qaum teb thiab qab sib npaug.

Leonardo da Vinci *n.* ib tug kws yees duab uas yog Italian Renaissance, yug thaum A.D. 1452, uas yees tau ntau daim duab uas zoo tshaj plaws, xws li daim Mona Lisa thiab The Last Supper, thiab tseem tshaj lij rau fab tshawb nrhiav txhua yam hauv ntiaj teb.

longbow / rab hmuv *n.* ib tug hmuv uas tua tau hneev uas mus chob tau rau ib tug tub rog cev khaub ncaws hlau.

longitude / txoj kab khiav tav toj *n.* ib qho kev ntsuas ntawm sab hnub tuaj los sis sab hnub poob ntawm txoj kab uas faib lub ntiaj teb kom sab hnub tuaj thiab sab hnub poob sib npaug.

lord / tus thawj tub rog *n.* ib tug thawj tub rog uas muaj av uas muaj zog tshaj plaws.

Luther, Martin *n.* ib tug German uas kawm txog lub ntiaj teb, yug thaum A.D. 1483, uas yog ib tug thawj coj ntawm Reformation thiab qhia txog kev ncaj ncees los ntawm kev ntseeg Tswv Ntuj dua qhov uas ua zoo tau zoo.

M

Magna Carta *n.* ib daim ntawv uas muaj cov cai uas sau los ntawm England kev ncaj ncees thiab kos npe rau los ntawm King John thaum A.D. 1215.

maize *n.* ib hom pob kws uas cog los ntawm cov neeg Qhab.

Mali *n.* ib thaj av uas muaj ntau lub teb chaws hauv Sab Hnub PoobAfrican uas tsim los ntawm cov neeg Malinke.

Manchu *n.* ib tug neeg koom ntawm cov neeg Suav uas nyob sab qaum teb sab hnub tuj uas txeeb tau Suav Teb thaum A.D. 1644 thiab pib nws lub zim txwv kawg nkaus hauv keeb kwm Suav, hu ua Qing Dynasty.

manor / lub tsev loj *n.* lub tsev ntawm ib tug tus nom, feem ntau muaj ib lub tsev uas muaj riam phom los sis ib lub tsev loj heev.

Mansa Musa *n.* ib tug nom ntawm Mali uas ua ib qho kev ncig nrov npe heev mus rau Mecca thaum A.D. 1324.

maritime / txog haiv txwv *adj.* hais txog hiav txwv.

Maya *n.* kev coj noj coj ua ntawm sab qab teb Mev Teb thiab sab qaum teb Central America, uas siab tshaj thaum A.D. 250 thiab 900.

Mbanza *n.* lub nroog hauv lub hauv paus loj hauv lub teb chaws African txheej thaum ub ntawm Kongo.

mercantilism / cai hais txog nyiaj txiag *n.* ib tsab cai hais txog nyiaj txiag raws lub tswv yim tias lub teb chaws lub zog yog nyob los ntawm kev muaj nyiaj.

mercenary / tus tub rog uas raug ntiav *n.* ib tug tub rog uas raug them nyiaj rau kom mus sib tua.

Meso-America *n.* ib cheeb tsam uas muaj ib feem ntawm sab qab teb hauv Mev Teb thiab feem ntau hauv Central America.

Michelangelo *n.* ib tug kws kho duab uas yog Italian Renaissance, yug thaum A.D. 1475, uas ua txoj hauj lwm ua ib tug uas txua ub no tiam sis kos ib co duab uas muaj koob nto npe xws li lub ru tsev hauv Sistine Chapel hauv Rome.

Middle Ages *n.* lub sij hawm ntawm European keeb kwm thaum Rome thiab Renaissance poob, kav ntev li ntawm A.D. 500 txog 1450.

missionary / qhia txog lus zoo *n.* ib tug neeg uas mus ncig teb chaws txawv es thiaj li ua tau cov hauj lwm ntseeg ntuj.

monastery / chaw teev hawm *n.* ib qho chaw uas cov neeg koom ntawm ib qho kev teev hawm xyaum thov ntuj thiab teev hawm.

Mongol Ascendancy *n.* lub sij hawm uas cov Mongols tswj tag nrho Central Asia, uas rau kev ua lag luam hauv teb chaw thiab kev mus los muaj kev ruaj ntseg.

monotheism / ntseg ib tug tswv *n.* ib qho kev ntseeg tias muaj ib tug Tswv Ntuj xwb.

Montezuma II *n.* Aztec tus nom kawg, uas kav thaumA.D. 1502 txog 1520 thiab raug rho tawm los ntawm cov Mev.

mosaic *n.* ib daim duab uas ua los ntawm ntau cov xwm fab xwm meem los sis cov iav uas muaj ntau cov yeeb yuj.

mosque / tsev teev hawm *n.* ib lub tsev rau cov neeg Muslim mus teev hawm, ua kom ntsias ntsoov lub nroog Mecca.

mother culture / thawj qhov kev coj noj coj ua *n.* ib qho kev coj noj coj ua uas kho thiab yaum tau cov kev cai lij choj thiab tswv yim ntawm cov kev coj noj coj ua tom qab ntawv.

movable type / hlau txav *n.* ib qho hlau los sis ib thoob ntoo me me uas muaj ib tug ntawv uas sawv xwb, siv los luam cov ntawv.

Murasaki Shikibu, Lady *n.* ib tug kws sau ntawm uas yog Japanese thaum ntxov ntawm A.D. 1000s, uas sau The Tale of Genji, uas pom tau hais tias yog ntij teb thawj cov phau ntawv.

Muslim *n.* ib tug neeg uas caum cov kev ntseeg ntuj tnawm Islam, uas txais Allah uas tib tug Tswv Ntuj xwb.

Mutapa *n.* ib lub teb chaws txheej thaum ub uas tam sim no yog lub teb chaws Zimbabwe, tsim los ntawm Shona king li thaum A.D. 1440; ntxiv thiab, ib tug neeg kav ntawm lub teb chaws no.

N

Nam Viet *n.* Vietnamese ib lub teb chaws uas txheeb tau los ntawm cov neeg Suav thaum 111 B.C.

natural rights / cov cai ib txwm muaj *n.* cov cai ntawm tag nrho cov neeg uas yug los—xws li cov cai muaj neej, kev ncaj ncees, thiab vaj tse raws li tus neeg kawm txog txhua yam thaum tiam (century) 18 John Locke.

Noh *n.* ib hom dab neeg Japanese uas tsim thaum A.D. 1300s, feem ntau muaj cov kev rov qhia piav txog cov dab neeg qub qub thiab cov dab neeg uas ua los ntawm cov neeg uas tim tsav yeeb yam hauv ib lub looj ntsej muag uas pleev yeeb yuj.

nomad / tus neeg tsis muaj tsev nyob *n.* ib tug neeg uas txav ib qho chaw mus rau ib qho chaw uas tsis nyob ruaj rau ib qho chaw xwb.

O

oasis / ib qho chaw uas muaj dej nyob tom taj suab puam *n.* ib thaj av uas zoo ua noj hauv ib lub thaj av nkaus xwb.

Olmec *n.* haiv neeg uas puag thaum ub uas paub tias yog thawj haiv neeg Meso-American cov kev coj noj coj ua, uas nthuav dav thaum 1200 txog 400 B.C. thiab nyob nruab nrab ntawm sab qab teb sab hnub tuaj hauv Mexico.

Omar Khayyám *n.* ib tug neeg Mulsim uas hais paj huam uas yug tim Persian uas feem ntau sau paj huam uas ua plaub seem thiab tseem nyog ib tug neeg tshaj lij rau fab zauv.

oral history / hais keeb kwm *n.* ib qho kev hais txog tej yam uas tshwm sim yav dhau los uas tsis sau rau hauv ntawv, xws li cov dab neeg uas hais ib tiam dhau ib tiam.

Orthodox *adj.* hais txog lub tsev teev hawm Christian uas tsim los hauv Byzantine Thaj Av Uas Muaj Ntau Lub Teb Chaws thiab tsis yog nyob qab tswj hwm ntawm cov thawj coj hauv lub tsev teev ntuj.

Osman *n.* ib tug thawj coj Turkish uas tsim tau lub Ottoman Thaj Av Uas Muaj Ntau Lub Teb Chaws thaum ntxov thaum A.D. 1300s.

P

Pacal II *n.* ib tug huab tais uas kav lub nroog Mayan hauv Palenque tau ze 70 xyoo (thaum A.D. 615)—Mayan cov huab tais uas zoo tshaj plaws.

Pachacuti *n.* Inca tus neeg kav zus cuaj, uas tau lub zog kav thaum A.D. 1438 thiab nthuav lub Inca Thaj Av Uas Muaj Ntau Lub Teb Chaws.

parliament / pej xeem kav *n.* ib pawg neeg uas sawv cev uas muaj ib co zog kav hauv tsoom fwv.

patron / tus txhawb nqa *n.* ib tug neeg uas txhawb nqa cov kev ua los sis cov tsev uas tau nyiaj los pab.

Peace of Westphalia *n.* ib qho kev cog lus uas tau kev pom zoo thaum A.D. 1648, uas pom zoo rau ib feem ntawm sab hnub poob hauv Europe mus ua Catholic thiab Protestant cov teb chaws thiab xaus kev sib ntaus sib tua ntawm qhov kev ntseeg ntuj.

perspective / kev pom *n.* ib qho kev kos duab, tsim thaum lub sij hawm Renaissance, uas sawv cev tau qhov pom ntawm ib qho khoom mus ua peb sab.

philosophe *n.* ib tug ntawm cov neeg xav thaum lub sij hawm tiam (century) 18 uas sim siv qhov kev kawm xog ib puas yam tsawv hauv ntiaj teb nov rau cov teeb meem ntawm neeg.

pilgrimage / kev dawb huv *n.* ib txoj kev mus rau ib qho chaw uas dawb huv los sis ib qho chaw teev hawm.

Pizarro, Francisco *n.* ib tug neeg ncig teb chaws uas yog Mev uas tau tuaj txog rau hauv Peru thaum A.D. 1532 thiab tau txeeb lub Inca Thaj Av Uas Muaj Ntau Lub Teb Chaws thaum 1535.

Polo, Marco *n.* ib tug Venetian ua lag luam uas thaug Silk Roads thiab mus txog rau hauv Suav Teb li thaum A.D. 1275. Nws ua ib tug neeg pab rau Kublai Khan thiab tom qab sau tau ib phau ntawv uas muaj koob nto npe txog nws cov kev mus ncig.

porcelain *n.* ib cov xis mas uas dawb thiab taws, feem ntau hu ua suav.

predestination / paub ua ntej *n.* ib daim ntawv tias Tswv Ntuj xaiv cov neeg rau kev ncaj ncees thiab kev phem ua ntej lawv yug los thiab cov neeg tsis muaj peev xwm los hloov qhov uas Tswv Ntuj tau ua cia.

primary source / qhov kev paub uas nyob ntawv *n.* ib daim ntawv los sis ib qho khoom uas tsim rau thaum ib lub sij hawm twg yav dhau los.

printing press / kev luam ntawv *n.* ib lub tshuab siv los nias cov ntau ntawm ib qho txav tau uas muaj kob.

projection / qhov pom *n.* ib txoj kev los sawv cev lub Ntiaj Teb no qhov nkhaus ntawm daim kab lig teb uas tiaj tiaj yam uas tseem ceev tau qhov uas nkhaus ntawm kom zoo ib yam thiab tswj tau.

Protestant *n.* ib tug neeg koom hauv pawg neeg Christian uas tawg ntawm Roman Catholic Church thaum lub sij hawm los sis tom qab tiam (century) 16.

Q

quipu *n.* ib tug twj suav ntawm Inca kev coj noj coj ua txheej thaum ub, uas xuas cov hlua uas khib uas pob ntawm tej ntu.

Qur'an *n.* Muslim phau ntawv dawb huv, uas muaj cov lus qhia los ntawm Allah uas ceev los ntawm cov neeg caum Muhammad tom qab nws tuag.

R

rationalism / kev sib tswv yim *n.* lub tswv yim tias neeg yuav tsum muaj tej yam dab tsi, los sis muaj kev xav uas meej pem, thiaj li yuav nkag siab txog lub ntiaj teb.

Reconquista *n.* ib co kev tawm tsam, kawg thaum A.D. 1492, uas cov tub rog Christian tshem tawm cov neeg kav Muslim tawm hauv Spain.

Reformation *n.* ib qho kev txav tawm tsam Roman Catholic Church, pib thaum tiam (century) 16.

regent / tus neeg kav *n.* ib tug neeg uas kav ib qho uas ncua uas tsis muaj tus tswj fwm teb chaws.

religious order / kev teev ntuj *n.* ib pawg neeg uas nyob raws cov cai hauv kev ntseeg ntuj.

Renaissance *n.* ib lub sij hawm rov qab yug dua thiab muaj tswv yim txog kev kos duab, sau ntawv, thiab kev xav thaum kws yees li A.D. 1300 txog 1600, pib hauv Italy thiab nthuav mus thoob Europe.

republic *n.* ib hom nom tswv uas cov zog kav nyob ntawm cov pej xeem, uas xaiv tsa thiaj li xaiv tau cov thawj coj.

reunify / ua ke *v.* coj los ua ke.

Roman Catholic *adj.* hais txog Christian church ntawm Sab Hnub Poob uas nyob qab tswj hwm ntawm tus thawj coj hauv lub tsev teev ntuj.

S

Sahara *n.* ib thaj av loj ntawm sab qaum tebAfrica, nthuav ntawm sab ntug dej Atlantic mus rau Nile Valley.

Saladin *n.* ib tug thawj coj tub rog uas coj cov Muslims mus sib ntaus nrog cov Christians hauv Palestine thaum lub sij hawm tiam (century) 12 A.D.

salon *n.* ib qho kev sib sau cov neeg xav thiab cov kws kos duab los tham txog cov teeb meem thiab sib pauv tswv yim thaum lub sij hawm Enlightenment.

samurai *n.* ib tug tub rog tua rog ua tau uas tau kev xyaum ntawm pawg Japanese.

savanna / nyom ntsuab *n.* ib thaj nyom ntsuab uas tiaj tiaj, uas muaj ntoo tsawg, hauv ib cheeb tsam uas los nag heev.

schism / cais *n.* ib qho kev sib cais ntawm ob pawg neeg.

scholar-official / tus neeg txawj ntse *n.* ib tug neeg uas muaj kev kawm ntawv siab uas tau ua hauj lwm hauv tsoom fwv.

scientific method / ib hom kev siv cov kev paub hauv lub ntiaj teb no *n.* ib qho kev mus rau kev tshawb nrhiav tej yam uas paub hauv lub ntiaj tb no uas muaj cov kev soj ntsuam kom zoo, ua thiab sim cov kev xav, thiab xaus lus uas yuav qhia tau los sis hloov tau ib qho kev xav.

Scientific Revolution *n.* ib lub sij hawm, pib thaum A.D. 1500s, uas European cov neeg txawj ntse pib nug txog cov tswv yim txog tej yam hauv ntiaj teb thiab cov kev ntseeg ntawm Christian.

secondary source / kev paub yam tsis nyob ntawv *n.* ib qho kev ua uas tsim txog tej yam tshwm sim hauv keeb kwm los ntawm ib tug neeg uas tsis nyob ntawv lub sij hawm ntawv.

Seljuk Turk *n.* ib tug neeg koom hauv cov neeg Turkish uas tswv qhov nruab nrab thiab sab hnub poob hauv Asia thaum tiam (century) 11 mus rau tiam (century) 13.

serf / neeg ua liaj ua teb *n.* ib tug neeg ua liaj ua teb hauv ib qho chaw uas muaj kev sib ntaus sib tua, uas ua hauj lwm rau ib tug neeg muaj koob nto npe los pauv qhov uas muaj kev tiv thaiv thiab ib co cai.

Shakespeare, William *n.* ib tug kws sau ntawv uas yog English uas muaj koob nto npe thaum lub sij hawm Renaissance, uas neeg paub zoo tshaj rau nws zaj play Romeo and Juliet thiab Hamlet.

Shi'a *n.* ib pawg Muslim uas tsis kam uas raws li Umayyads txoj cai, uas ntseeg tias tus kav ntxuas ntxiv yuav tsum txheeb tus saub Muhammad.

Shinto *n.* ib hom kev ntseeg ntuj hauv Japan, raws li kev teev hawm thiab kev hwm rau tej yam ua yeej ib txwm xeeb txawm los li thiab caj ces.

shogun *n.* ib tug thawj coj tub rog Japense—ib pawg uas xub muaj zog kav thaum A.D. 1192 thiab kav sawv cev tus nom tiam sis feem ntau ua raws li lawv nyiam.

Shona *n.* ib haiv neeg uas hauv lus Bantu-uas thriving rau hauv qhov chaw ua tam sim cov teb chaws ntawm Botswana, Mozambique, thiab Zimbabwe nyob thaum A.D. 1000.

Shotoku, Prince *n.* ib tug nom uas kav Japan thaum A.D. 593 txog 622 thiab yuav cov kev ua ntawm haiv neeg Suav—feem ntau, yog Buddhist qhov kev ntseeg ntuj—mus rau lub teb chaws.

Silk Roads *n.* cov kev ua lag luam txheej thaum ub uas txuas Europe nrog China.

slash-and-burn agriculture / ntov ntoo thiab hlawv *n.* muaj feem txog ib hom kev ua liaj ua teb uas tej thaj av yog npaj rau kev ua qoob loo uas muab cov ntoo ntov thiab hlawv.

Songhai *n.* cov neeg nyob Sab Hnub Poob African uas lawv cov thawj coj tsim ib thaj av uas muaj ntau lub teb chaws uas zoo tshaj plaws thaum tiam (century) 15 thiab 16 A.D.

sponsor / tus txhawb nqa *n.* ib tug neeg uas muab nyiaj mus pab ib tug neeg los sis ib qho dab tsi.

standing army / pawg tub rog uas npaj tos *n.* ib pawg tub rog uas tswj thaum muaj kev ywj pheej thiab thaum uas muaj kev tsov rog.

stele *n.* ib qho cim hauv lub pob zeb txheej thaum ub uas cim txog cov hnub uas tseem ceeb los sis tej lub sij hawm uas zoo.

Stoicism *n.* Greek ib tug neeg uas paub txog txhua yam hauv lub ntiaj teb uas hais txog qhov tseem ceeb ntawm kev ncaj ncees, txoj hauj lwm, thiab kev uv thiab tshwj xeeb tshaj yaum tau hauv Rome txheej thaum ub.

Suleyman I *n.* tus thawj coj hauv Ottoman Thaj Av Uas Muaj Ntau Lub Teb Chaws thaum A.D. 1520 txog 1566, ua txhawb cov duab thiab tswj tus cai.

Sundiata *n.* ib tug neeg kav txheej thaum ub ntawm cov neeg Malinke, uas txhom tau lub hauv paus loj hauv Ghana thiab nthuav thaj av uas muaj ntau lub teb chaws.

Sunnah *n.* Muhammad cov lus thiab cov kev ntseeg, uas ua ib tug qauv pab cov Muslims mus rau kev ua neej kom zoo.

Sunni *n.* ib tug neeg koom hauv pawg neeg Muslim uas txias txoj cai ntawm cov kav txuas mus uas xaiv tau thiab tsis yig cov Umayyads.

Swahili *n.* ib hom lus African uas xyaw nrog Bantu thiab Arabic cov kev siv.

T

Tenochtitlán *n.* Aztec ib lub nroog txheej thaum ub, nrhiav tau thaum A.D. 1325 ntawm ib lub menyuam pov txwv hauv Lake Texcoco.

Thomas Aquinas *n.* ib tug Italian uas txhawj ntse uas ua ib qho kev kawm ntawm kev kawm txog txhuam yam hauv lub ntiaj teb thiab Christian cov kev qhia thaum ub.

Timbuktu *n.* ib lub nroog hauv qhov nruab nrab ntawm Mali hauv Sab Hnub Poob Africa, uas nrhiav tau thaum tiam (century) 13 thiab yog qhov nruab nrab ntawm kev ua lag luam thiab haiv neeg.

Tokugawa Shogunate *n.* txoj cai ntawm Tokugawa Ieyasu thiab nws cov neeg hauv Japan, uas pib thaum A.D. 1603 thiab yuav ib lub sij hawm uas yog 250-xyoo ntawm kev ruaj khov rau lub teb chaws.

Treaty of Tordesillas *n.* ib qho kev cog lus ntawm Spain thiab Portugal thaum 1494, tsim ib txoj kab uas qhov muag tsis pom pib sab qaum teb rau sab qab teb ncig lus ntiaj teb thiab cia Spain tau cov av nyob sab hnub poob ntawm txoj kab thiab Portugal tau cov av uas nyob sab hnub tuaj ntawm txoj kab.

triangular trade / kev ua lag luam peb sab *n.* qhov sib pauv khoom noj thiab qhev ntawm lub pav dej Atlantic Ocean ntawm Americas, Europe, thiab Africa.

tribute / kev hawm *n.* ib qho kev them ntawm ib lub teb chaws mus rau lwm lub teb chaw uas ua ib qho kev hwm.

U, V, W, X, Y, Z

universal gravitation / kev nqus thoob teb chaws *n.* Isaac Newton qhov kev xav tias cov kev nqus nqus tag nrho cov khoom thoob plawv lub qab ntuj no.

vassal / tus tau txais kev pab *n.* hauv ib lub zej zos uas muaj kev sib ntaus sib tua, ib tug neeg uas tau txais av thiab kev tiv thaiv los ntawm ib tug thawj coj vim nws qhov kev ncaj ncees.

vegetation zone / thaj chaw ua qoob loo *n.*
ib cheeb tsam uas, vim tias nws cov av thiab huab cua,
muaj ntau hom roj ntsuag uas txawv.

vernacular / ib hom lus *n.* ib tug neeg hom lus
uas nws hais.

weather / huab cua *n.* qhov txawv ntawm lub ntiaj
teb rau tej qhov chaw thiab sij hawm.

**wood-block printing / kev xuas lub thawv
ntoo los sau ntawv** *n.* ib qho kev luam ntawv uas
tsim los ntawm cov neeg Suav txheej thaum ub, uas siv
cov ntoo uas ua thawv uas kos uas muaj ntau tus ntawv
los luam tag nrho cov nplooj ntawv.

Yucatán Peninsula *n.* ib cheeb tsam uas nyob sab
qaum teb sab hnub tuj ntawm Mev Tes uas extends mus
rau Caribbean Sea thiab Gulf of Mexico.

Zen *n.* ib hom Buddhism ntawm cov neeg Japenese,
uas hais txog kev qhuab qhia tus kheej, kev ua yooj yim,
thiab kev zaum xav.

Zheng He *n.* ib tug nom Suav uas nws mus ncig heev
thaum A.D. 1405 thiab 1433 uas nthuav Suav Teeb kev
lag luam thiab lub koob lub npe.